PRAISE FOR

15 New Testament Words of Life

Nijay Gupta is artful and accessible in his effort to take a single word from a New Testament book and explore that theme at length. Gupta explores themes on God, salvation, and the life of faith. A very rare kind of New Testament theology, eminently readable and enjoyable.

MICHAEL F. BIRD, academic dean and lecturer in theology,
Ridley College, Melbourne, Australia

Not only does Nijay Gupta define important New Testament terms and illustrate their significance for today, he also models a strategy for how a Bible reader might approach the exploration of biblical ideas. *15 New Testament Words of Life* is an introduction to New Testament theology that invites readers to study the Bible by investigating key concepts that frequently appear in books, sermons, and even casual conversations. Gupta's scholarship and cultural awareness combine to make the work a necessary resource for preachers, teachers, and all other curious Bible readers. I am eager for my students to read it.

DENNIS R. EDWARDS, associate professor of New Testament,
North Park Theological Seminary

Gupta imaginatively engages in biblical theology by focusing on fifteen words that embrace vital theological themes in the New Testament that also connect with the Old Testament. These words had a momentous impact on the rough and tumble life in the ancient world by conveying God's vision for a just, compassionate, and harmonious world. Gupta's captivating presentation shows how they can continue to leave their marks on hopeful living in a world still wracked by sin. This book provides a great resource both for teaching and for fashioning a preaching tour through the major story lines of Scripture.

DAVID E. GARLAND, professor of Christian Scriptures,
George W. Truett Theological Seminary

Nijay Gupta has provided the church and its pastors with a remarkable resource. Wearing his deep learning lightly, he winsomely portrays how the New Testament writers draw on the Old Testament to theologize in ways that are immensely hopeful and intensely practical. A book like this is just what the church needs today—a rich biblical theology that speaks words of life to the lives of the people of God in our increasingly fraught and complex world.

TIMOTHY GOMBIS, author of *Power in Weakness*

Nijay is a gift. He's a brilliant New Testament scholar with a pastor's heart. His passion is to see people transformed by the gospel so they can embody the life of Christ in the real world. This will be a book you buy for others and revisit frequently.

DERWIN L. GRAY, cofounder and lead pastor of Transformation Church, author of *How to Heal Our Racial Divide*

Do you suspect there's more to the Christian faith than what you're hearing? Dr. Gupta brings the best of biblical scholarship to the pews, where standard Christian ways of talking about things have grown stale. By highlighting these fifteen key words, he opens a whole new world of understanding that will reinvigorate Christian practice. If you are hungry to move beyond clichés, this book is your invitation to a nourishing feast.

CARMEN JOY IMES, associate professor of Old Testament, Biola University, author of *Bearing God's Name*

Into a parched landscape, Nijay Gupta offers these refreshing words of life. Beautifully written, his reflections on each word invite us to consider anew concepts that are central to our Scriptures and to our daily life with God. With the need for deep Christian formation apparent all around us, Gupta invites us not only to think more faithfully about these words but to live them. This book will find wide use in the classroom, in churches, and in the lives of disciples young and old who want their faith to shape their lives as they are seeking the good of the world.

KRISTEN DEEDE JOHNSON, dean and vice president of academic affairs, G. W. and Edna Haworth Chair of Educational Ministries and Leadership, Western Theological Seminary, Holland, Michigan

While the New Testament is full of depth and complexity, its most important ideas have a profound simplicity to them. In this collection of word studies, Nijay Gupta explores foundational themes in New Testament theology, but in a very accessible way. If you're looking to deepen your understanding of some of the most essential concepts in Christian belief, this book is for you.

TIM MACKIE, cofounder, the BibleProject

Accessible and engaging yet rigorous, *15 New Testament Words of Life* offers readers a way to learn and then live the theology of the Scriptures. The consistent format facilitates confident movement through the terms, even as it allows Gupta to engage with a wide range of biblical and historical texts without becoming encyclopedic. I will certainly be putting this book into the hands of my students and parishioners alike.

AMY PEELER, associate professor of New Testament,
Wheaton College, and associate rector at St. Mark's
Episcopal Church, Geneva, Illinois

Everything Nijay Gupta writes is accurate, clear, accessible, and helpful to the church. This little gem is no exception, a study of key themes in New Testament theology through some of its most important words. By linking each theme to the message of a New Testament book, Gupta provides a model on how to do biblical theology and its real life application for today.

MARK L. STRAUSS, university professor of New Testament,
Bethel Seminary

15
NEW TESTAMENT
WORDS *of* LIFE

A NEW TESTAMENT THEOLOGY FOR REAL LIFE

NIJAY K. GUPTA

ZONDERVAN
ACADEMIC

ZONDERVAN ACADEMIC

15 New Testament Words of Life
Copyright © 2022 by Nijay K. Gupta

Requests for information should be addressed to:
Zondervan, *3900 Sparks Dr. SE, Grand Rapids, Michigan 49546*

Zondervan titles may be purchased in bulk for educational, business, fundraising, or sales promotional use. For information, please email SpecialMarkets@Zondervan.com.

Library of Congress Cataloging-in-Publication Data

Names: Gupta, Nijay K., author.
Title: 15 New Testament words of life : a New Testament theology for real life / Nijay Gupta.
Other titles: Fifteen New Testament words of life
Description: Grand Rapids : Zondervan, 2022. | Includes bibliographical references and index.
Identifiers: LCCN 2022009692 (print) | LCCN 2022009693 (ebook) | ISBN 9780310109051 (paperback) | ISBN 9780310109068 (ebook)
Subjects: LCSH: Bible. New Testament--Terminology. | Bible. New Testament--Theology. | Theology, Doctrinal--Popular works.
Classification: LCC BS2385 .G87 2022 (print) | LCC BS2385 (ebook) | DDC 225.6/6--dc23/ eng/20220330
LC record available at https://lccn.loc.gov/2022009692
LC ebook record available at https://lccn.loc.gov/2022009693

Cover design: Thinkpen Design
Cover image: © Shutterstock
Interior design: Kait Lamphere

Printed in the United States of America

22 23 24 25 26 27 28 29 30 31 32 /TRM/ 15 14 13 12 11 10 9 8 7 6 5 4 3 2 1

To Amy, a beautiful model of lived theology

Contents

Foreword

"Of making many books there is no end . . ." says the author of Ecclesiastes (12:12) with, one infers, a certain sense of weariness, a sense reinforced by the second half of the sentence: "And much study is a weariness of the flesh." When it comes to written theologies of the New Testament, I can, at times, feel a level of sympathy for this sentiment. Over the years there have been countless attempts to produce "a theology of the New Testament" that answers all questions, weaves everything into a seamless whole, and provides a lens through which everything in the New Testament can be read. I have numerous of these volumes on my shelves and although I, as a rule, have appreciated the insights they bring, I do not feel the need to add to my collection.

This book, however, is a very different kind of New Testament Theology, and it will make a very welcome addition to my bookshelves. It doesn't try to be the "last word" on anything, nor indeed to provide a single framework for understanding the whole. Instead, it takes fifteen key words—those that mean so much but which we often struggle to define—and explores them. Even better than that, it begins with a bird's-eye view looking at how the word can be traced throughout the Bible and then zooms in, looking at the word in a book from the New Testament where it plays an especially important role and then comparing that usage with usage in another key book from the New Testament.

The effect is that, as you read, you get a sense both of the sweep of the whole Bible as well as an in-depth reflection of the words and phrases that bear the theological weight of what the New Testament writers were trying to say. In all of this, the importance of words and their meaning comes to the fore. It is easy to imagine that once we have translated the New Testament from Greek into English the hard work is over: anyone can come along and pick up the New Testament, read and understand. This wonderful book reminds us that transferring a text from one language to another is only the very first step in a long process of translation for better understanding. Words—just like people—have backstories; they function differently in different places, and if we want to understand what they mean we need both to step back to see the whole as well as to step in to see the detail.

The genius of this book is its focus on words—the words that we need to understand in depth in order to understand the theology of the New Testament. Most importantly of all, it drives you back to the New Testament itself, armed with new insights into its words and the theology that lies behind them, to read it afresh. Once you have read this book, you will wonder why no one has thought to do it before. It is readable, helpful, thought-provoking, and inspiring.

I would say that this book will be a welcome addition to my bookshelf—it will be—but I suspect I will have it open on my desk more often than on the shelf itself.

Dr. Paula Gooder
Chancellor of St. Paul's Cathedral, London

Introduction

Words of Life

One of my favorite stories of Jesus in the Gospels involves his "bread of life" teaching (John 6:35–59). Jesus's popularity was at an all-time high, his followers were eager to learn more about his ministry and mission. So what does he tell them? *You must eat my flesh and drink my blood* (6:53–58). Keep in mind, he gave this teaching *before* any kind of last meal upper room banquet with bread and wine. We, the readers of John's Gospel, already know how the whole story goes, but the characters were pretty confused. This must have sounded like some strange lesson on cannibalism, human sacrifice, or vampire etiquette. "This teaching is difficult; who can accept it?" (6:60). John notes that many followers gave up on Jesus that day. Jesus turns to the Twelve and asks, "Do you also wish to go away?" Simon Peter answers, "Lord, to whom can we go? You have the words of eternal life" (6:68). Peter didn't deny that Jesus's teachings were enigmatic, even off-putting at times. But he knew that there was something special about Jesus, that he was "the Holy One of God" (6:69).

I have always been intrigued by Peter's description of Jesus's teaching as "words of eternal life." The words Jesus used were not *themselves* life, but they communicated, translated, conducted God's gospel life. In John 6:68, the term for "words" is *rhēma*, which refers to individual words. More commonly throughout the New Testament we find the term *logos* used to describe the gospel message as the "word of God,"[1] the "word of the Lord,"[2] the "word of faith,"[3] the "word of Christ,"[4] the "word of truth,"[5] and the "word of life."[6] The gospel word, "the Message" (as Eugene Peterson calls it) is a communicative event that God uses to bring restoration and life to the world through Jesus Christ and the Spirit.

So, words are important. Sticks and stones can break bones, yes, but words move whole worlds. And what is incredible about Peter's response to Jesus is that words can lead to life, the life of God. This book, *15 New Testament Words of Life*, looks at fifteen important words in the New Testament, inspired by this idea that the gospel is greater than the words we use to describe it; and yet those words are still the way we give and receive that life.

Words for Real Life

But why write a book about these words? Because the goal of the New Testament writers was not to wax eloquently about "theology," but to prepare Christians to live well in the real world. Of course, they did talk about "theology," the study of the things of God, but the endgame all along was formation. When I tried to describe this book project to friends over the year I was writing it, I refered to it as a "New Testament theology for real life." So many of the books I have read on New Testament theology keep the discussion focused on the ancient past or talk about "theology" in an abstract way. Can we connect this "theology" to life today? *Real* life today?

I get frustrated when my students, friends, or neighbors refer to the Bible as irrelevant or antiquated. Just because something is *old* or

---

1. Acts 4:31; 6:2, 7; 8:14; 11:1; 12:24; 13:5, 7; 17:13; 1 Cor 14:36; Eph 6:17; Col 1:25; 1 Thess 2:13; 2 Tim 2:9; Titus 2:5; Heb 13:7; 1 Peter 1:23; Rev 1:9; 6:9.
2. Acts 8:25; 11:16; 13:44–48; 1 Thess 1:8; 4:15; 2 Thess 3:1.
3. Rom 10:8.
4. Rom 10:17; Col 3:16.
5. Eph 1:13; Col 1:5; 2 Tim 2:15; James 1:18.
6. Phil 2:16; 1 John 1:1.

relates to a previous generation doesn't mean it can't be captivating, thought-provoking, or worldview-shaping. Take *Hamilton: The Musical*. From one perspective it is a tale of politics, skirmishes, and legal debates from over two centuries ago. From another perspective it is all about family, ambition and hope for a better world, love, friendship, and forgiveness. This book, *15 New Testament Words of Life*, is my attempt to make a case that the New Testament is a riveting, divinely inspired collection of writings on love, peace, hope, friendship, generosity, and more. The stuff we most prize in life—beauty, justice, goodness—this is the stuff that fills the onionskin pages of our Bibles. Is the gospel a timeless message of eternal salvation and eternal life? Yes, of course. Is it a message about and for real life—making a difference in the little things like shopping, dealing with health and wealth, and mending broken relationships? It is!

Approaching New Testament Theology

I mentioned that I think of this book as an exercise in New Testament theology (or, as some scholars say, New Testament "theologizing"). What does that mean? To me that means the New Testament writers shared common beliefs about God and his world, and they wanted to shape the imaginations, identities, communities, virtues, and behaviors of their readers, the church, to conform to the gospel of Jesus Christ. There have been many proposals over the years for how one might go about writing a New Testament theology. Howard Marshall focuses on the distinct contributions of the individual writings in his *New Testament Theology: Many Witnesses, One Gospel*.[7] Frank Matera, also attentive to the diversity of the New Testament documents, concludes his book with an account of the "diverse unity" of these texts through a master story told in the New Testament.[8] The basic elements of this

---

7. I. Howard Marshall, *New Testament Theology: Many Witnesses, One Gospel* (Downers Grove, IL: IVP Academic, 2004).

8. Frank Matera, *New Testament Theology: Exploring Diversity and Unity* (Louisville: Westminster John Knox, 2007).

story include (1) humanity in need of salvation, (2) the bringer of salvation, (3) the community of the sanctified, (4) the life of the sanctified, and (5) the hope of the sanctified.

James D. G. Dunn's short contribution on New Testament theology examines the unity and diversity in the New Testament through four key themes: God, Salvation, Israel, and Torah.[9] Craig Blomberg has written *A New Testament Theology* with a focus on the theme of "fulfillment."[10] Joshua Jipp argues that a "messianic" theology (Jesus as the Messiah) connects (almost) all the New Testament books.[11]

My goal here isn't to arbitrate between these books. I affirm, along with virtually all the scholars mentioned above, that there are both unifying threads throughout the New Testament as well as clear distinctives in each text. *Jesus is Lord. The gospel is the message. The end is at hand. The church is the missional agent empowered by the Spirit.* But in *this* book we will take a different, though I hope complementary, approach to thinking about the theology of the New Testament. Our focus will be on fifteen important theological words in the New Testament: righteousness, gospel, forgiveness, life, cross, faith, grace, fellowship, hope, salvation, peace, religion, holiness, love, and witness. I don't think that I need to convince you that these are significant concepts in the New Testament. These words have deep meaning in the theological lexicon of the New Testament writers. But at the end of the day, words are still just words. It is crucial that words be understood within context. In this book, we will ground each of these words in a key New Testament text—for example, we will use 1 John as the primary case study or focal text for looking at "love." Hebrews will help us think about "peace." And Galatians and Romans are important texts to process the idea of "faith." But we will also try to understand how these words were used by particular writers in particular contexts to shape Christian identity, Christian community, and Christian life for the good of the world. We will be interpreting these important theological

---

9. James D. G. Dunn, *New Testament Theology* (Nashville: Abingdon, 2010).

10. Craig L. Blomberg, *A New Testament Theology* (Waco, TX: Baylor University Press, 2018).

11. Joshua W. Jipp, *The Messianic Theology of the New Testament* (Grand Rapids: Eerdmans, 2020).

words in view of three contexts: canonical context (especially how the New Testament is grounded in the Old Testament), literary context (the meaning developed within a key focal New Testament text), and historical context (attentive to the social and cultural "encyclopedia" of the apostolic age, the Jewish and Greco-Roman world of the first century).

Fifteen Words of Life

GOSPEL

Righteousness *Life*

Forgiveness

cross

salvation

FAITH

Grace

Fellowship hope

Love

PEACE

RELIGION

holiness witness

These are the terms and concepts we will focus on in this book. From my experience studying and teaching the New Testament, these words have stood out to me as "load-bearing" concepts. To be honest, we use them *a lot* in preaching and teaching of Christian Scripture, Christian life, and Christian ministry, but they can get overused and become overfamiliar, such that they get flattened into "Christianese." All too easily, we domesticate these powerful concepts, and they lose their ability to challenge us as part of Scripture's testimony. In the following chapters, we will address each of these in turn, exploring their meaning in the context of Scripture, and then also reflecting on how these concepts can find fresh meaning and bring challenge and inspiration to our lives today in the twenty-first century.

The Plan of the Book

We will devote a chapter to each theological concept listed above. We will "ground" the concept in one particular New Testament book, as a focal text. Otherwise, if we tried to perform a "whole New Testament" examination of the concept, this book could easily become a thousand pages long and we would risk turning this into a boring dictionary—we want to help bring these ideas to life! But tying each theological concept to only one New Testament book also has its limitations. So, after discussing the nature of the concept at length in one book, we will look briefly at the same concept in another New Testament text or book for comparison. This offers some balance and gives the concept more texture and depth. Each chapter will begin with a brief look at the background of the concept in the Old Testament and Jewish tradition, and sometimes also how the term was used and understood in the wider Greco-Roman world of the New Testament writers.

Each chapter ends with an extended set of reflections on how we can conceive of the theological concept in the rough and tumble of life today. The theology of the New Testament means *nothing* for believers today if it does not grab us and challenge us and direct us and bring hope to our real lives here in the twenty-first century. Too often "New Testament theology" is treated as this static thing, an object to analyze, dissect, and analyze some more. Now, I am *all* for rigorous analysis of the New Testament. I have written books and articles with all the sophisticated tools and methods that reflect the state of biblical criticism. But this book is not for the ivory tower. It is for Christians who are interested in what the New Testament has to say about God, God's people, God's world, and a great big, beautiful gospel mission that can make all the difference. But reading the Bible is hard. It is an ancient and foreign text. Even when we translate it into English, it is still a cross-cultural experience to read and interpret the New Testament. We have work to do to "translate" not only the language into our mother tongues, but also to relay the theological concepts at the heart of Scripture. Our goal is not to *change* these concepts, but to locate them meaningfully within our own cultural lexicon. In one sense the words of Scripture *are* words on the page. But they are meant to be more than inked words; they can be *words of life* if we take the time to reflect on their formative dynamics for our lives today.

TABLE OF SECTIONS

Old Testament Background

Greco-Roman World (as Relevant)

Focal Text

Other New Testament Voices

For Today

CHAPTER 1

Righteousness

Integrity, Justice, and Mercy before God and in the World

The Gospel of Matthew

Imagine seeing a web advertisement for a managerial job.

> Restaurant manager wanted. Strong skills in leadership and communication. Proficient in Excel or other spreadsheet programs. Must be righteous.

You wouldn't see that kind of ad, would you? Why not? Because the language of "righteous/righteousness" has fallen out of use in modern English. It sounds old-timey, King-James-y. Probably for many modern people, it sounds like a religious word—like someone who goes to church. Or maybe it sounds so ancient it only applies to people who had long beards and wore robes and sandals.

I'm kind of disappointed that we don't use this word in English anymore. Not because I want America to be more "religious" per se, I'm not nostalgic like that. I am disappointed because we actually could use a single word to describe someone who innately does what is good and right out of the purity of their heart and care for the other. How would you describe such a person in one word? Hebrews would say *tzedek*, Greeks would say *dikaios*—righteous.

Old Testament Background: Righteousness

There are three notions about religion in our popular consciousness today that ancient people did not share: (1) religion is optional (not obligatory), (2) religion is private (not public), (3) religion is spiritual (not material). The biblical writers and the people of God did not associate "salvation" with heaven, inner peace, or spiritual enlightenment per se. They saw the redemption vision of the gospel in the Old and New Testaments as a world restored to righteousness. Not souls and spirits rescued and reclaimed, but bodies and communities, trees and forests, sky and earth restored to health and vitality. All things made right from the utter wrongness of sin and wickedness. Before we get to how all this is worked out in the biblical story, we ought to begin with the simple question—what is "righteousness"?

What Is Righteousness?

Again, the first thing to affirm is that this is not a religious word or concept. To be righteous is to live and behave according to a standard of what is good and right toward the other. Gordon Wenham puts it succinctly when he says that the Hebrew word *tzadik* "is the most general Hebrew term to describe good people."[1] When Genesis 6:9 claims that "Noah was a righteous man," that means he cared about having a clean conscience, living faithfully according to a standard of what is right, and caring about justice in the world. Today, we might say he was a person of *integrity* (Genesis 6:9 describes him as "blameless among the people of his time" [NIV]). Here are some words and characteristics in the Old Testament that are often associated with righteousness.

> **PURE HEART:** we would liken this to having a clear and clean
> conscience (Prov 20:9).

---

1. Gordon Wenham, *Genesis 1–15*, WBC (Waco, TX: Word, 1987), 170.

INNOCENCE: irreproachable, blameless, unable to be accused
of wrongdoing (Ps 18:24).

FAIRNESS: caring about and holding to a just and fair standard
for all (Ps 9:8).

JUSTICE: maintaining a standard of morality for all, offering fair
and equal judgment and treatment (Ps 33:5; Lev 19:15).

It is worth dwelling a bit on the last item, the notion of "justice." In the last century or so, theologians have debated whether the Christian gospel is primarily about saving the soul or caring about social justice. The ancient people of God would have seen all of this as one thing. Knowing God and being saved by God was directly connected to social and political justice, because there is one God who wants to redeem the whole world to truth, grace, and new life. The Old Testament talks far more about interpersonal justice than it does about "the afterlife."

One might get the impression from the above description that "righteousness" is all about legalistically checking boxes and obeying laws and rules. Laws and rules are good, but there is more to righteousness. It is also about faithfulness and loyalty in relationships ("being there" for the other person, keeping your word) and even showing mercy to others. God is often described in the Old Testament as *both* "righteous" *and* "merciful" (Isa 55:7). He is faithful to his promises and committed to his people, he cares for them, so one form that his righteousness takes is compassion and mercy (Exod 34:7). Walter Brueggemann talks about how Israel's mandate from God toward righteousness is all about faithful and generous engagement with the community.

> Righteousness is an ethical term used to mark people who live generatively in the community in order to sustain and enhance the community's well-being. The "righteous person" is characteristically one who invests in the community, showing special attentiveness to the poor and the needy.[2]

---

2. Walter Brueggemann, *Reverberations of Faith: A Theological Handbook of Old Testament Themes* (Louisville: Westminster John Knox, 2002), 177.

Brueggemann goes on to describe the righteous Israelite as someone who lives with "integrity and gravitas, who by their presence and their actions lend[s] stability to the community."[3]

The Old Testament Story of Righteousness

We might conceive of the whole Old Testament as telling a *story of righteousness*—lost and longed for. The first thing to say is that the Old Testament begins with a covenant God who is righteous. After the infiltration of sin into the world and the resulting devastation, God hatches a plan to restore his creation, but it must begin with a special relationship with one people: Israel. As a righteous God, he pledges loyalty to them and demonstrates his character as good and just: "For the LORD is righteous, he loves justice, the upright will see his face" (Ps 11:7 NIV; cf. Ps 50:6).

As part of the covenant, Israel is called to be righteous as well, faithful to God and his law, but also just and good in the world. Israel is meant to be a light to the other nations, a model of a new humanity that does right, seeks justice, defends the oppressed, cares for the orphan, and advocates for the poor widow (Isa 1:17). We catch brief glimpses of Israel trying to fulfill this destiny (e.g., 2 Sam 8:15), but by and large Israel struggles and sins and deviates from this calling. For example, in Isaiah, Israel is described as a vineyard tended by the Lord. But when he went to examine this precious vineyard, "he expected justice, but saw bloodshed; righteousness, but heard a cry" (Isa 5:7). So the gospel of God must be both a promise to restore the whole world, and also a promise to restore his people who minister to that world. The prophets give us the most vivid vision of what this redemption will look like. Thanks to Handel's *Messiah* many of us are familiar with Isaiah's promise of a new leader: "He is named Wonderful Counselor, Mighty God, Everlasting Father, Prince of Peace" (Isa 9:6). He is not depicted as a deity swooping down and snatching people up to heaven. He establishes a good government of peace for his people, a Davidic kingdom "uphold[ing] . . . justice and righteousness from this time onward and forevermore" (Isa 9:7; cf. Amos 5:24).

---

3. Brueggemann, *Reverberations of Faith*, 177.

Surely this was the *good news* (= gospel) that Israel was longing for. Surely this was the solution to the problem of sin, infidelity, wickedness, dishonesty, corruption, and injustice in the world. But *when* would this happen? And how? These are the questions that many Jews had in the years just before the birth of Jesus.

Focal Text: The Gospel of Matthew

Jesus was born into this Jewish world of longing for the righteousness of God (in all its dimensions) for Israel and the world. Suffice it to say that Matthew is fully aware of this, as righteousness is a master theme of his Gospel. As early as chapter 3, we have this story.

> Then Jesus came from Galilee to John at the Jordan, to be baptized by him. John would have prevented him, saying, "I need to be baptized by you, and do you come to me?" But Jesus answered him, "Let it be so now; for it is proper for us in this way to fulfill all righteousness." Then he consented. And when Jesus had been baptized, just as he came up from the water, suddenly the heavens were opened to him and he saw the Spirit of God descending like a dove and alighting on him. And a voice from heaven said, "This is my Son, the Beloved, with whom I am well pleased." (Matt 3:13–17)

So, Jesus began his ministry by identifying with Israel through the baptism of John, and this to "fulfill all righteousness." Why did Jesus talk about "righteousness" here? If you use your imagination, you could fill that space with so many other words Jesus could have used: "fulfill the *plan of salvation*," "fulfill the *gospel*," "fulfill the *hope of eternal life*." Why does Jesus say "righteousness"? Honestly, we don't quite know, but it seems to be his signal to John that Jesus was ready to initiate his plan to spread the gospel of the kingdom of God, and this would bring God's righteousness—his dynamic activity of "right-making"—to bear on his world. But Jesus was not only the herald of righteousness; he also embodied it himself. As Donald Senior remarks, "The entire purpose of Jesus's mission is to 'fulfill' or faithfully carry out all that his Father asks. In Matthew's perspective Jesus is God's Son not only because of his mysterious origin from God but also because of his faithful and loving obedience. This commitment to doing God's will is a powerful ethical motif of Matthew's Gospel, one demonstrated finally in Jesus's obedient death."[4] Part of what Senior is saying here is that Jesus's calling for disciples to be righteous means stepping into a relationship of trust with God by faith where his people trust and obey him.

This perspective on "righteousness" is established clearly in the famous Matthean Beatitudes (Matt 5:1–12). Jesus pronounces blessings on all different kinds of people, but in 5:6 he refers to those who "hunger and thirst for righteousness, for they will be filled." It is instructive, at the head of the Sermon on the Mount, that Jesus makes it a point to idealize and honor such people. They are starved by the wickedness of the world, bereft of justice, weary from corruption, longing for a sensible world. When I read about those who yearn and hunger for righteousness, for integrity and justice, I remember Isaiah's vineyard vision where the owner hungered for ripe grapes and sweet juice, but tasted the blood of malice; "he expected justice, but saw bloodshed" (Isa 5:7). But Jesus believed in hope—they who hunger for righteousness will taste that delicious fruit because the kingdom is near. God is making all things new and righteousness and justice will follow him like the train of a robe.

I am reminded of how this notion of hungering for righteousness and fulfilling all righteousness coheres with Matthew's version of the Lord's Prayer: *Your kingdom come, your will be done on earth as it is in heaven* (6:10). Both of these things belong together: longing for the kingdom and seeking to do God's will. In fact, that is exactly what righteousness entails. It is about living faithfully as a part of the gospel kingdom of Jesus Christ, where the people live rightly according to the will and ways of God. In fact, once I heard someone say that the "kingdom of God" is the place where God's will is done. In other words, it is a restored and renewed *righteous* kingdom.

---

4. Donald Senior, *The Gospel of Matthew*, Interpreting Biblical Texts (Nashville: Abingdon, 1997), 94.

When we look at it that way, it is no wonder that Jesus told his disciples not to worry about all the little things in their lives, but rather to "strive first for the kingdom of God and his righteousness, and all these things will be given to you as well" (Matt 6:33). The kingdom is not about this abstract thing called "heaven" or "salvation" or "justification." It is a society and a people that are about righteousness—living rightly toward God and each other in honesty, fairness, compassion, and justice. Jesus calls his followers to put this above any other concern, even worries over their food, their clothes, and their health. If the kingdom were embodied in a banner, it would say "righteousness," because the true and just king is righteous.

There is a shadow side to the pursuit of right living in the Gospel of Matthew. A people's desire to do what is "right" can lead to all kinds of wrongs, especially when there is no righteous ruler to guide them. In Matthew, the antitypes of true righteousness are the Pharisees. Now, it is important to note that popular portrayals today of the ancient Pharisees are misleading caricatures. They were not all hypocrites or legalists. What they were largely known for was passionate devotion to obeying God's word, a noble commitment indeed. But Jesus did denounce and criticize them for focusing only on selective ways of being "righteous" before God and in the world.

They had become used to regulating their behavior by following certain righteous practices of tithing. But Jesus accused them of failing at hungering and thirsting for righteousness (Matt 23; see also ch. 12 in this book). They had become comfortable with the way things were; they did not really want the disruptive, upheaval-causing, in-breaking kingdom of God. Jesus exclaims that John reached out to the religious leaders, showing them the "way of righteousness"—a new kingdom path to the fulfillment of all righteousness—but they refused to believe. But the tax collectors and prostitutes took notice, their ears perked up, and they followed (Matt 21:32). Why? Despite the fact that the religious elite called them "sinners," these "sinners" *knew* they were enmeshed within systems of injustice and wickedness. They knew they were broken people in a broken world. The Pharisees were blind to this. So it is with a smack of irony that Jesus said, "I have come to call not the righteous but sinners" (Matt 9:13). The so-called "righteous" do not hunger for the just kingdom. The sinners listen to Jesus and dream of that blessed world.

From this perspective, it makes all the sense in the world that Jesus called his followers to pursue a righteousness that "exceeds that of the scribes and Pharisees" in order to enter the kingdom of heaven (5:20). This might shock us because we might (mistakenly) think that "righteousness" is about being very religious. But by now hopefully it is clear that Jesus's "righteousness" is about the unpredictable, dynamic, Jesus-centered, justice-seeking, compassion-and-mercy-filled, anyone-and-everyone-is-welcome, heart-and-soul piercing kingdom come on earth as it is in heaven. The Pharisees believed they had arrived at a destination of pleasing God in their righteousness. The sinners who followed Jesus knew there was a long road ahead, but the kingdom door was open to them and hope shined forth.

So, for Matthew, "righteousness" was the word that often came to mind when pondering Jesus Christ (the Messiah-king), the kingdom, and the gospel. If Isaiah and the prophets were right, that God would bless the world with a new kingdom ruled by the Prince of Peace, then Jesus would be God's power and wisdom to reform the fractured world back into the shalom of the garden.

OTHER NEW TESTAMENT VOICES

2 Corinthians 5:21; 6:7; Galatians 2:21; Ephesians 4:24; 6:14; Philippians 3:9; 1 Timothy 6:11; James 1:20; Revelation 19:11

Romans

Sometimes Paul is portrayed as the "apostle of justification," teaching the imputed righteousness of Christ, not a gospel of righteousness and works. It is true that Paul did not believe anyone is made right with God by their personal righteousness. But to argue that Paul was not *interested at all* in personal and communal righteousness would require a severely reductionistic reading of his letters. Romans, for example, explains plainly that God alone saves, only God justifies and makes righteous, and this only by faith (Rom 1:16–17). But Romans also has much to say about God's vision for a just world.[5]

In Romans, Abraham is held up as an example of a believer who trusts God, and this trust is credited *as* covenantal righteousness (Rom 4:3, 9). The believer in Jesus is humble and surrendered to God, desiring to be transformed by the Spirit and to conform to the Son of God. It is true that in the first part of Romans (1–4), Paul's discussion of righteousness is about being right with God, reconciled by faith in Jesus Christ. But as we journey further into Paul's message in this letter, a wider perspective comes in view. Redemption is portrayed as a new life of service to God; believers are no longer in bondage to sin and death, but to *righteousness* (Rom 6:16). Surely Paul has in mind here the opposite of sin and death, portraying righteousness *as* an obedient and meaning-filled, justice-filled life. In 6:19, Paul explains that the righteous life is a consecrated life, a sanctified life that reflects the holiness of God.[6]

Toward the end of Romans, Paul casts a vision of the gospel kingdom life, the world redeemed and renewed by the living God. We might fight over matters of "food and drink" now (and such elements are necessary and good for our embodied selves), but the kingdom is all about peace, joy, and *righteousness* in the Holy Spirit (Rom 14:17). This verse is something like the Romans version of the fruit of the Spirit (see Gal 5:22–23). This messianic kingdom will be a perfect place *because* God will have brought all things into alignment and right purpose in Jesus Christ. Joy—because sin will not frustrate work, friendship, and play. Peace—because problems will be solved with honesty and integrity. And righteousness—because sin will not hold us back from seeking to do good and right for God and neighbor.

---

5. See Douglas Harink, *Resurrecting Justice: Reading Romans for the Life of the World* (Downers Grove, IL: InterVarsity Press, 2020).

6. On holiness, see chapter 13 of this book.

Righteousness for Today

The New Testament is all about righteousness, and righteousness is not religious piety. It is about honesty, transparency, personal integrity, faithfulness in relationships, justice-seeking in the world, and compassion and mercy toward the other, especially concern for the marginalized in society.

We have looked back to Isaiah for insight and wisdom on this, and it is helpful here to reflect once again on the eschatological vision of the prophet found in Isaiah 11:4–10. It is hailing the coming era of a great Davidic king who will bring peace and justice to the world. He will take concern for the poor "with righteousness" and "with justice" consider the meek of the earth (11:4 NIV). You may be familiar with some of the natural and animal imagery from 11:6–9:

> The wolf shall live with the lamb,
>> the leopard shall lie down with the kid,
> the calf and the lion and the fatling together;
>> and a little child shall lead them.
> The cow and the bear shall graze,
>> their young shall lie down together,
>> and the lion shall eat straw like the ox.
> The nursling child shall play over the hole of the asp,
>> and the weaned child shall put its hand on the adder's den.
> They will not hurt nor destroy
>> on all my holy mountain;
> for the earth will be full of the knowledge of the LORD
>> as the waters cover the sea.

These are not just playful images, but snapshots of a whole planet that lives in harmony, peace, and gentleness. But it is crucial to keep in mind that for Isaiah (and Matthew) the blessed hope of peace on earth will not happen by chance, magic, or sheer human grit. It will take leadership and guidance, judgment and reckoning—it will take a king. And as Isaiah says, "Righteousness shall be the belt around his waist, and faithfulness the belt around his loins" (11:5).

As we reflect on what the New Testament's theology of righteousness means for today, it is important to begin with "a right relationship with God."

Right with God in Jesus Christ

Solomon once said, "The fear of the LORD is the beginning of wisdom" (Prov 9:10). We might adapt that for this chapter and say, "The love of the LORD is the beginning of righteousness." Part of Jesus's message about the gospel of the kingdom is that seeking what is "right" as of first importance actually leads people down the wrong path. Just read the news or listen to the radio. There are too many problems to solve in the world—it's overwhelming. And there are so many proposed "solutions" to all these world problems. Who knows who is right? Jesus says, *don't worry*. Turn your attention away from worry and toward God. Seek his kingdom and righteousness. That means, trust Messiah Jesus, walk with him, follow in his footsteps. Then, all the other things will fall into place. You won't solve all the problems of the world with the snap of a finger, but you will know you are going in the right direction when it comes to "righteousness."

Upright Lives of Honesty and Integrity

Sometimes scholars have argued that the Greek word *dikaiosynē* (which is the word most often translated into English as "righteousness" in the New Testament) is better translated as (social) "justice" rather than (personal) "righteousness." This is only partly true.[7] Often when we talk about justice today, we think of something social or external, something we *do* out there in the world. The biblical use of *dikaiosynē* sometimes has that connotation. But often it describes a character trait, an innate and personal quality of what we call integrity today. It involves this idea that "I" am not two different persons, two-faced, hypocritical, chameleon-like. Rather, "I" am just me, trying to be my best self all the time, whether people are around or not. "I" try to live by conscience and a standard of innocence according to the moral commitments I

---

7. For those who want to follow the more intricate nuances of the lexical and theological debate about this, see Nicholas Wolterstorff, *Justice: Rights and Wrongs* (Princeton: Princeton University Press, 2010), 109–31.

have. Paul, for example, was under character attack by some people in Thessalonica. And he could plainly and boldly state that no one had any basis to accuse him: "You are witnesses [you, Thessalonian Christians], and God also, how pure, upright, and blameless our conduct was toward you believers" (1 Thess 2:10).

Yes, *dikaiosynē* relates to doing (justice), but at its core it is about *being*. It is a "who am I?" kind of characteristic. The Bible sometimes separates people into the categories of "righteous" and "wicked." The "righteous," of course, have committed to knowing, following, and loving God, but also they seek to cultivate the virtues of integrity and honesty in their hearts and souls.

Right with Others

Isaiah's righteousness, the psalmist's righteousness, Jesus's righteousness, they are not abstract activities of doing good and right things in the world. Those things are important (see below), but in many cases the righteousness they are referring to focuses on having "right" relationships with others. This is eminently modeled by God himself. As often as Israel praises God's righteousness, they especially recognize his covenant faithfulness toward them. For example, in Psalm 143 David calls upon God to be merciful and not to judge him for his sins, "for no one living is righteous before you" (143:2). David dares to ask for compassion and forgiveness from the Lord because he is the covenant God. So he says, "Give ear to my supplications in your faithfulness" (143:1). Sometimes we misunderstand righteousness by thinking it is a kind of robotic commitment to rules and moral laws. But because it is deeply relational, it is also messy. That leads us to the next dimension of righteousness—"right compassion."

Right Compassion

I used to think of righteousness as the objective and stoic judge on a pedestal with a gavel, perhaps with a blindfold, judging legal cases according to the letter of the law. But the Bible presents the image of a leader pursing righteousness that *includes* love, clemency, and compassion. The psalmist claims, "The Lord is gracious and righteous; our God is full of compassion. The Lord protects the unwary [i.e., the vulnerable]; when I was brought low, he saved me" (Ps 116:5–6 NIV). And when Jesus introduces the Beatitudes, he probably has the same blessed people in mind who are both hungering for righteousness (Matt 5:6) and showing mercy and compassion (Matt 5:7). Unfortunately, we too often put these things at odds. On social media I hear people screaming about how horrible and immoral "those people" are and how they should be shunned or punished, all in the name of justice. There is no love, charity, or compassion in these comments. There is judgment, rage, and malice masquerading as "righteousness." But then I think about Paul—also passionate about justice—who says to the Philippians, "Let your *gentleness* be known to everyone" (Phil 4:5). A better translation of the Greek word *epieikes* ("gentleness") here is something like "kindness" or "generous patience." Paul would say true justice must also be compassionate to all, generous and kind in patience and grace. There is no place in the Bible for coldhearted righteousness or angry justice.

"Right-Seeking" in an Unjust World

Finally, we come to the nature of biblical righteousness as justice and "right-seeking" in a dark and unjust world. The great big vision of the gospel taking root and growing in God's world is one of transformation of all of society—including relationships, economics, business, and politics. The tired, old polarization of the "spiritual gospel" vs. the "social gospel" resembles nothing of what Jesus, Paul, and the rest of the New Testament writers thought about righteousness. The social gospel carries the danger of caring for people but not doing it with worship of God at the center. The spiritual gospel turns the eye inward to one's own soul and is blind to the pitiable state of God's world, where creation groans for the body of Christ to bring healing. Righteousness is not just a status of being "right with God." It is not being a "good rule-follower," either. Transformed and transformative Jesus-following righteousness is on a mission to right the wrongs of the world to the glory of God. In a former house I lived in, we used to have a magnet of a Klimt painting that intentionally looks a bit crooked. We had it attached to a metal vent by our bed. Every now and again, we would notice that "someone" had turned the magnet to try and make it look right. Eventually, we realized our two-year-old daughter could not stand to see (what she thought was) a crooked magnet. She was compelled to make it "right." Would that we all would be like this child and hunger and thirst for making crooked things right!

Suggested Reading

Michael F. Bird. *The Saving Righteousness of God*. Eugene, OR: Wipf & Stock, 2007.

Walter Brueggemann. *The Prophetic Imagination*. Minneapolis: Fortress, 2018.

Katherine Grieb. *The Story of Romans: A Narrative Defense of God's Righteousness*. Louisville: Westminster John Knox, 2002.

Douglas Harink. *Resurrecting Justice: Reading Romans for the Life of the World*. Downers Grove, IL: IVP Academic, 2020.

Cynthia Long Westfall and Bryan R. Dyer, ed. *The Bible and Social Justice: Old Testament and New Testament Foundations for the Church's Urgent Call*. Eugene, OR: Pickwick, 2016.

N. T. Wright. *Evil and the Justice of God*. Downers Grove, IL: IVP Academic, 2013.

CHAPTER 2

Gospel

God's Good News for the
Life of the World

The Gospel of Mark

In high school, I was in our drama club's production of *Godspell*. Most people in the pews or on the streets probably don't know that "Godspell" is an old English translation of the Greek word *euangelion*, which is rendered today as "gospel" or "good news"—God + spell (news/announcement). You don't hear people use the language of "gospel" much in popular society today, except perhaps as a relic of Christian usage. So we have "gospel music," or we might say "it's the gospel truth," meaning the idea or story is completely reliable. While to us "gospel" sounds like a technical religious term, when the earliest Christians used *euangelion* in relation to Jesus, they were communicating in ordinary, plain language. *Euangelion* just means "good news," or "announcement of good fortune." Think about it this way. In the late 1930's, confectioner Ben Myerson named his new candy bar "Good News" to announce the birth of his son. The style and wording of the wrapper was meant to look like a newspaper headline, and the only other key word on the front of the wrapper was "Celebrate!"

So, for the first Christians, "gospel" was not about religion per se, heaven, or the Bible. It was all about the great news that God was fulfilling his plan to save the world. Even though "gospel" is not a technical term, it is still more than worthwhile to explore the nuances of how "good news" language appears in the Old Testament, and its connotations in the Greco-Roman world as well.

Old Testament Background

"Good news" is all over the Old Testament. Despite many misleading popular assumptions today that the people of God in the Old Testament period lived in misery and drudgery, we find celebration of God's goodness and his covenant faithfulness from Genesis to Malachi. But once we get into the Major Prophets, we see a particular conception develop for how Israel thought about "good news" on a larger scale—the redemption of divided, broken, homeless, and downtrodden Israel. The clearest and most important case study for this "gospel" hope of Israel is the book of Isaiah. More specifically, Isaiah 40–66 offers the prophet's vision of Israel's consolation.

For example, Isaiah 40:9 projects a vision of a messenger sent to announce a special report to weary Israel.

> Get you up to a high mountain,
>   O Zion, herald of good tidings;
> lift up your voice with strength,
>   O Jerusalem, herald of good tidings,
>   lift it up, do not fear;
> say to the cities of Judah,
>   "Here is your God!"

Isaiah did not use "good news" as a technical term for "the gospel," that is, salvation through Jesus Christ. The "good news" prophesied by Isaiah was all about the great promises of the covenantal God coming together with the reassuring word, "Here is your God!" Israel struggled deeply with being strangers in a strange land, their home and temple destroyed. The question echoed in their minds and hearts, "Where is our savior God?" I mentioned *Godspell* earlier, one of my favorite musicals (with incredible music, I must add). When I think of Israel's plight in exile, I cannot help but remember the *Godspell* song, "On the Willows," transparently a rendition of Psalm 137. Here is the complete Old Testament psalm.

> By the rivers of Babylon—
>> there we sat down and there we wept
>> when we remembered Zion.
> On the willows there
>> we hung up our harps.
> For there our captors
>> asked us for songs,
> and our tormentors asked for mirth, saying,
>> "Sing us one of the songs of Zion!"
>
> How could we sing the LORD's song
>> in a foreign land?
> If I forget you, O Jerusalem,
>> let my right hand wither!
> Let my tongue cling to the roof of my mouth,
>> if I do not remember you,
> if I do not set Jerusalem
>> above my highest joy.
>
> Remember, O LORD, against the Edomites
>> the day of Jerusalem's fall,
> how they said, "Tear it down! Tear it down!
>> Down to its foundations!"
> O daughter Babylon, you devastator!
>> Happy shall they be who pay you back
>> what you have done to us!
> Happy shall they be who take your little ones
>> and dash them against the rock!

It is against this kind of backdrop that the "good news" of God's herald is so refreshing. The beatific vision of the restoration of Israel is even more vivid in Isaiah 52; the vibrant "gospel" for Israel is on full display.

> How beautiful upon the mountains
>> are the feet of the messenger who announces peace,
> who brings good news,
>> who announces salvation,
>> who says to Zion, "Your God reigns."
> Listen! Your sentinels lift up their voices,
>> together they sing for joy;
> for in plain sight they see
>> the return of the Lord to Zion.
> Break forth together into singing,
>> you ruins of Jerusalem;
> for the Lord has comforted his people,
>> he has redeemed Jerusalem.
> The Lord has bared his holy arm
>> before the eyes of all the nations;
> and all the ends of the earth shall see
>> the salvation of our God. (Isa 52:7–10)

Israel's "gospel" is not about heaven and the "afterlife." It is not about appeasing a wrathful God. It's about a new creation and the renewal of all things. God swoops in and comes to his people. He frees them from bondage; he restores them to their home and rebuilds their city. He battles against their oppressors and brings justice and peace to a chaotic world.

You are probably aware that eventually Israel was permitted by the Persian ruler to send a group back to their land to rebuild their city and temple. *Was this the "good news" Isaiah was talking about?* Certainly Israel rejoiced at the work of God in all of this, but history reveals that the years ahead—under Greek and eventually Roman rulers—were not especially kind. The Jewish people did rebuild the temple and reestablish their worship practices as prescribed in their Scriptures (more or less). But most Jews felt that life after exile did not quite live up to Isaiah's grandiose dream.

The Greco-Roman World

When Jesus or the apostle Paul went around preaching about "good news," almost certainly the ears of fellow Jews would have perked up, conjuring up again Isaiah's depiction of the full renewal of Israel. But I wonder: what if a pagan, a non-Jew, happened to be listening? What would come to mind when Paul (for example) said, "I am here to proclaim *the good news* to you"? Keep in mind, the Greek word *euangelion* ("good news") was not technical religious language. Just like Myerson's candy bar, it could refer to any kind of happy report. The pagan would *not* have had Isaiah in mind, of course. But could there have been some kind of grandiose conception of salvation connected to *euangelion* in their own cultural consciousness? Perhaps.

While "good news" did not have a particularly *religious* connotation for pagans, it may have evoked political ideas of the security and peace of the Roman empire. The word *euangelion* (and related forms) were sometimes found in public and political writings. For example, an inscription in Priene (western Asia Minor) was displayed by local subjects of the Roman emperor Caesar Augustus, celebrating his rulership. It affirms that divine providence gave Emperor Augustus as a gift of imperial leadership to the people. It names him as a "savior" (*sotēr*) who ends wars and strife. He is hailed as the climax of Roman hope (*elpis*). So the year of Augustus's birth ought to be commemorated as "the beginning of good news."[1] Less than a century after the Priene Inscription was posted, Mark began his story with "The beginning of the *good news* about Jesus the Messiah, the Son of God" (Mark 1:1 NIV). In the ancient world, there was no sharp divide between religion and politics. In fact, many imperial subjects revered the emperors as godlike figures or honored them alongside the gods.[2] This makes a world of a difference when the early Christians preached, sang, and confessed a "gospel" about their own "savior" who ruled as "Son of God."[3]

---

1. *Orientis Graeci Inscriptiones Selectae* 458, lines 32–42, as cited in Daniel Lynwood Smith, *Into the World of the New Testament* (London: Bloomsbury, 2015), 40.

2. See Bruce W. Winter, *Divine Honours for the Caesars* (Grand Rapids: Eerdmans, 2015).

3. In the Roman world, sometimes rulers were referred to as "son of [a] god"; see Smith, *Into the World of the New Testament*, 45.

Focal Text: Mark

The beginning of the good news about Jesus the Messiah, the Son of God.
(1:1 NIV)

The language of "gospel" technically appears more frequently in other Gospels (especially the Gospel of Luke), but what is especially intriguing about Mark is that *euangelion* is found in his first sentence (in fact, it is the third word of that sentence, in Greek). That first sentence probably serves as a guiding note for the whole gospel— "The beginning of the good news about Jesus the Messiah, the Son of God" (1:1 NIV). David Garland explains that Mark chose to offer this prescriptional note, as it were, at the head of his work to signal what was most important in what followed. "He focuses . . . on the facets that form the basis of the belief that Jesus is the Christ and the Son of God. In this introduction, the audience alone receives vital, behind-the-scenes information that remains hidden in various degrees to all of the human characters when the rest of the drama begins."[4] In other words, the prescript serves as a kind of "cheat sheet," identifying Mark's main concerns.

What does Mark mean when he writes, "The beginning"? *The beginning of what?* Looking ahead at the introductory portion of the Gospel of Mark, it could be a reference to the ministry of John the Baptist (Mark 1:2–8) or to the first major section of Mark (1:2–13). But there is also a case to make that Mark 1:1 serves as a title or summary of the entire gospel story. The ending of the Gospel of Mark is abrupt. Mary Magdalene, Mary the mother of James, and Salome go to the tomb, intending to anoint the dead body of Jesus. After seeing the open tomb, they are commanded by an angel to go to Galilee and proclaim the resurrection of Jesus to Peter and the others. Mark's Gospel simply ends with this report: "So they went out and fled from the tomb, for terror and amazement had seized them, and they said nothing to anyone, for they were afraid" (Mark 16:8). This might seem like a strange way to end a gospel, but Mark intended the readers to connect the dots

---

4. David Garland, *A Theology of Mark's Gospel* (Grand Rapids: Zondervan Academic, 2015), 183.

and realize that the women *did* proclaim the risen Jesus and a great movement exploded. Mark's gospel story, then, is "just the beginning." The plan was set into motion to see the whole world transformed by the "good news."

But what *is* the "news" that Mark wanted to proclaim in his story? Of course, it took sixteen chapters for him to tell that story, but in one word it is about *Jesus*. He is the object and substance of Mark's *good news*. Jesus is at the center of the plan of Israel's God to rescue and restore his people. Alongside the name and person of Jesus, Mark also connects "the beginning of the good news" to Jesus *as* "Messiah" (or Christ). Now is not the time to go into great depth about how Israel came to hope in a messiah and why, but suffice it to say this figure was expected to do much more than escort them to heaven.[5] Not all Jews in Jesus's time kept hopeful watch for the arrival of a messiah, but some did. For example, the Jewish text titled the Psalms of Solomon offers a vivid picture of what the messiah would accomplish. He would be a great king, like David, to reign over Israel. In this role, he would "shatter unrighteous rulers" (17.21–22). He would purify Israel and destroy wicked nations (vv. 23–25). He would unite a fractured Israel and lead them into righteousness (v. 26).

This royal messiah would be a man of integrity and honesty, not lusting after money or power. His singular focus would be to please God and serve his people "with wisdom and gladness" (17.35). He would teach with godly wisdom and serve as a trustworthy judge. He would be so aligned with the wisdom and purposes of God that it is as if the Lord himself ruled as king again over Israel (v. 46).

One can see that the Jesus of Mark's Gospel comfortably fits into so many features of this kind of messianic portrait (but not all of them, as we will see later). It is also no wonder that Jesus associated the "good news of God" with the kingdom. "The time is fulfilled, and the kingdom of God has come near; repent and believe in the good news!" (Mark 1:15).

---

5. See Andrew Abernethy and Gregory Goswell, *God's Messiah in the Old Testament* (Grand Rapids: Baker, 2020); Stanley E. Porter, ed., *The Messiah in the Old and New Testaments* (Grand Rapids: Eerdmans, 2007); Michael F. Bird, *Are You the One Who Is to Come? The Historical Jesus and the Messianic Question* (Grand Rapids: Baker Academic, 2009).

Kingdom of God → Messiah → Good News

This all seems to invoke that beautiful vision that Isaiah talked about—a restored and unified Israel basking in the presence, goodness, and glory of God. For Isaiah, for Jesus, for Mark, the "good news" was not simply a condition (saved, happy, blessed), nor just a place (Zion, heaven); it was a kingdom with a good king. Mark describes the kind of kingdom that Jesus announces as unified (3:24), prosperous (4:32), glorious and full of power (9:1), generous and humble, caring for and attentive to all (10:14, 23–25), and full of love for God and neighbor (12:32–34). Wouldn't the arrival of such a kingdom and community be *good news?*

But notice that Jesus called for repentance and faith. Such a glorious kingdom could not come without a cost. After all, the Roman emperor thought *he* ruled the world. The prefect Pontius Pilate thought *he* governed over Judea. And the puppet king Herod laid claim to the throne of Israel. Some Jews allied themselves to Herod in hopes of power and reward. Others gave up hope altogether. It would have been both stirring and challenging, then, to hear Jesus proclaim, *the time has come, a new kingdom must confront the incumbent.* Everyone would be able to read between the lines or hear what was not said—*this means war.*

Anyone who subscribed to a messiah and kingdom ideology similar to what is found in Psalms of Solomon 17 would have seen this as a signal to take up arms. But Jesus taught an entirely different way to challenge the worldly kingdoms. Not with the weapons of war, but with the weapons of truth, love, and covenantal obedience to God. Salvation does not come from destroying the other, but from giving oneself to God and loving one's enemies. Notice how good news/gospel appears in this key statement from Jesus in Mark 8: "For those who want to save their life will lose it, and those who lose their life for my sake, and for the sake of the gospel, will save it" (8:35; cf. 10:29). For some disciples, this actually might have involved martyrdom: "You must be on your guard. You will be handed over to the local councils and flogged in the synagogues. On account of me you will stand before governors and kings as witnesses to them. And the gospel [*euangelion*] must first be preached to all nations" (13:9–10 NIV). Being a part of this "good news" kingdom of God is a privilege and blessing, but it also comes at a price. Most kings seek a kingdom where they can be exalted. And they often take that kingdom by force. In order for Jesus to establish a truly righteous and benevolent kingdom of God, his kingship must be different. So, in Mark we hear Jesus say, "The Son of Man came not to be served but to serve, and to give his life a ransom for many" (Mark 10:45). This was meant as a model also for others to imitate: "Whoever wants to be my disciple must deny themselves and take up their cross and follow me" (Mark 8:34 NIV).

It should go without saying (but I will say it anyway) that the "good news" of Jesus's kingdom of God comes to a climax in his self-sacrifice on the cross. The kingdom *will* be a resurrection kingdom, but death cannot be circumvented or pushed aside. So the "good news" that will change the world carries "bad news" for Jesus—he will be betrayed, he will suffer, and then he will die. We ought not to underestimate the weight of this darkness. In the garden of Gethsemane, he tells his disciples that the anguish of the moment and his fate is suffocating him (14:34).

The "gospel" of Jesus Christ, as Mark helps us to see, is not a theological formula for salvation. It is not a road map to heaven. It is the message of what God has done, is doing, and will do in fulfillment of his promises to bring a glorious, beautiful, just, and unifying kingdom, a kingdom with Jesus as Lord and Messiah.

A final thing to emphasize about the "gospel" as Mark conceives of this word: It is not only good news for the people of Israel but a proclamation of good fortune for the *whole* world. In Mark 14 we find the story of the woman who anoints Jesus's head with fragrant oil. Some of the men who were with Jesus rebuked her, but Jesus praised her. She saw beyond the present moment and recognized that she was pre-anointing the body of Jesus that would soon be dead. But anointing was also a ritual performed to consecrate a king. According to Mark, this unnamed woman is one of the wisest characters in his story; she sees the gospel summed up in the presence and person of Jesus. Just as she rightly recognizes him, so *she too* will be remembered: "Truly I tell you, wherever the good news is proclaimed in the whole world, what she has done will be told in remembrance of her" (14:9). But *why* would people retell this woman's story? Because she looked at the simple, humble Galilean Jesus and saw Israel's true king and messiah, Israel's hope and consolation. And, even more, she saw that the path to and through the cross was *part* of his kingship, a leader leading through service, a sage demonstrating wisdom through foolishness, a prophet prophesying his own death and new life for those with ears to hear.

OTHER NEW TESTAMENT VOICES

Matthew 4:23; 11:4–5; 13:31–33; Luke 2:10–11; 4:18–19; Acts 8:12; Romans 16:25–26; Galatians 3:8; 2 Thessalonians 2:13–14; 2 Timothy 2:8–9

Philippians

Paul's apostolic ministry began *after* the death and resurrection of Jesus, but the apostolic era was still in that exciting beginning phase of God's gospeling work he was performing through the church. Paul could have referred to his own ministry as part of "the beginning of the good news." Scholars have sometimes highlighted the differences between Jesus and Paul, but it is obvious they both focus on the fulfillment of the "good news" work of God.

There is something peculiar about the way Paul uses the language of gospel (*euangelion, euangelizō*) in Philippians. Yes, it is a message, but it is so much more. He uses this language as if it is also representative of an ethos to embody and a mission (or task) to complete. For example, Paul challenges the Philippian Christians to live their lives in community in a manner worthy of the "gospel of Christ" (1:27). Here "gospel" is conceived of as much more than a story of God's activities; it is a standard, an oath, an ethos, a guide for the *way* Christians should live. High standards. Best practices. The "gospel" represents something valued and Christians anywhere and everywhere are expected to contribute positively to the nobility or sanctity of that standard.

Second, the gospel is a task. It is not simply a doctrine. It is a worldwide mission. Allow me to use a bit of a strange example. Take the

Google Maps cars. They have a job to map the whole world. It's not enough to do half the world. They have a task to cover the globe. Some places are easy to reach and map, while other places are hard, but the job ain't done until it's done. Of course, the gospel is more important than creating "Street View Maps," but I hope it helps to give us a sense of how Paul thinks about the apostolic duty he shares with his churches. He talks about *advancing* the gospel (1:12) as if it is something special that all people need in their lives (like "upgrading" their lives, though it is much more important than a new iOS version).

One way that Paul talks about the gospel mission is as if it were a series of wars waged to conquer the whole world (Phil 4:3). One might shudder at the notion of a type of colonizing war, but keep in mind that Paul's weapons are love and goodness. When Paul claims this message, ministry, mission, and ethos is "good news," he really means it; it is vivifying and conducive to flourishing for all people everywhere, Jew or gentile, male or female, Roman or non-Roman, rich or poor, slave or free.

The Gospel for Today

What would Mark think about how we use the word "gospel" today? I am afraid Mark might be disappointed. Modern Western Christians tend to relate the term "gospel" to the concept of salvation. That's fine. But we also tend to relate "salvation" to religious conversion and the afterlife. When I was a teenager, I was trained to do door-to-door evangelism. In this training, I was told to ask strangers, "How sure are you that you will go to heaven when you die?" This was meant to be my lead-in to share "the gospel." In that context, the "gospel" was telling people to accept Jesus into their hearts, say the Sinner's Prayer, and connect them with a church. We also encouraged people to pray and to read and obey the Bible. These are all fine things, but is that what Jesus (and Mark) meant by "gospel"? By focusing on the gospel as leading to a heavenly home and a set of religious practices, it was still "good news" to many people, but often it was not holistically transformative. I remember reading a story in which a Jewish person was explaining the difference between his religion (Judaism) and that of a Christian from his perspective. He said, "We Jews practice our religion every day, and Christians practice their religion only on Sunday." When I read this, it stung; it may be inaccurate for some Christians, but all too often modern Christians have a Sunday faith, and sometimes not even that. At the core, those who have an afterlife faith or a Sunday faith just don't understand the gospel—certainly not how Mark and the other New Testament writers understood it.

But where are we to begin in enlarging our understanding of the gospel? I think we must start with confronting the bad news. The greater our awareness of the deep darkness, evil, and brokenness that has affected the whole world, and our individual lives as well, the more it will become relevant that there is a problem in need of a solution. In the summer of 2012, my family moved from Seattle to Philadelphia. We took a long but wonderful road trip across the country. But on the way, our youngest daughter got sick with a fever. Long story short, we took her to the doctor in Philly, and she was diagnosed with leukemia. Talk about "bad news." If you are a parent, it is pretty much the worst news imaginable (she was fifteen months old at the time). Even though we were strangers in a new city, didn't yet have a place to live, and I was starting a new job; even still, everything in our lives got sucked into the vortex of chemotherapy. The bad news not only cut our hearts to the deepest place but also consumed our thoughts almost every minute. We needed a bigger and stronger word than "bad" for this bad news.

BUT—there was good news (bigger and greater than good news). Yes, cancer is bad. It sucks. But once you get into the "cancer club," there is "good cancer" and "bad cancer." Our daughter had the good kind, because it was treatable with a reasonably high rate of success. And the good news got better. Before we moved to Philly, we knew nothing about the hospitals there. But we found ourselves basically living in Children's Hospital of Philadelphia (CHOP) for a few weeks. I remember logging on to their Wi-Fi in our little hospital room on the oncology floor. I typed in something like "ranking children's hospitals." That year (2012) CHOP was the #1 children's hospital for pediatric oncology in the entire United States. Out of hundreds of institutions, it was the best. *That was good news.* That wasn't pie-in-the-sky good news. It was not Sunday good news with hymns and a cup of cheap coffee.

It meant *everything* to us. Can you imagine "good news" on a scale and magnitude that your heart is forever taken to a whole other level of hope and joy? Our daughter is now ten years old and cancer free. We see such a bright radiance in her life, especially because we know the deepest, blackest darkness of 2012.

When we think about the backstory before the "good news" of Jesus Christ in the Bible, we have to understand that Jews in particular knew and felt that the whole world was marred, corrupted, and desolate. In Psalm 14, David confesses, "The LORD looks down from heaven on humankind to see if there are any who are wise, who seek after God. They have all gone astray, they are all alike perverse; there is no one who does good, no, not one" (14:2–3). For Jesus to come running through the streets, yelling, "It's happening! It's happening! Good news! Good news! Isaiah was right"—that is a world-changing event.

If Mark is right, the gospel is good news to a people who see and experience a world devastated by sin, evil, and corruption.

If Mark is right, the gospel is the announcement of the hope of change that does not focus on a religious formula, but on a living relationship with the Lord Messiah Jesus.

If Mark is right, the gospel as he recorded it is just the "beginning," a holy mission that is meant to spread out and consume the entire cosmos, bringing light, joy, and goodness to every person and place.

Suggested Reading

Matthew W. Bates. *Salvation by Allegiance Alone*. Grand Rapids: Baker Academic, 2017.

Michael F. Bird. *Evangelical Theology: A Biblical and Systematic Introduction*. Grand Rapids: Zondervan, 2013.

David Garland. *A Theology of Mark's Gospel*. Grand Rapids: Zondervan, 2015. Pages 188–94.

Suzanne Watts Henderson. "The 'Good News' of God's Coming Reign: Occupation at a Crossroads." *Interpretation* 70.2 (2016): 145–58.

N. T. Wright. *Simply Good News: Why the Gospel Is News and What Makes It Good*. New York: HarperOne, 2015.

CHAPTER 3

Forgiveness

Releasing and Restoring to Make Whole

Luke-Acts

One of my pet peeves is that feeling of being restrained or held back by something. Have you ever started driving your car, and something feels off, sluggish, or slow, and you realize that you were driving with the parking brake on? Once you take that brake off, all of a sudden the car moves forward faster and more freely. In a way, that is how the Bible portrays forgiveness. Today we often think of forgiveness primarily in terms of guilt and freedom—like when a car insurance company offers "first accident forgiveness" so your premiums don't go up the first time you get into a fender bender. Sure, that is technically a type of forgiveness, but you don't *really* have a relationship with your insurance company, so it is not a personal kind of forgiveness; it's a business deal.

In the Bible, forgiveness has to do with sin, of course, but ultimately it is something that happens in the context of a personal relationship with God. Human sin causes us to carry around this burden, this weight of having harmed the relationship, broken trust. Forgiveness on God's part is not just "forgive and forget." God's love and grace frees sinful mortals from the burden of guilt and shame—much like releasing that parking brake. The author of Hebrews didn't have a Toyota, so he couldn't have used my analogy, but the one he *did* use is pretty good, too.

> Let us throw off everything that hinders and the sin that so easily entangles. And let us run with perseverance the race marked out for us, fixing our eyes on Jesus, the pioneer and perfecter of faith. (Heb 12:1b–2a NIV)

Notice what Hebrews assumes: freedom doesn't mean roaming "freely" but rather running the race fixed on Jesus. Forgiveness draws us closer to God.

Old Testament Background: Forgiveness

Before we can talk about the theological importance of forgiveness in the Old Testament, we need to begin with God's relationship with his people Israel. God heard the cries of his people who were suffering as slaves in Egypt. He freed them from their bondage and led them away (the word "exodus" means "path out of [slavery]"). More important than Israel's merely escaping Egypt was God giving Israel its own land and establishing a temple and kingdom. First, though, they camped at Mount Sinai, God set his covenant expectations for obedience before them, and Israel agreed to the terms (Exod 24:7). But as the story goes, Israel did not keep God's commandments—they worshiped a calf-idol only shortly after this covenant ratification (32:7–8). Now, it would have been within God's covenantal rights to reject and abandon his people—they knew the risks (Josh 24:20). But because of his righteousness, his mercy, and his love, he committed himself to them (Deut 31:6). In fact, over the years the Jewish people came to associate their God with this foundational covenantal affirmation of the divine identity:

> The LORD, the LORD,
> a God merciful and gracious,
> slow to anger,
> and abounding in steadfast love and faithfulness,

> keeping steadfast love for the thousandth generation,
> forgiving iniquity and transgression and sin,
> yet by no means clearing the guilty,
> but visiting the iniquity of the parents
> upon the children
> and the children's children,
> to the third and the fourth generation. (Exod 34:6–7)

There is a lot of messy-relationship reality in this long identity statement, but notice how the very *first* thing said about the Lord is that he is "compassionate and gracious," quick to forgive sin and disobedience. Hundreds of years after this post-exodus testimony of the forgiving God, having returned from Babylonian exile, Israel reflects on the ongoing mercy-filled faithfulness of God:

> They refused to obey, and were not mindful of the wonders that you performed among them; but they stiffened their necks and determined to return to their slavery in Egypt. But you are a God ready to forgive, gracious and merciful, slow to anger and abounding in steadfast love, and you did not forsake them. (Neh 9:17)

So *this* God forgives, that is an essential part of his identity. That seems pretty amazing, but what exactly does this "forgiveness" entail? After all, the Lord often punished his "forgiven" people (see again Exod 34:7).

Atoning Forgiveness

One way to look at the whole matter of forgiveness in the Old Testament is through the sacrificial system that was an essential part of Israel's worship. Some forms of sacrifice were about celebration and thanksgiving, but other offerings were due to sin. The biblical language of "atonement" is all about "covering" over sin (cf. Pss 32:1; 85:2). The Old Testament does not express the logic of what exactly is covered, how, and why, but one sensible guess is that the blood of an animal stands as a temporary substitute for the life of the covenant breaker (i.e., the sinner; see Heb 9:22). We must keep a few things in mind, though, when it comes to Old Testament sacrifice. First of all, God does not eat food, so the sacrifice is not a bribe. It is an important act of repentance and remorse. Secondly, it is not the sacrifice itself that solves the problem of sin; it is the gracious, forgiving nature of Israel's God (see 1 John 1:9). Along these lines, we can make the following statements about forgiveness according to the Old Testament and the Mosaic covenant:

- God's forgiveness does not prevent punishment.
- God's forgiveness expects repentance.
- Israel often questioned and pleaded with a silent or angry God.

God's Forgiveness Does Not Prevent Punishment

We have a modernistic assumption today that forgiveness means there will be no negative consequences for bad decisions. But this is not always the case, even today. Sometimes, forgiven people still have the responsibility to make things right, to repair what was broken or ruined. For example, according to the book of Numbers, God showed mercy to his rebellious people when they sinned in the wilderness as they wandered for forty years. In his love and care, he forgave them (14:18a): "Yet he does not leave the guilty unpunished" (14:18b NIV). He promised not to abandon them, but he expects to discipline them as his children who need to learn from their mistakes (Deut 8:5).

God's Forgiveness Expects Repentance

A related point to make about the merciful nature of Israel's God is that, although he is quick to forgive, he also expects his people to confess their sins and repent. When Solomon built the temple for the Lord, God agreed to make this a special place for his glory to reside. But he also warned Solomon that his presence would be contingent upon Israel maintaining a faithful relationship with him. If this people sinned, they would have to make things right: "If my people who are called by my name humble themselves, pray, seek my face, and turn from their wicked ways, then I will hear from heaven, and will forgive their sin and heal their land" (2 Chron 7:14; cf. Ps 7:12).

Similarly, the prophet Ezekiel warned Israel that penalties were about to come for a wayward people. So, they should repent and turn away from sin, or face consequences from the Lord. They were warned that failure to act would result in *death*! Repentance is not about simply saying sorry or showing remorse. It is a whole-life change. Turning around from going the wrong way, and then moving intentionally in the *opposite* direction. To truly accomplish this, Ezekiel explained that Israel needed a new heart and spirit (18:31). The situation was dire: "Turn, then, and live" (18:32).

Israel Often Questioned and Pleaded with a Silent or Angry God

Human relationships are complex—and so is a relationship with a personal God. Even though the Lord, God of Israel was essentially known as a merciful, loving, patient God, the people of Israel also developed in the Old Testament a sense of fear, anxiousness, and grief that this same God was absent or silent. The Psalms are a helpful place to look for Israel's ruminations on this paradoxical phenomenon: divine anger and and divine comfort. Psalm 130 expresses Israel's confident hopes in the clemency of God.

> Out of the depths I cry to you, O Lord.
>> Lord, hear my voice!
> Let your ears be attentive
>> to the voice of my supplications!
>
> If you, O Lord, should mark iniquities,
>> Lord, who could stand?
> But there is forgiveness with you,
>> so that you may be revered.
>
> I wait for the Lord, my soul waits,
>> and in his word I hope;
> my soul waits for the Lord
>> more than those who watch for the morning,
>> more than those who watch for the morning.

O Israel, hope in the LORD!
> For with the LORD there is steadfast love,
> and with him is great power to redeem.
It is he who will redeem Israel
> from all its iniquities. (130:1–8)

Look at the sense of confidence and assurance here, that Israel will meet a gentle and tender God. This resonates with a text like Micah 7:18: "Who is a God like you, pardoning iniquity and passing over the transgression of the remnant of your possession? He does not retain his anger forever, because he delights in showing clemency." And yet, in the Old Testament there are also occasions where Israel senses the unforgiving silence or judgment of God. For example, in the aptly named book of Lamentations, the people confess, "We have transgressed and rebelled, and you have not forgiven. You have wrapped yourself with anger and pursued us, killing without pity; you have wrapped yourself with a cloud so that no prayer can pass through. You have made us filth and rubbish among the peoples" (Lam 3:42–45). Similarly, the Lord commanded the prophet Hosea to call his daughter "Lo-Ruhamah" (not loved), "For I will certainly not forgive their guilt" (Hos 1:6 NET). *How can God be both merciful and also obstinately unforgiving?*

Breaking the Cycle of Sin

It may be helpful to distinguish between two kinds of forgiveness: "maintenance" forgiveness and "transformative" forgiveness. Maintenance forgiveness involves "letting go" of the wrong and releasing the sinner from guilt (though some punishment may still be involved). Maintenance forgiveness allows the relationship to continue. This is what often happens in the Old Testament through confession, sacrifice, and penitence. But we can also talk about transformative forgiveness, where God changes their hearts and spirits to enable them to enter into a deeper union with him and bring a greater healing to their relationship. This "transformative forgiveness" was promised by God as part of a "new covenant." This was not a *whole new deal* but a transformation of their previously established covenantal relationship.

The law would be written on their hearts and they would experience intimacy and trust like never before (Jer 31:33). It was precisely this transformative "forgiveness of sins" Israel longed for. Again, it was far more than the wiping away of a charge or accusation—it would pave the way forward for a richer, deeper, more fruitful life with God in covenant. When would this happen? And how?

Forgiveness in Luke and Acts

He Preached a Baptism of Repentance for the Forgiveness of Sins

Sometimes I hear a popular myth repeated that Luke wrote a gentile-oriented Gospel (vs. Matthew's more "Jewish" Gospel). While it is true that Luke gives special attention to Jesus's care for the outsider, it is simply wrong to state that Luke's Gospel is "less Jewish" than Matthew's. Notice, Luke's Gospel begins with the life of a Jewish priest (Zechariah). Luke was also interested in the fulfillment of Jewish Scripture (Luke 2:23; 3:4; 4:4, 8, 10, 17; 7:27; 19:46; 24:46). He cared deeply about what the gospel of Messiah Jesus would mean for Israel's salvation (Luke 1:16, 54, 68; 2:25, 32; 24:21). This matter is crucially important for looking at the Third Gospel (and Acts) when it comes to understanding what Luke means when he refers to the "forgiveness of sins." It is no coincidence that Luke is more interested in "forgiveness" as a gospel concept than any other New Testament writer. There is a rather straightforward reason for this—Luke wants to pick up where Jeremiah 31 left off. Jeremiah imagines a new day and a new (or renewed) covenant with Israel, when the bondage of sin no longer infects and toxifies their relationship with God. When that happens, "I will forgive their iniquity, and remember their sin no more" (Jer 31:34). We sometimes associate forgiveness with "freedom"—releasing someone from a penalty. But as Luke sees it, there is much more to it than that. It is "Jeremiah forgiveness," "The Big One," the kind of transformative forgiveness that shifts the relationship to another level of blessing, union, and intimacy. Later Jeremiah describes the aftereffect of this forgiveness as the foundation of a new city of God that bustles with life and joy.

And this city shall be to me a name of joy, a praise and a glory before all the nations of the earth who shall hear of all the good that I do for them; they shall fear and tremble because of all the good and all the prosperity I provide for it. (Jer 33:9)

I want you to think about what Jeremiah is saying here. Imagine it in your head—the sights, smells, sounds, and celebrations of blessed Zion. Now imagine Israel waiting. Waiting hundreds and hundreds of years. Longing and dreaming and waiting. And waiting. And then . . .

Luke's opening scene is of a Jewish priest, Zechariah, and his wife, Elizabeth. They are meant to have a special child. All children are special, of course, but inspired by the Holy Spirit, Zechariah prophesies that this child will be a turning point toward the Jeremiah fulfillment of God's redemption. This child will catch Israel's attention in preparation for the coming king (Luke 1:76). This child who will be called "John" will bring to light the hope of "salvation through the forgiveness of their sins, because of the tender mercy of our God, by which the rising sun will come to us from heaven to shine on those living in darkness and in the shadow of death, to guide our feet into the path of peace" (1:77–79 NIV).

Once we transition to seeing John the Baptist in action, he goes around all of Judea "proclaiming a baptism of repentance for the forgiveness of sins" (3:3). Now, Jesus had not yet even launched his ministry, so what exactly did this baptism mean? John's baptism was not the Christian rite of initiation into faith in Jesus Christ. Yet, it was an important period for Israel, because it was *the beginning of the beginning of the gospel*. It is like standing out in the rain, waiting for your ride home to show up. You are cold and miserable, shivering and looking in the far distance for headlights. Then you *finally* see a car coming, hurray! That car is John. You are so happy to get in and close the door—you're not even close to home yet, but the journey has begun.[1]

That is the beginning. But before we make our way through the middle of Luke, it is worth looking ahead to the end his first book (the Third Gospel). Just as it commences with the hope of forgiveness, so it

---

1. For more on John the Baptist, see Darrell Bock, *Luke 1–9:50*, Baker Exegetical Commentary on the New Testament (Grand Rapids: Baker, 1994), 289.

ends too, when the risen Jesus says to his disciples: "Thus it is written, that the Messiah is to suffer and to rise from the dead on the third day, and that repentance and forgiveness of sins is to be proclaimed in his name to all nations, beginning from Jerusalem. You are witnesses of these things" (24:46–48). These are essentially the final words of Jesus before he ascends, so the path is cleared to begin the story again with Acts 1:1.

What does all this mean for Luke? It means that the grand story the Old Testament tells about God's covenant with Israel, one devastated by sin and rebellion, has begun a new chapter and is moving toward the glorious vision painted by the prophets of joy, peace, and prosperity in communion with the God who is present (remember Jer 33:9). This is transformative forgiveness.

No Forgiveness without Repentance

Notice too that Luke includes John's and Jesus's emphasis on *repentance*. Luke dwells on forgiveness more than any other New Testament writer does—and the same applies to repentance. According to Luke, when Jesus called sinners, he did not call them to forgiveness per se, but to *repentance* (5:32). The angels do not rejoice over forgiveness, they rejoice over *repentance* (15:10). Though we might find it a bit awkward to say, there is no good news for sinners without repentance, because there is no forgiveness without repentance (Luke 13:3; cf. Acts 5:31).

The Messiah Who Heals and Forgives

Much of the main story of Jesus's ministry work involves healing: the leper, the paralytic, the centurion's slave, the Gerasene demoniac, the boy with a demon. This would have been an impressive sight, no doubt. But what would have been astonishing for Jews was not just that Jesus could cure diseases, but that he also pronounced *forgiveness* to the afflicted. To the paralytic who sought physical restoration Jesus said, "Friend, your sins are forgiven" (5:20). Of course, he also healed the man and sent him home walking on his own two feet. But how are the two connected? Psalm 103 offers a helpful clue. David praises God for his many good works for Israel. It is worth visualizing this massive list: *love, compassion, goodness, renewal, righteousness and justice, mercy and grace, tender care.* The first thing David mentions, though, is that the LORD "forgives all your [Israel's] iniquity and heals all your diseases" (Ps 103:3). Given the rest of the things David is thankful for, he connects these by linking all problems and benefits to Israel's relationship with God. Away from God's holy presence, God's people step into dangerous spaces where they are vulnerable to all manner of evil and they also get lost in their own sinfulness and rebellion. Like a sheep who has wandered off, they end up with scrapes from thorns and cuts from sharp rocks. But the good shepherd finds the sheep, takes pity, and restores them to the fold.

For Luke, the relationality of covenantal forgiveness is best portrayed in the story of the unnamed woman whom Jesus forgives and blesses (7:36–50). The Pharisees are offended that Jesus would let her touch him by kissing his feet and pouring perfume on him. But Jesus tells them the story of her love for him—that it's so profound because he forgave her and released her from her sins. The appropriate response to covenantal forgiveness is not the "freedom" to do anything, and certainly not to take offense at Jesus, but affection, because the love of God has finally come to restore the world. So Jesus said to her, "Your faith has saved you, go in peace" (Luke 7:50).

The Forgiven Forgive

If we carry with us into Luke the Old Testament backdrop depicted above of Israel's hopes for restoration, renewal, new creation, and new life, then it not only brings to light Jesus as the "forgiveness of sins" for God's people, but it also rachets up Jesus's teaching on how and why disciples should forgive. This matter is not only important in Luke's Lord's Prayer—"Forgive us our sins, for we also forgive everyone who sins against us" (11:4 NIV)—but also in chapter 17 where Jesus teaches his followers to be generous in relationships (17:3–4). Forgiveness is *not* doormat theology; Christians are not called to let others step and stomp all over them. In fact, Jesus says, "Rebuke them!" (Today we would say, "Call them out on it!") He also says, *watch for their repentance*. So, there is a process; forgiveness itself is not instantaneous. But we see in 17:4 the (implicit) call to forgive others like God has forgiven us: "Even if they sin against you seven times in a day and seven times come back to you saying, 'I repent,' you must forgive them" (17:4 NIV). *Why would anyone keep asking for forgiveness after sinning against someone SEVEN times in one day? And why would they continue repenting?* Clearly, there is a relationship in place. Just as the covenant God is forbearing (valuing the relationship), so disciples need to be generous forgivers—with remorse and confession as features of the process for weightier matters.

All of that makes sense. There is a process for forgiveness, and with repentance and confession of the sinner in place, relationships can be restored. That seems right and good. Until we get to the cross. This is not a scene of friends or relatives in disagreement or dispute. This is execution with torture. It was normal for the accused to spit out cries of vengeance and hatred toward their executioners.[2] But Jesus did quite the opposite. He said, "Father, forgive them; for they do not know what they are doing" (23:34). There is no confession of sins by those hostile to Jesus; there is no remorse or repentance. But Jesus's final words model what he taught:

- Love your enemies and bless those who curse you—*radical love and forgiveness* (6:27–28).
- Be loving and generous toward your enemies without expecting something back—*radical love and forgiveness* (6:35).
- Be merciful, because your Father is merciful—*radical love and forgiveness* (6:36).

Who is sufficient for these things? No one. But Jesus taught it and lived it and believed the world could not finally be redeemed unless the church became a forgiving and loving and blessing institution—even toward those who hate it.

The Spirit-Church Lives the Forgiveness of God

In Luke's second book, the book of Acts, the story of the gospel of the forgiveness of sins continues. Jesus brought the new covenant of transformative forgiveness, but what we see in Acts is the gift of

---

2. See David Garland, *Luke*, Zondervan Exegetical Commentary on the New Testament (Grand Rapids: Zondervan Academic, 2011), 922.

the transforming and empowering Spirit to lead the Spirit-church to embody the forgiveness of God in the world. The apostles (like Peter) went out with this message: "Repent, and be baptized every one of you in the name of Jesus Christ so that your sins may be forgiven; and you will receive the gift of the Holy Spirit" (2:38).

What is the link between the Spirit and forgiveness? Probably the prophetic words of Ezekiel as he imagines a new covenant where Israel has a new heart and a new spirit: "I will put my spirit within you, and make you follow my statutes and be careful to observe my ordinances. Then you shall live in the land that I gave to your ancestors; and you shall be my people, and I will be your God" (Ezek 36:27–28). Forgiveness means for Luke the fulfillment of this kind of prophesy, the new creation of Israel to live rightly before and with God.

Just as Luke capped off his Gospel with forgiveness in the words of Jesus, Paul announces forgiveness in Acts. But Paul not only becomes an apostle, extending divine forgiveness, he is also the transformed recipient of God's clemency and liberation himself. If the Gospel of Luke moves to a climax with the ascension of the risen Jesus—the king of forgiveness, then Acts moves toward the church's ever-expanding mission to share the king's message and ministry with the whole world. In Acts 26, Paul professes to King Agrippa how he was commissioned by Jesus to be a forgiveness-delegate: "I am sending you to them [Jesus told me] to open their eyes and turn them from darkness to light, and from the power of Satan to God, so that they may receive forgiveness of sins and a place among those who are sanctified by faith in me" (Acts 26:17–18 NIV).

I used to think that biblical forgiveness was all about liberation, setting captive sinners free. This element is there, yes, but instead of linking forgiveness and freedom, thanks to Luke I now associate forgiveness with *reconciliation*, because for him it is all about healing the relationship, not just releasing a debt.

OTHER NEW TESTAMENT VOICES
Matthew 6:12–15; Mark 2:5–10; John 20:23; James 5:15; 1 John 1:9

2 Corinthians 2:7

The apostle Paul had a thoughtful theology of forgiveness, even if his usage of the technical terminology was not as frequent as Luke's (see Rom 4:7; Col 3:13; Eph 4:32). Twice in his letters he sums up divine redemption through Christ as "the forgiveness of sins" (Col 1:14; Eph 1:7). An important case study of Christian forgiveness appears in 2 Corinthians, when Paul talks about how to treat someone in the church who has been disciplined. In this case, there was someone who needed to be called out, and he was (2 Cor 2:6). But it appears that their punishment of him was harsh, bordering on excommunication. Paul wrote to them to say, "Enough is enough!" Paul proceeds with a *now what?* transition. "Now instead, you ought to forgive and comfort him, so that he will not be overwhelmed by excessive sorrow" (2 Cor 2:7 NIV). And also, Paul adds, affirm your love for him (2:8). When we extend forgiveness, Paul teaches, we don't do so because we are naturally gracious people, but because we forgive as we stand before Christ (2:10). How can we look Christ in the eye and accept his forgiveness, and then withhold it from someone else, another sinner like us? Paul warns the Corinthians that Satan rejoices when we deny forgiveness in the name of justice as we see it (2:11). This is one of Satan's most clever schemes, and it requires our deepest humility to rob him of that joy. So, as Christians we are exhorted to reprimand the stubborn sinner, as is sometimes necessary, all the while acting on a sense of compassion for their humanity and extending grace, ultimately seeking to welcome them back.

Forgiveness for Today

Forgiving as Holding On, Not Letting Go

My friend got a traffic violation recently. It was a bit of a gray-area kind of situation, but she wanted to make her case that she was not in the wrong by going to the court hearing. The city sent her a video of the incident, and from the footage it became clearer to her that she had made a mistake. But she was hopeful that the judge would show leniency. Long story short, he was not merciful. She had to pay the fine. What she wanted was for the judge *not* to hold her accountable for this mistake—she wanted forgiveness. In that situation, it would mean "letting it go." And that is how we often view some kinds of transactional forgiveness. We want the other person to "let go."

For the covenant God, though, forgiveness is not so much about letting go of sin as it is about *not letting go of the sinner.* When it comes to divine forgiveness, I used to have the image in my mind of a judge releasing a criminal. But a better metaphor from Luke's standpoint would be a father who cares for his children. We who are forgiven are not convicts let loose on society. We are sons and daughters, welcomed in embrace: "While he was still a long way off, his father saw him and was filled with compassion for him; he ran to his son, threw his arms around him and kissed him" (Luke 15:20 NIV). Forgiveness is not merely your name etched in ultrasmall print in the big Book of Life. It is the feeling of kisses on your cheek mixed with the wet tears of joy from your worried Father's eyes. You were lost. You are found. Welcome home.

Becoming the Forgiveness of God

In 2 Corinthians, Paul talks about believers becoming the "righteousness of God," thanks to Jesus. This includes being "right with God" (reconciled to God), but also becoming like Christ such that we share the right-making gospel throughout the world. I wonder: perhaps Luke might say that Christians are destined to become the *forgiveness of God.* Not just that we are forgiven, but also that we embody and express the power of mercy and forgiveness in our world; like a match lighting a candle, that candle can light another, and another, and yet another. There are many kinds of forgiveness—sometimes the relationship can be healed and restored immediately; sometimes it is about forgiving after the other has agreed to restitution. And on other occasions still it may mean the relationship *cannot* be restored (as in forgiving someone who has passed away). But the heart of forgiveness is compassion and affection for a fellow human, even one's enemy.

Many theologians have pondered what keeps us from forgiving others. Often it is a sense of condoning injustice, that letting go means evil has won. But there is a saying often attributed to Nelson Mandela that has stuck with me: "Resentment is like drinking poison, hoping it kills the other person."[3] Hatred is the darkness of the soul. Metropolitan Kallistos Ware has taught me much through the practices and liturgy of the Orthodox Church. At the end of Lent (mid-April), the Orthodox observe the Vespers of Forgiveness. The next day ("Clean Monday") they celebrate the mercy, freedom, and joy of the Lord. Ware explains,

> In many places it is still the custom to go out on the hills and have a picnic; and on this, the first open-air festival of the year, both children and grown-ups fly kites in the spring breeze. Such can also be our inner experience when we begin to forgive one another. To forgive is to enter spiritual springtime. It is to emerge from gloom into the sunlight, from self-imprisonment into the liberty of the open air. It is to ascend the hills, to let the wind blow on our faces, and to fly noetic kites, the kites of imagination, hope and joy.[4]

I like Ware's notion here of "spiritual springtime." That is just it. Resentment is cold and opaque, spiritual winter. Forgiveness for others inspired by divine mercy shines the light and heat of God on our life and that of our enemy. It may feel like it comes at a cost to us, but in tandem we must remember the debt of love we owe to the forgiving God.

Suggested Reading

Mark J. Boda. *'Return to Me': A Biblical Theology of Repentance*. Downers Grove, IL: IVP Academic, 2015.

Mark J. Boda and Gordon T. Smith, ed. *Repentance in Christian Theology*. Collegeville, MN: Liturgical Press, 2006.

Tim Carter. *The Forgiveness of Sins*. Cambridge: James Clarke, 2016.

David Konstan. *Before Forgiveness: The Origins of a Moral Idea*. Cambridge: Cambridge University Press, 2012.

Miroslav Volf. *Exclusion and Embrace: A Theological Exploration of Identity, Otherness, and Reconciliation*. Nashville: Abingdon, 2019.

---

3. David Horsey, "Nelson Mandela Transformed Himself and Then His Nation," *Los Angeles Times*, December 6, 2013, www.latimes.com/opinion/topoftheticket/la-xpm-2013-dec-06-la-na-tt-nelson-mandela-20131206-story.html.

4. See https://incommunion.org/2012/04/05/forgive-us-ware/.

CHAPTER 4

❧

Life

Health, Growth, and Fulfillment

The Gospel of John

When I was growing up, sitting in waiting rooms and public libraries, I would often come across a photo magazine called *Life*. It is not in print anymore (ask your parents or grandparents about it), but in the late twentieth century *Life* captured impression-making snapshots of human moments, big and small. Thinking back now about the substance and contents of the magazine, it gives a telling definition of what we (the human race) think about this word "life." Put another way, if an alien picked up this periodical to understand what humans think "life" is all about, they would learn that it has little to do with subsistence. It is not pictures of bagels, bathrooms, sleeping, or commuting to work. We see these things every day and it is hardly "snapshot" worthy. Often the most iconic or memorable images from *Life* have been moments of great emotion, sometimes elating, sometimes harrowing. While we mortals can refer to "life" as the (mere) continuation of biological existence, we can also speak of "life" as something more transcendent—peace, joy, fulfillment, love. I don't want to put too fine a point on this, but I have been thinking a lot lately about why we love watching movies and reading novels. It is not simply to pass the time—we are all *way* too

43

busy for that! Fiction, *good* fiction, is designed to trigger deep emotional responses in us, feelings of grief, anguish, delight, even fear. Why are we so determined to engage with experiences, even fictional ones, that draw these feelings out? My theory: because we want "life." And we think it is found in more than just drawing air into our lungs and keeping blood moving in our bodies. We innately believe what Jesus says: *Life is more than food and clothing* (Luke 12:23).

This is important to keep in mind when we think about "life" as a theological concept. When Jesus offers "life" to his followers, this goes beyond adding minutes, hours, or days to physical life. Now, to be sure, Jesus did *not* preach about a soul that floats around freed from a body-prison. Resurrection life is still a *physical* life, even if that body is transfigured. Nevertheless, Jesus brought the hope and fullness of *life* as the substance of his gospel. What did this mean for God's special people, Israel? How did Jesus's followers take this notion of receiving "life to the full"? And what does this promise and fulfillment mean for us today?

Old Testament Background: Life

The Old Testament doesn't waste any time before getting to the issue of "life." Obviously, Genesis begins with the glorious divine act of creating life, including God breathing life into humans (Gen 2:7). The point here is that there is no life without divine power. God doesn't just redeem life or raise people from the dead. Every living plant, tree, fish, emu, and every mortal human owes their entire existence to the life-giving God (see Gen 1:30; Ps 104:29). In the garden of Eden was a tree of *life* (Gen 2:9; 3:22, 24). Apparently, this tree represented God's life-giving relationship with the first humans. When they sinned, this created a rupture in that relationship and they were driven out of the garden and put at a distance from that special tree. The clever serpent, as we all know, questioned God's warning to Adam and Eve—if you eat from the tree of knowledge, you will die (Gen 3:1)—and it is true that they didn't drop dead on the spot like poor Ananias and Sapphira did before Peter (Acts 5:1–11). However, the death of Adam and Eve did become inevitable because sin created a distance between God and his human creatures, and so they became cut off from the source of life. In a sense, the tree of life would have protected them from the enemy called Death, but east of Eden they would spend the rest of their days, waiting to die.

Not long after the story of the Bible gets started, humans barely get a chance to see the fullness of life before it all goes wrong. By the end of the first book of the Bible, you see the fading glory of the patriarchs; eleven verses into Exodus, God's people Israel are labor slaves in a foreign land (Exod 1:11).

The covenant that God made with Israel offered a new lease on life; it would not be life in the garden; it would be on the move, as it were. But it would be life with God, by God's grace (Deut 30:19). Israel came to know but struggled to fully embody the notion that "one does not live by bread alone, but by every word that comes from the mouth of the LORD" (Deut 8:3). Because of their up-and-down experience of trusting God, listening to his voice, and obeying with faith, they were constantly punished and rebuked. This came to a head in exile, with their city destroyed and their home far away.

For me, nothing sums up better the hopelessness of Israel than the image of the "Valley of Dry Bones" in Ezekiel 37. Israel's degrading experience in exile is likened to a desolate place filled with dry, blanched bones. Have you ever been in a relationship that has experienced such hard times and broken trust that it feels like this? *Dark, arid, lifeless?* The Lord says to the prophet: *Can these bones live?* Ezekiel says, "O Lord GOD, you know" (37:3), but the Lord's question is a rhetorical one. *These bones are lifeless. It would take a miracle to animate them.* But as the story goes, God is in the business of challenging Death. God rolls up his sleeves and says, "I will cause breath to enter you, and you shall live. I will lay sinews on you, and will cause flesh to come upon you, and cover you with skin, and put breath in you, and you shall live; and you shall know that I am the LORD" (37:5–6). Once this "person" was reconstituted, the final step was new life: "Prophesy to the breath, prophesy, mortal, and say to the breath: Thus says the Lord GOD: Come from the four winds, O breath, and breathe upon these slain, that they may live" (37:9). When this breath filled them, "They came to life and stood up on their feet—a vast army" (37:10 NIV).

The book of Ezekiel goes on to explain that this parable-like prophesy represents the death and life of Israel. But it is not about their physical existence only; it is about the meaning and calling of their lives: "I am going to open your graves, and bring you up from your graves, O my people; and I will bring you back to the land of Israel. And you shall know that I am the LORD, when I open your graves, and bring you up from your graves, O my people" (37:12–13).

It is in that exilic and post-exilic period of Israel's life that they came to develop more concretely a theology of resurrection and new life. But, again, these images of new life are not primarily about an "afterlife." It is focused on new life with and from God. Notice the language used in Hosea of covenantal reconciliation.

> Come, let us return to the LORD;
>> for it is he who has torn, and he will heal us;
>> he has struck down, and he will bind us up.
> After two days he will revive us;
>> on the third day he will raise us up,
>> that we may live before him.
> Let us know, let us press on to know the LORD;
>> his appearing is as sure as the dawn;
> he will come to us like the showers,
>> like the spring rains that water the earth. (6:1–3)

In Isaiah and Daniel we see movements toward more of an actualization of this hope in the form of physical resurrection.

> Your dead shall live, their corpses shall rise.
>> O dwellers in the dust, awake and sing for joy!
> For your dew is a radiant dew,
>> and the earth will give birth to those long dead.
>> (Isa 26:19)

Many of those who sleep in the dust of the earth shall awake, some to everlasting life . . . (Dan 12:2)

Much more could be said about Israel's hopes of resurrection and new life, but suffice it to say here the hope of "life" promised to God's people would be much greater and more impactful than simply adding days or years to physical life. We can identify God's promises of life with the following:

Restored relationship with God (notice the "knowing" language in Hos 6:3)
Deeper sense of meaning and purpose in life
Joy and strength, not fear and shame
Unity in community, not enmity and division
Harmonious living in a place called "home," not wandering and isolation

Focal Text: John

"This bread is my flesh, which I will give for the life of the world."
(John 6:51 NIV)

John is sometimes called the "maverick" Gospel—his story of Jesus focuses on some different things and takes a bit of a fresh perspective on the Son of God when compared to Matthew, Mark, and Luke. One way that John does this is through his interest in the language of "life," "living," and "eternal life." At the risk of oversimplification, the Jesus of the Synoptic Gospels came to proclaim the *kingdom of God*, but according to John, Jesus offered himself as *new life for the world*. But what is this "life" he offered? It is a big mistake to assume that this is only about "eternal life," if by that we mean going to heaven and having a long afterlife with God while we strum harps perched on fluffy clouds, chubby angels soaring around us. John was not concerned with the Jesus who adds days, months, years, or even centuries to mortal life. Part of the problem is the English translation of the word "eternal" for the Greek adjective *aiōnios*. When this kind of language was used of gods or special figures (like Roman emperors), the focus was not on *time* (endless life) per se, but on *power* (such glory and grandeur that death and time held no sway over them). To be *eternal* was to be *greater than time and decay itself*. While "eternal" is a fair translation, the meaning of *aiōnios*, when related to God and life, comes closer to the idea of "immortal"—*immortal life* is what Jesus offers.

This perspective helps us greatly when we look at how John describes Jesus: "In him was life, and the life was the light of all people" (John 1:4; cf. 5:26). The "life" Jesus offers is the power and quality of his *own* life; he is LIFE walking around, the source and vitality of LIFE in the flesh, and it is something that *anyone* can share with him. For those who walk with Jesus, who abide in Jesus, who believe in and trust in Jesus, he promises this kind of life:

> *Life that shines a light on one's path* (John 8:12; 14:6)
> *A sense of fullness, satisfaction, and contentment in life*
>   (John 4:10, 14; 6:35, 48–58; 7:38)
> *A life free from fear of weakness or death* (5:21–29; 11:25)

There are a few other things we can say about what "life" means in Jesus according to John.

Umbilical Life: Life through Relationship

Sometimes we falsely conceive of eternal life or salvation as if it were God handing over some kind of object to us, like a gift or resource. Perhaps we might conceive of this like a heart or kidney transplant. But a better image—certainly a more Johannine one—is that of how a fetus "shares" the life of the mother. Life can only happen for that baby because they are connected to the vitality of the mother. Notice a similar idea in John 6: "Just as the living Father sent me and I live because of the Father, so whoever eats will live because of me" (6:57; cf. 6:53–54). And again: "Because I live, you also will live" (14:19). So we are back to the notion that Jesus is not just the *giver* of life, but he is in fact LIFE itself.

While John doesn't develop a baby–mother image of life, he does offer his famous portrayal of Jesus as the "true vine" (John 15). Those who live in a way that is vitally connected to Jesus will have his life flowing through them (15:4–5). This not only brings strength and energy to the branches, but—most importantly—enables them to produce fruit. For John, that "fruit" is love (15:8–9).

Bold Faith: Life through Belief

All this talk of life in John sounds pretty good: bread of life, living water, life to the full. But the fact of the matter is that many people who engaged with Jesus did not like him or his message, and some tried to kill him (John 11:53). Truth be told, Jesus *said* some strange things and *did* some strange things (e.g., cf. John 6:60). But he called for bold and trusting faith from those who were willing to follow him and see what he was all about. For example, when a royal official appealed to Jesus to save his dying son, Jesus forced him into a position of bold faith: "Go; your son will live" (4:50). The official had to go back home *without* Jesus and trust him at his word. John tells us that the healing happened at the exact time Jesus pronounced those words. Faith, for John, is not about filling the mind with theological information; it is a commitment of the whole self to something. *Believing is dependence on Christ* (John 6:35; 17:2–3), much like the old hymn, "Leaning on the Everlasting Arms." So, life with God is a relationship that disciples participate in by *faith* in Jesus.

Sacrificial Faith: Life through Death

There's a catch (there's *always* a catch). This exciting, vibrant, immortal, eternal, resurrection gift of life in the Son has a price tag: death. Not physical death (although John assumes that Christians will still die; 11:25), but followers of Christ are to give up their own lives willingly for the sake of others. This is, of course, a paradox, but the best case study is Jesus himself, the Son of God. Jesus says to his followers, "This bread is my flesh, which I give for the life of the world" (6:51 NIV). Somehow, according to John, Jesus is "life" in himself, and he gives "life" to the world, but it requires him to sacrifice himself, to give up his flesh. This is not some kind of unfortunate coincidence or accident; rather it is the only way transforming life in a sick world is possible. Jesus's self-sacrifice for the sake of life is also a model to his followers and an invitation to do the same.[1]

---

1. See chapter 5 on the cross.

"I am the good shepherd. The good shepherd lays down his life for the sheep." (10:11)

"Those who love their life lose it, and those who hate their life in this world will keep it for eternal life." (12:25)

"No one has greater love than this, to lay down one's life for one's friends." (15:13)

You may have been put off by Jesus saying that believers must "hate" their life. This is not to be taken as self-loathing. This would have been understood as a poetic way of drawing out a contrast: *infatuation with self-glory and self-preservation kills, but sharing life and investing in the well-being, honor, glory, and joy of another results in more blessing on my own life.* And, again, in 15:13 we see the emphasis on love. For John, love is not just a feeling of warmth and affinity for another; it is above all a disposition of care and generosity for others, giving and serving, even in self-sacrificial ways (John 13:1). This counteracts the work of the Thief who desires to steal, kill, and destroy life through hatred, fear, resentment, and darkness. Jesus has opened a path to new life, but it must come through death.

Resurrection Life

One of the most profound reflections on life comes in John 11, when Jesus and Martha are discussing death and life. Martha complains to Jesus that he could have prevented Lazarus's death, but didn't. Jesus comforts her by saying, "Your brother will rise again" (11:23). Martha assumes that Jesus is talking about a day of resurrection (e.g., Dan 12:2) where Lazarus and all the other righteous ones will awake from their sleep to everlasting life. Jesus challenges her thinking and her assumptions about life and resurrection by boldly stating: "I am the resurrection and the life. Those who believe in me, even though they die, will live" (11:25–26). This is quite an unusual expression, even for Jesus! Jesus draws Martha's attention away from death, and even away from the hope of resurrection, and he directs her to himself as the embodiment of the power and vitality of God's salvation. For Jesus to say "I am the resurrection" is quite profound, because Martha did not have to wait until the day of resurrection—all of her hopes could turn to joy in the presence of Jesus. Interestingly, the only two mentions of "resurrection" (*anastasis*) in the Gospel of John appear in this passage (11:24–25). While Jesus no doubt affirms that a mass resurrection event would happen someday in the future (John 5:28–29), it is far more comforting and important to recognize the experience of LIFE in the presence of the living Jesus Christ—something Christians later experience through the Advocate, the Spirit of Christ (John 14:16).

OTHER NEW TESTAMENT VOICES
Matthew 7:13–14; 10:32–39; Mark 8:34–37; Luke 12:15; Romans 6:4; 7:6, 9–10; 8:12–13; 1 Corinthians 15:22–23; Philippians 1:21; 2 Peter 1:3; 1 John 4:9

---

1 Thessalonians

John's discussion of "life" is clearly rich and profound, but it can run the risk of staying in the abstract. We are able to reflect on more concrete examples of receiving "life" by looking at a glimpse of Paul's usage in 1 Thessalonians. (I fully admit, though, Paul can be abstract as well!) In chapter 3, Paul shares how he was concerned for the Thessalonians' well-being in the midst of their persecution and because he had to leave them in a hurry. So, he stopped in Athens and sent Timothy to check on them. In 1 Thessalonians he shares how relieved he was when Timothy returned with the good news of their strong faith and ongoing love and support for Paul. In that moment of hearing this update, Paul admits to feeling relieved: "For now we live, if you continue to stand firm in the Lord" (1 Thess 3:8). The New Living Translation puts it this way: "It gives us new life to know that you are standing firm in the Lord."

It reads as if Paul's heart had stopped when he feared for their well-being, and it was jolted back into action again when he came to know they were okay. This is a small reminder to us that life is often found in the vitality and health of a community where the group shares its ups and downs—where the life of the other is my own life and vice versa. This is also a beautiful reminder that "life" isn't something we are waiting to experience in an "afterlife." (Notice the irony of trying to wait until "after life" to have "life.") Jesus Christ gives new life today, in communion with himself and others, and we can look forward to an even *greater* experience of life in the consummation of new creation.

Life for Today

When I was in college, eBay was one of the coolest new things on the Internet (and Napster, *remember that?*). I recall reading about an interesting guy named John Freyer.[2] He was young, single, and a pack rat. He had lots of stuff, and one day he decided to sell it all on eBay for $1 each. He sold *everything*. Personal photographs (even undeveloped film), his used kitchen spatula, his winter coat (in winter), half a bottle of mouthwash—he even sold his sideburns, shaved and ziplocked. In the auction descriptions, he would put a bit of "life story" related to each object. To his surprise and delight, people were interested in buying these pieces of his life. One man bought his ashtray, even though the buyer didn't smoke (he used it as a coin tray). Buyers would reach out to Freyer and try to meet him, or they would invite him to their houses to "visit" his former possessions.[3] By the end of this experiment, Freyer's "life" sold on eBay for about $6,000. But Freyer didn't do it for the money, obviously. So why did he do it? And why did so many strangers find value in his used junk? The heart of this story goes beyond the transfer of possessions and goods. Life is not found in an asset audit. Freyer did not come right out and say this (I am reading between the lines), but I think he was searching for fulfillment in life, and he knew his belongings had meaning to him, but it was not owning them that brought him meaning. Life is most deeply felt in experiences and relationships. And many would add that fulfillment comes from bringing happiness to others.

---

2. You can read an article on his story here: www.theguardian.com/books/2002/dec/08/art.

3. Freyer eventually wrote about his story in his book, *All of My Life for Sale* (London: Bloomsbury, 2002).

Searching for Meaning and Fulfillment

According to a 2017 Pew research report, Americans are searching for a sense of fulfillment in life, and when asked, they often point to family life, a good career, meaningful friendships, and good health.[4] But many people can have most or all of these things and still struggle with anxiety, depression, loneliness, and emptiness.[5] Many of life's "highs" are fleeting. So people alternate between high highs and low lows, going up and down. This is not just a modern American phenomenon. Jesus's disciples were also searching for "life." Like Freyer, they knew that a fulfilled life could not be found in collecting objects and possessions. There is something that humans long for that transcends the satisfactions of basic needs. (I love that memorable line from C. S. Lewis: "If we find ourselves with a desire that nothing in this world can satisfy, the most probable explanation is that we were made for another world."[6] Actually, this is a very Johannine perspective!) According to John's Gospel (aka, "The Gospel of Life"),[7] humans can only find true fulfillment, abundant life, in Jesus Christ who is life himself. We will conclude with reflections on three key images of life in John.

Life on the Vine: Living in Community

The most important association that John wanted to make for his readers was that, insofar as Jesus is life himself, true human life must be connected to him. He is the vine, and his people are living branches. More than any other Gospel, John's is the Gospel of living communion.[8] Even John's repeated language of eternal life is centrally about a vibrant, rich, fulfilled, and indelible life rooted in union with God.

---

4. See "Where Americans Find Meaning in Life," Pew Research Center, November 20, 2018, www.pewforum.org/2018/11/20/where-americans-find-meaning-in-life/.

5. Alice G. Walton, "Why the Super-Successful Get Depressed," *Forbes*, January 26, 2015, www.forbes.com/sites/alicegwalton/2015/01/26/why-the-super-successful-get-depressed/#7e569b938509.

6. C. S. Lewis, *Mere Christianity* (London: HarperCollins, 2017), 136–37.

7. See Andrew T. Lincoln, "'I Am the Resurrection and the Life': The Resurrection Message of the Fourth Gospel," in *Life in the Face of Death*, ed. Richard N. Longenecker (Grand Rapids: Eerdmans, 1998), 122–45, at 143.

8. See Rekha Chennattu, *Johannine Discipleship as a Covenant Relationship* (Peabody, MA: Hendrickson, 2006); Michael J. Gorman, *Abide and Go: Missional Theosis in the Gospel of John* (Eugene, OR: Cascade, 2018).

For us to experience this kind of life today, we need to seek to really know God in prayer, worship, and communion.

Life Is Light: Direction and Wisdom

The Bible as a whole has a tendency to associate life with light. This makes good sense, as we think about entering fresh light out of the dark womb, the work done in daylight, the way we open our eyes every morning. But light isn't just about seeing; it is about moving and doing, as illumination lights the path of life. The deeper life is full of purpose and direction. When we feel the most "alive," we are often thriving as we pursue God's calling for our lives. As Christians, we come to experience new life by knowing our place in this world and recognizing the gifts God has given us, then using them to work and serve as a part of society to better the lives of others.

Life Is Bread and Water: Satisfaction and Peace

If I had to guess, I would say that our modern language of "fulfillment" in life (even as it is now used in the secular realm) can be traced back to John's imagery of heavenly bread that fills, and a Christ-well that satisfies. Each of us knows, I hope, the feeling of having a delicious meal. Every year, on my birthday, my thoughtful wife goes out and picks up a delicious dinner from my favorite Vietnamese restaurant and we feast at home. I look forward to that every year—but that feeling fades quickly (and then I have to wait another 364 days). We also know that feeling of being parched when we are out and about and have no water handy. That sometimes happens to me when I forget to refill my water bottle at the airport after security, and I get up in the air on the plane. When the dry air eventually gets to me at 35,000 feet, I am out of luck. As mortals, we have constant physical needs, and we are always fluctuating between fulfillment and neediness. Jesus doesn't offer a physical meal plan. We still need a social, geological, political, and economic ecosystem of food production. But Jesus knows that we have a deeper need for satisfaction and peace in our lives. We can have food and money and still be restless. We can have friendships and a good job and not be at peace. Alternatively, if we have a living communion with the God of peace, we can endure other depravities. We can be physically sick but find that "it is well with my soul."

Suggested Reading

Jaime Clark-Soles. *Reading John for Dear Life: A Spiritual Walk with the Fourth Gospel*. Louisville: Westminster John Knox, 2016.

Jon D. Levenson. *Resurrection and the Restoration of Israel: The Ultimate Victory of the God of Life*. New Haven: Yale University Press, 2008.

Richard N. Longenecker, ed. *Life in the Face of Death*. Grand Rapids: Eerdmans, 1998.

CHAPTER 5

The Cross

New Life through Sharing Christ's Death

1–2 Corinthians

Why did Jesus die on a cross? If you are reading this book, I am sure you have thought about this question before. And probably you have heard many popular or classic answers. The most simplistic answer is "for our sins" (1 Cor 15:3)—and this is a very biblical answer. But the actual rationale or mechanism behind this often remains unstated in the New Testament. Perhaps the most common answer you will find for the operation of these "death for us" statements is "Jesus was a sacrifice." In ancient religion, a sacrifice was about the death of an animal given to atone for (or cover) sin. So, Jesus is the perfect sacrifice for human sin. That might provide one explanation for how and why "Jesus died for our sins," but it doesn't really explain why Jesus died *on a cross*. If God's intent in the incarnation and the activity of the Son was simply to "die" to atone for sinners, then couldn't Jesus have died in his sleep or on a battlefield? *Why the cross?*[1]

What we come to learn, when we read the Bible carefully and notice

---

1. See the excellent little study by Donald Senior, *Why the Cross?* (Nashville: Abingdon, 2014).

how cross and crucifixion language is used by the apostles, is that the "cross of Christ" is not just a wooden object, neither is it just a place; it is a context in which God uses the life, suffering, death, and new life of Jesus to teach believers a whole new way to think and live.[2] You see, the "problem" of sin is not just that it is wrongdoing. It is like an infection that has so corrupted the person that they must be retrained to think, to will, and to live.

Let's say we asked the question, *How do you find new life in God?* There is a certain way the world thinks and acts that leads it to certain kinds of answers: *power, strength, wisdom.* None of these things are inherently bad, but sin has corrupted our understanding of them. Thus, it takes something disruptive and transformative to redeem our imagination and activity in the world and our orientation toward God. There is a biblical answer to how we find new life in God, but it will be counterintuitive to our fleshly minds: our "life" can only be found in our "death." The reality of the impact of sin and death in the world is that our death cannot be circumvented. So, when we say, "Jesus died for my sins," we are *not* saying, "Therefore, I don't have to die." This paradox appears in Paul letter to the Galatians: "I have been crucified with Christ, and I no longer live, but Christ lives in me" (2:20 NIV). The path to new life is not around death. It is as if Jesus says to us, "The bad news is that you will have to die; the good news is that I have made a path *through* death if you live in me and if I live in you. It will hurt like hell, but resurrection and new life will win out."

If you grew up with a "magic wand" theology, this might seem like a strange, new way of looking at Christianity. A "magic wand" theology sees the gospel as a religious "trick" that blinks away your sin with an easy move. It leads to a simple and easy faith but does not lead to true discipleship where one seeks to become like Jesus. I think of that haunting line from David Crowder, "Everybody wants to go to heaven,

---

2. For me to say this is not to deny that sacrificial theology is present in the New Testament; rather, the biblical writers used a host of images and metaphors to communicate the rich nature of salvation in Jesus Christ; see Brenda Colijn, *Images of Salvation in the New Testament* (Downers Grove, IL: InterVarsity Press, 2010); Michael F. Bird, *Evangelical Theology: A Biblical and Systematic Introduction*, 2nd ed (Grand Rapids: Zondervan, 2020); Joshua M. McNall, *The Mosaic of Atonement: An Integrated Approach to Christ's Work* (Grand Rapids: Zondervan, 2019).

but nobody wants to die."[3] For those of you who have not been introduced to a robust theology of the cross (and "cruciformity"—we will define this term below), this will be the major focus of this chapter. Typically in this book we have journeyed chronologically from Old Testament to New, but in this case, because "cross" is not a key topic of the Old Testament, we will begin with Paul. But, of course, Paul was heavily influenced in his thinking by the Old Testament, so we will eventually explore scriptural resonances later. Briefly, though, let us look at why people were crucified in the first century and the cultural importance it held in Roman society.

Greco-Roman Context

Romans were not the first people to hang "criminals" on a cross as a form of punishment and execution—but they perfected the cruel practice with classic Roman efficiency.[4] Other capital punishments were used by the Romans, such as beheading and strangling. Crucifixion was considered the *summum supplicium*, the most violent form of punishment (Cicero, *Against Verres* 2.5.168). So gruesome and grotesque was crucifixion that it became a kind of curse word. We have found Pompeian graffiti that reads "go crucify yourself," along the lines of our modern "go f**k yourself." Crucifixion was reserved for the worst of criminals, widely known as execution fit for slaves and traitors (Cicero, *Against Verres* 2.5.169; Plautus, *Poenulus* 347).

When we see Renaissance and Baroque paintings of Jesus's crucifixion in history, it appears to us as if there were just a few people put on a cross that fateful day, Jesus and the two "thieves" (better understood as insurrectionists or rioters). But we have ample evidence that the Roman state disciplinary machine crucified victims in the hundreds on a regular basis (Paulus Orosius, *Seven Books of History against Pagans* 5.9.4), so there were probably many more then three that hung on a

---

3. David Crowder Band, *A Collision*, produced by David Crowder Band (Atlanta: Sixsteps, 2005).

4. On ancient crucifixion, see Martin Hengel, *Crucifixion in the Ancient World and the Folly of the Message of the Cross* (Philadelphia: Fortress, 1989); John Granger Cook, *Crucifixion in the Mediterranean World* (Tübingen: Mohr Siebeck, 2015).

Roman cross the same day Jesus died. You might remember the story of Spartacus, but you might not know that, according to Appian, praetor Crassus had more than six thousand slaves crucified between Capua and Rome in the aftermath of that revolt (Appian, *Civil Wars* 1.120).

When Rome spent money and manpower on crucifying someone, they wanted to send a message to the whole empire's inhabitants. They chose the most crowded highways to post crosses on to instill fear and dread among passersby (Quintilian, *Decl.* 274). Rome demanded order and cooperation, conformity to Roman control. The crucified, like Spartacus's comrades, like Jesus of Nazareth, were given Rome's bloody stamp of rejection. More than just ending their existence, their honor and dignity were obliterated. And, given that social standing and status were the most prized possessions in the ancient world, you could easily see how anyone would have wanted to avoid the cross at all costs. *What fool would get themselves crucified?*

Focal Text: 1 Corinthians

From what we can gather about the Corinthian church, there were many believers who came to put their trust in Jesus Christ, but struggled to allow Jesus's way to transform their values and perspectives. In Roman Corinth, we know that dominant cultural values of the Roman empire prevailed, which hailed the significance of power and social status. To be honorable and praiseworthy meant (1) having the right friends, (2) following the leaders/heroes who were moving up in the world, and (3) incrementally moving up the ladder of status and success oneself.[5] Perhaps some were even attracted to the religion and message of Jesus Christ because of the promises of empowerment and "resurrection." We see that one can create a very lopsided Christian faith by picking and choosing which elements of the faith to focus on, and this can have disastrous effects on a church community, just as we see with the Corinthian church.

Paul begins his first letter to the Corinthians by pointing out the

---

5. For an illuminating perspective on this value system, see Joseph Hellerman, *Embracing Shared Ministry* (Grand Rapids: Kregel, 2013).

folly of their hero debates. Some say, "I am of Paul" (remember, this is about aligning oneself with the best leader to increase one's own status), others "I am of Apollos" or "I am of Cephas" (1 Cor 1:12). Paul was absolutely horrified by the thought that Christian leaders might be treated as competing heroes. *Take me off your pedestal, you idiots!* (Paul doesn't say that exactly, but it's there if you read between the lines of 1:13–14). Some of these Corinthians wanted Christ to bring them power and status—one way or another. So, Paul had to disrupt and subvert their whole way of thinking about the way of Jesus.

Paul reminds the Corinthians in 1 Cor 2:2 that he had already anticipated this problem when he was with them before, so "I decided to know nothing among you except Jesus Christ, and him crucified." Put another way, Paul was saying that they needed to have it sink in that the Lord they honored was *crucified*. Jesus had died in shame and pain because of his love for others. This is what Paul meant when he talked about the "message of the cross" in 1:18–25. Paul wrote "the message of the cross is foolishness for those who are perishing, but to us who are being saved it is the power of God" (1:18 NIV). Somehow, Paul explained, God's great strength is found in Jesus's humility, and God's perfect wisdom is found in Jesus's willingness to suffer the highest form of shame in this world. Preaching "Christ" means preaching "Christ crucified" (1:23). Paul is not just teaching a theology of how to get saved but is affirming that the process of God's work changing us involves becoming like Christ *in his crucifixion*. Paul explains it to the Philippians in this way: to be righteous and to truly know God in Christ requires that we enter the life of Christ by participating in his sufferings and becoming like him in his death (Phil 3:9–10).

This is a good place to pause and introduce the theological concept of "cruciformity."[6] Michael J. Gorman has been a leading voice in the subject of Pauline theology, and he has brought this term cruciformity to the center of the discussion. Gorman defines cruciformity in this way.

---

6. The root word *cruciform* literally means "in the shape of a cross," and in the nineteenth and early twentieth century this term was most commonly used in reference to an architectural form. Later, in the twentieth century, it began to appear in theological works in reference to becoming like the crucified Christ in character and obedience to God.

"Cruciformity" . . . means conformity to the cross, to Christ crucified. Cruciformity is the ethical dimension of the theology of the cross found throughout the New Testament and the Christian tradition. Paradoxically, because the living Christ remains the crucified one, cruciformity is Spirit-enabled conformity to the indwelling crucified and resurrected Christ. It is the ministry of the living Christ, who reshapes all relationships and responsibilities to express the self-giving, life-giving love of God that was displayed on the cross. Although cruciformity often includes suffering, at its heart cruciformity—like the cross—is about faithfulness and love.[7]

So, cruciformity means becoming like the Jesus who went to the cross willingly, out of love. I have my own definition of cruciformity which I will offer below, but it is largely resonant with Gorman's formulation. Cruciformity means believers are Spirit-led and Spirit-enabled to give of self to the needy other for the sake of love. This is clearly *not* what the Corinthians were doing, by and large, so Paul had to remind them of this as a matter of primary concern.

There are many illustrations of cruciformity in 1 Corinthians, but we will limit ourselves to just three: rethinking rights, rethinking the social table, and rethinking love.

Rethinking Rights

In 1 Corinthians 9, Paul addresses his God-given rights as an official apostle. As an apostle, he had certain powers and privileges—like receiving money from his churches to support his work (9:6–7). In fact, not only did this make good economic sense, but indeed the Lord Jesus *commanded* this, "that those who proclaim the gospel should get their living from the gospel" (9:14). Even though Paul's arguments in favor of this were ironclad, he is also insistent that he made a personal choice *not* to take up this right with the Corinthians. He refused that right in order to live free from financial attachments to churches, but also to be a bona fide servant to them (9:19; cf. 1 Thess 2:9). Cruciformity

---

7. Michael J. Gorman, "Cruciformity," *Dictionary of Scripture and Ethics*, ed. Joel B. Green (Grand Rapids: Baker, 2011), 197; see Gorman's important book, *Cruciformity: Paul's Narrative Spirituality of the Cross*, 20th Anniversary Edition (Grand Rapids: Eerdmans, 2021).

means that sometimes we forgo what belongs to us in order to be a special blessing to others. At one of my workplaces, we had allotted to us a certain number of "sick hours" we could spend per year. But there was a benevolent policy put in place which allowed us to "bank" the sick hours we didn't use, and "gift" them to another employee who had exceeded their sick hours. All too often we live in a world of hoarding our rights, privileges, and gifts, but the grace of the cross teaches us that if God is a generous giver (with something to lose), we too can let go of those rights, privileges, and gifts sometimes to show that same kind of generosity. This Paul did in many ways, not least when he offered the gospel free of charge. We embody the theology of the cross when we give up, give over, or suspend a prerogative to support someone else.

Rethinking the Social Table

In the ancient world, meals were not just occasions to fill bodies with sustenance. Yes, food was a physical necessity then as it is now, but in the Roman world meals were often social events where status was contested, displayed, and reinforced. It mattered greatly *who* was invited to meals, *where* they sat, and *what* they ate. At social dinner parties, which Greeks and Romans loved, you learned a lot about where you fit in the pecking order. The most important people (1) were invited to the party early (or hosted), (2) sat in the seats of honor, and (3) had access to the most expensive and most delicious food—and they had plenty of it.

We get the impression from 1 Corinthians that some of these believers turned what should have been a very welcoming, hospitable experience of the Lord's Supper into another competitive and exclusive social gathering. As Paul says, "Your meetings do more harm than good" (11:17 NIV). Paul talks about this experience reinforcing "divisions" (11:18). God is not honored at such occasions (11:20). Apparently, they reinforced special times and places of eating for the "more important" people (11:21) while others were not getting enough food or drink. Paul implies here that the lowly and poor were being humiliated while the wealthy and elite were satiating themselves (11:22).

Paul longed for a whole new social table, where each person was equally honored and cared for, both in terms of respect and nourishment. Cruciformity means thinking of the other, especially of those who have little or nothing. Cruciformity means *sometimes I choose to give up the part or the whole of something given to me (even if I "deserve it") to care for someone who does not have enough.*

Rethinking Love

Here we can turn to the famous "love" passage of 1 Corinthians 13, a popular Scripture reading for weddings. It is well and good to be reminded of this in romantic settings, but in the context of 1 Corinthians, it is most probable that this was a *corrective* teaching. Paul was instructing them about the nature of love because they were being *unloving*. We will not belabor the point here, but suffice it to say that Paul was painting a picture of love that is cruciform—the kind of affection, care, and sacrifice that is costly and generous. The Corinthians apparently put much emphasis on gaining and growing in impressive spiritual gifts like prophesy. But Paul held up genuine love as greater than any other spiritual blessing. Christian love is the opposite of being protective of *my own* rights, privileges, and power. Christian love seeks to bless the other, to be gentle, to forgive (13:4–5). Put another way, if Paul were evaluating various churches over which he had oversight, the quality he would have been most interested in was generous love. This is the single most significant indicator of the transformative work of Christ and the believer's conformity to the cross of Christ.

Cruciformity and Benevolent Ignominy

For about ten years, I followed Gorman's definition of cruciformity, but in recent years I have developed my own version with a few small differences. Here is mine:

> Cruciformity is the biblical pattern of discipleship, demonstrated by Jesus's obedience to God and his love for others, which came to a climax in his willingness to suffer and be crucified.

We can supplement this with four points.

1. **CRUCIFORMITY** is, first and foremost, an attitude toward God: believers prioritize obedience to God's will, whatever the cost.
2. **CRUCIFORMITY** is a worldview: believers see reality in a whole new way through the cross of Christ, where losing is winning, weakness is strength, and foolishness is wisdom.
3. **CRUCIFORMITY** is an attitude toward humanity: God's human creatures are of such worth and value that believers ought to be willing to accept shame, weakness, and insult to stand with the broken, condemned, forgotten, and hated. In that sense, cruciformity is a tribute to the incarnation.
4. **CRUCIFORMITY** is a form of hope: it is a protest against the ways of the broken world and an affirmation that God will make all things right one day.

Another way that I explain cruciformity is in a formulation I call "benevolent ignominy." Ignominy involves facing disgrace, insult, and rejection. Believers must endure these things. But not just for the sake of being rejected. Rather, believers can do these things out of benevolence—I like to define benevolence as becoming a *force for the good of the other*. Cruciformity is all about facing rejection, disgrace, insult, and weakness in order to be a force for good for the other, in imitation of Jesus Christ, our crucified and risen Lord.

Benevolent Ignominy in 2 Corinthians

Paul does not use cross language much in 2 Corinthians, but the cruciform concept of what I call "benevolent ignominy" is vividly prominent throughout. In this lengthy follow-up letter, it is clear that the Corinthian believers needed further instruction on living in the way of Jesus. Paul holds the apostles up as models, not as "superhumans," but as broken and humble vessels carrying the treasure of the gospel (2 Cor 4:7). What the apostles carry into the world is not a quick-fix solution to life's problems, but "the death of Jesus, so that the life of

Jesus may also be made visible in our bodies" (2 Cor 4:10). Those ready to hear and understand the gospel will see past the "ugliness" of the dead body of Jesus to perceive life-giving power in his love-filled self-sacrifice (4:11). Paul explains to the Corinthians that, yes, he and his ministry sometimes look ugly, like "death," but one has to look past the external to the impact of his cruciform ministry—"Death is at work in us, but life in you" (4:12). Paul is willing to accept the world's mockery, labels, spite, all for the purpose of carrying out his calling to bring the good news of resurrection life, a life hidden to those who only care about things that glitter and shine on the outside (4:16–18).

Old Testament Background

As mentioned above, we cannot say that cruciformity is present in a *formal* or overt way in the Old Testament, but I believe when people like Paul came to a realization of the power of the cross as a way of life, naturally he would have looked back to the Jewish Scriptures. We could ponder many examples of self-sacrificing love in the Jewish Scriptures, but here we will only briefly look at two. First, let us direct our attention to Moses. He never died on a cross, but he did take radical steps to identify with his suffering people, Israel. Once he came to the full realization of the plight of his slave people, he stepped out of the comfort of his palace home and stood with and for Israel. Hebrews 11:24 offers an apt summary of Moses's faith and sacrifice: "By faith, Moses . . . refused to be called a son of Pharaoh's daughter." This was not just about a last name. More importantly, it was about the prestige, security, and power he was abdicating to align himself with a small, impoverished "slave nation." Moses did this by faith in God, and out of compassion for his people; that is a good example of *cruciform* loyalty.

Another profound example from the Old Testament is the famous Suffering Servant passage of Isaiah 53. This mysterious figure was destined to be utterly rejected, despised, mocked, jeered, and afflicted (53:2–3). But he was not guilty of any crime, eminently undeserving of such treatment. He willingly bore *our* transgressions, was crushed for *our* iniquities. *We* are the wayward sheep, but *he* accepted the punishment. He did this with a purpose, to make "many righteous" (53:11). He showed *cruciform* love, even to the point of death.

OTHER NEW TESTAMENT VOICES

Matthew 27:32–37; Mark 10:43–45; Luke 2:30–32, 34; 23:32–34; Romans 6:1–11; 8:1–39; Galatians 5:24; 6:14; Philippians 2:1–11; 3:7–4:1; Colossians 1:20; 2:13–15; Revelation 5:9

John 13:1-17

I mentioned above that the Gospels don't offer an extensive explanation of the meaning of the cross of Christ. But in the Gospel of John, we are provided with a crucial *clue* to its meaning: the foot-washing (John 13:1–17). The catalyst for this action is Jesus feeling the weight of his impending "hour" when he would depart from this world. So, "having loved his own who were in the world, he loved them to the end" (13:1). His love is shown in his great humility, taking the role of a slave, stooping down to wipe away the dirt and filth from their feet. Famously, Peter protests this, perhaps thinking it is a trick; *No, I should wash YOUR feet* (he must have thought). But Jesus takes his refusal as no light matter. "Unless I wash you, you have no share with me" (13:8). Jesus was setting an example of humble service, the very thing they would later see profoundly demonstrated on the cross. In the upper room, he gives them this instruction: "So if I, your Lord and Teacher, have washed your feet, you also ought to wash one another's feet. For I have set you an example, that you also should do as I have done to you. . . . Servants are not greater than their master" (13:14–16a). Jesus's lesson was not about feet, water, towels, and dirt per se. It was actually about the cross. It was about loving the other in such a way that sometimes we take on the role of the lowly slave to serve them.

Jesus washed the feet of his disciples because he wanted to burn the image into their minds that *this* was what leaders and teachers do. In a world of washers (slaves) and the washed (the free), the disciples ought not to be fooled into prizing the latter. He calls them to imitate his meekness and service, so they too will do this. And so too with the cross. Yes, it was a "once-and-for-all" activity in a sense (hence, "It is finished"), but that ending was just a beginning. Just as he suffered and laid down his life for them, so they too must do this for others in imitation of Jesus (see John 15:13; 1 John 3:16).

Cruciformity for Today

You can probably tell what family life stage I am in right now, because I am going to use an illustration from the book *Diary of a Wimpy Kid*.[8] In this story, there was a piece of old, moldy cheese sitting on the Westmore Middle School playground. As legend had it, whoever touched the archaic cheese was cursed with the "Cheese Touch" (i.e., "cooties")—they infected whomever they were in contact with, so people avoided this cheese and the Cheese Touch pariah like the plague. Anyway, one day a group of bullies confront protagonists Greg and Rowley (Greg and Rowley being "wimpy kids"). Rowley is forced to eat a bit of the cheese. Normally, that would have meant that he had contracted the Cheese Touch. But when they were asked later about it by other kids at school, in order to protect Rowley from the Cheese Touch embarrassment, *Greg* said *he* (Greg) had thrown it away. This got Rowley off the hook of being treated as cursed, but it meant *Greg* now had the dreaded Cheese Touch. I love this story, because this is cruciformity in action—someone risking difficulty, disgrace, and weakness in order to protect, love, and care for someone else. I think Paul would find this an apt parable of cruciformity!

I am often asked by students (when I introduce the concept of cruciformity to them) what it actually *is*? *What does it mean to become like the cross, to become like the Jesus who died on a cross?* In some ways, it defies definition; once you turn it into a method or philosophy, there is a risk of losing the mysterious essence of participating in the crucified Christ. But because we are trying to break big, theological words down

---

8. Hey, what's not to like? The story has a Gupta in it! See Jeff Kinney, *Diary of a Wimpy Kid* (New York: Amulet Books, 2007).

into bite-sized pieces in this book, I will take the risk and seek to define cruciformity for today.

Cruciformity Is about a Person

Cruciformity is not simply a religious view, a spiritual practice, or a moral philosophy. It is about me becoming like Jesus. In that sense, to borrow a term from Scot McKnight, it is really about *Christoformity*, becoming like *Jesus Christ*.[9] Just as Jesus says, "Take up your cross and follow me" (see Matt 10:38; 16:24; Mark 8:34; Luke 9:23; 14:27), Christians are called to become like Jesus in his character and ministry.

Cruciformity Is about Dying to Live

I think one of Jesus's (and Paul's) most profound teachings is the idea that giving up is the secret to getting more. This is often counterintuitive to our fleshly instincts. Too often we engage our self-protective mode and try to guard our piece of the pie; or worse, we hoard, thinking the world is going to end and the one with the biggest supply (of whatever) will win. But Jesus teaches that there is mystery in the grain of wheat that must fall to the ground and die to activate new life (John 12:24). The life "lost" is blessed with an even richer reward (12:25; Matt 16:25).

The world has its own definition of "winners" and "losers," but Christians see things differently through the lens of the cross. God, in fact, chose to use the so-called "losers" and "nobodies" as part of his redemptive plan to shift our perspective on how we put value in people and possessions (1 Cor 1:28). Those who want to live with and like Jesus must be willing to die to self and die to the world to find a deeper life in God.

Cruciformity Is All about Love

Living a cruciform life, yes, is about the hard work of becoming like Christ, but the orientation is all about love—love of God and love of neighbor. John talks about Jesus loving his disciples "to the end," which could mean *until the very end* or it could mean *to the fullest*

---

9. See Scot McKnight, *Pastor Paul: Nurturing a Culture of Christoformity in the Church* (Grand Rapids: Baker, 2019).

extent, and perhaps the language leaves it open to both interpretations (John 13:1). The New Testament writers repeatedly teach that real love is self-giving, spending of oneself to protect, preserve, and bless the other. Greed is, by nature, exploitative and retentive. Love, in its purest form, is generous and opens the self to the other. This is the greatest gift of the gospel of Jesus Christ. Not just that we can be "saved" from hell or sent to heaven. But that God has modeled redeemed humanity in the person of Jesus Christ to reorient us toward love as the greatest expression of God's own way of being.

Suggested Reading

James H. Cone. *The Cross and the Lynching Tree*. Maryknoll, NY: Orbis Books, 2011.

Timothy G. Gombis. *Power in Weakness: Paul's Transformed Vision for Ministry*. Grand Rapids: Eerdmans, 2021.

Michael J. Gorman. *Cruciformity*. 20th Anniversary Edition. Grand Rapids, Eerdmans, 2021.

Nijay Gupta. "Cruciform Onesimus? Considering How a Slave Would Respond to Paul's Call for a Cross-Shaped Lifestyle." *The Expository Times* (February 24, 2022). https://doi.org/10.1177/00145246221075897.

Richard B. Hays. *The Moral Vision of the New Testament*. San Francisco: HarperSanFrancisco, 1996.

Fleming Rutledge. *Crucifixion: Understanding the Death of Jesus Christ*. Grand Rapids: Eerdmans, 2017.

CHAPTER 6

Faith

Knowing and Becoming One with
God through Jesus Christ

Galatians and Romans

Mark Twain supposedly once said, "Faith is believin' what you know ain't so."[1] This captures well a popular (and misleading) assumption that "faith" is a set of beliefs or opinions that defies reason and lacks evidence. When I was in graduate school, one of the most popular TV shows was *Lost*, which took place on a tropical island and involved a mist monster and a polar bear. While I was truly "lost" when it came to the plot of the six-season series, I was interested in the show's deliberate juxtaposition of two of the main characters. John Locke represented a man of wandering spirituality, often acting in ways that seemed illogical, but he claimed to live by "faith," which apparently involved some sense of mystical intuition. Contrast that to Jack Shephard—the physician, the symbol of logic and empiricism. These two frequently locked horns, representing a primordial battle between faith and reason. Similarly, today religious people are sometimes portrayed as illogical, compared to those who live by fact, logic, and science. (I once read about a pastor who

---

1. As cited by James W. Fowler, *Stages of Faith* (New York: HarperCollins, 1995), 36.

felt he was called to test his faith by entering a lion enclosure at a zoo—there he died, Bible in hand.[2]) Faith is not about holding strange beliefs. For Paul, faith was absolutely *reasonable* (see 1 Cor 15:17). He believed there were credible historical and personal reasons to live the gospel. But I think Paul would say to us today that we are starting in the wrong place if we associate faith first and foremost with "thoughts," "doctrines," and "beliefs." The way this language is often used today, it can seem like "beliefs" are related to these ethereal, hypothetical questions we ask ourselves late at night like, "Are angels real?" "Do ghosts exist?" "Is there sentient life on other planets?" These are questions we might ponder at a pub or a coffee shop, but they seem removed from "normal life." For Christians, we might think of "beliefs" as things like, "I believe in the Trinity," "I believe in a thousand-year reign," or "I believe in soul sleep." *Is that what religion is all about? Is that what "faith" is, subscribing to a list of answers to hypothetical questions related to "spiritual" matters?*

Rethinking "Faith" and Religion: Greco-Roman Context

The first thing we need to do is revisit how people like Paul looked at the world. As a modern American, I come to questions of "faith" with a heritage and tradition of the separation of church and state, and a general siloing of the "sacred" and the "secular." Of course, you have Christians, Hindus, Jews, and Muslims today in America, but many Americans are either self-professed atheists/secularists, or they simply don't think about religious things much. But life was very different in the ancient world, where all people were "religious" and their whole lives revolved around "the will of the gods." Government, leadership, meals, education, work, leisure, family—everything related in some way to the divine. They simply took for granted that the gods existed and held sway over all aspects of human life.[3] But I hesitate to call

---

2. Kayode Imoleayo Israel, "Does Religion Blind Common Sense?," https://medium .com/@kayisrael3/does-religion-blind-common-sense-12ff65609cf1.

3. In the Greco-Roman world, you had *some* philosophers who pondered whether the gods existed, but these were rare, "ivory-tower" kinds of conversations, not inklings that made

these "beliefs" or "faith" because everyday people (1) didn't stop and wonder if such things were real or not and (2) did not treat these ideas as a matter of personal choice. It was simply considered *the way things are*.[4] Things began to change in the Hellenistic era (ca. 300–30 BCE) with the rise and widespread impact of Greek philosophy, which led to a clash of ideologies and perspectives and also to people adopting new ways of thinking about life. In the Greco-Roman world, yes, it was a "polytheistic" environment where many gods were worshiped, but people were drawn to different deities for different reasons. As foreign cults were introduced and incorporated into the Roman world, worship became more and more competitive, a marketplace of advocacy for the most beneficial or most powerful deity.[5] Luke recounts the chants of the crowds who proclaimed, "Great is Artemis of the Ephesians!" (Acts 19:27–28, 34; cf. v. 35).

And in the first century CE, we have the early Christians on a mission to change the outlook of different peoples toward seeing "god" in a new way.[6] Most people believed that the gods were involved in the affairs of mortals, but Christians took this to a whole new level with the incarnation. Sometimes the Olympian deities took pity on or cared for humans, but the Christians claimed a deep and selfless love from God demonstrated on the cross of Christ. To most inhabitants of the Roman empire, Christians were considered *atheoi*—not best translated "atheists," but rather something like "the godless," because they refused to revere the Olympians and the genius of Rome, the most powerful deities that safeguarded the welfare of the state and the people.

In any case, "faith" and "religion" were not hobbies to ancient people. They did not coalesce into a "statement of faith," and the prime motivation for most was not a "deeper spirituality." Religion was the glue that held together all of life in the universe. In Homer's *Iliad*,

---

it down to the lives and conversations of the common people; see Tim Whitmarsh, *Battling the Gods: Atheism in the Ancient World* (New York: Knopf, 2015).

4. See the wide-ranging study by Brent Nongbri, *Before Religion: A History of a Modern Concept* (New Haven: Yale University Press, 2013).

5. See Nathaniel P. DesRosiers and Lily C. Vuong, ed., *Religious Competition in the Greco-Roman World* (Atlanta: SBL Press, 2016).

6. See Larry W. Hurtado, *Why on Earth Did Anyone Become a Christian in the First Three Centuries?* (Milwaukee: Marquette University Press, 2016); and idem., *Destroyer of the Gods: Early Christian Distinctiveness in the Roman World* (Waco, TX: Baylor University Press, 2017).

the gods are portrayed as looking down from their celestial mountain, where they weave the fabric of mortal destinies.

> Two jars stand on the floor of Zeus' palace,
> full of his gifts, one of curses, one of blessings.
> Zeus the Thunderer gives some a mixed dowry;
> they encounter disaster at one minute, success at the next.
> (*Iliad* 24, 525–33)[7]

Christians would agree that God "causes his sun to rise on the evil and the good, and sends rain on the righteous and the unrighteous" (Matt 5:45 NIV). God is impartial in the sense that he does not unfairly play favorites. Where Christians would seem to go too far is in the way God crosses the lines of respectability, becoming *too* intimately involved in the troubles and affairs of mortals. But the general point we want to emphasize here is that "religion" was not an escapist affair for ancient people, Christian or otherwise. Life was living before and with the divine. There was no part of life where the gods' operations and impact were not felt.

A good example of this can be seen in the Old Testament psalms. Notice the range of topics and interests covered in the Psalter, a seamless interconnection of prayers and reflections on government, personal relationships, nature, grief, joy, education, war, traditions and communal activities, wellness, and suffering. "Faith" was not specifically something you set aside time for—it was *life*. With that, let us turn to the Old Testament.

Old Testament Background

For the reasons that I mentioned above, "faith" language is not pervasive in the Old Testament, not the way it is explicitly in the New Testament. But neither is it absent. Think about it this way: several of the key statements about "faith" in the New Testament actually point to the

---

7. As translated by John Ferguson, *Greek and Roman Religion: A Source Book* (Park Ridge, NJ: Noyes, 1980), 12.

Old Testament. For example, on three occasions in the New Testament we have Habakkuk 2:4 cited, "the righteous will live by their faith" (Gal 3:11 NIV; Rom 1:17; Heb 10:38). Obviously, Habakkuk 2:4 was not talking about *Christian* faith, but certainly it was not talking about adherence to religious doctrines. It reflected a call to trust in the one God in uncertain and difficult times (see Hab 1:2–4). It is true, this is one of the few times that Israel's relationship with its God is referred to using the language of *faith*, but this simply points to the fact that "faith" in the Old Testament is all about covenantal relationship and *that* is the main concern of the Old Testament as a whole. YHWH chose this nation Israel and said, "I will take you as my own people, and I will be your God" (Exod 6:7 NIV). According to Jeremiah, God says, "Obey my voice, and I will be your God, and you shall be my people; walk only in the way I command you, so that it may be well with you" (Jer 7:23). This is, in short, the nature of the covenantal relationship, a bond between two people that brings them together with the expectation of mutual trust, concern, and loyalty.

It tends to be when things are *not* going well that we catch glimpses of faith language. Israel is chastised for wandering away from trusting God while they were in the desert, "a perverse generation, children in whom there is *no faithfulness*" (Deut 32:20; cf. Josh 22:16). But as far as God is concerned, despite Israel's infidelity, he remains fully invested, committed, and faithful (Hos 2:19–23). So, to put it plainly, "faith" according to the Old Testament was all about committing to the covenantal God and trusting him with one's whole self—mind, heart, and body. And the platform or manual for this trust in the Old Testament period was the law of Moses.

Most of the time, Israel's "faith" involved simple trust and obedience in day-to-day life—in relationships, work, and service to God. But there were times when what God had commanded challenged their sense of what was good, right, or sensible. This is where we see occasions in the Old Testament of faith as *belief—do you believe God knows what is truly best for you?* The classic model for this involves the patriarch Abraham. Once upon a time, he hailed from Ur of the Chaldeans with his extended family, his clan of peoples, and his deities. Abraham's father Terah took Abraham and Lot's family to Harran and settled there. After Terah died, YHWH, a god foreign to Abraham, told him to leave Harran and start a new journey where he would leave behind his land and clan (something unthinkable for ancient people) and migrate to a new land. (Keep in mind that at this point Abraham was seventy-five years old!) Abraham listened and obeyed and uprooted his family at the word of this strange voice. In a new place, YHWH made a covenant with Abraham, promising him a great family (even though Sarah was barren), a great land, and a great name. "And he believed the LORD, and the LORD reckoned it to him as righteousness" (Gen 15:6). "Believing" isn't just about having "beliefs." It is a form of risk-taking that begins in our mind and will, then gets worked out in our bodies and social lives. Abraham took God at his word, and God acknowledged that trust. Israel would repeatedly look back upon and draw inspiration from that moment, when their father Abraham trusted these great but seemingly impossible promises, for their own relationship with God. To live by faith was to live in trust and hope.

Focal Text 1: Galatians

How does "faith" in the Old Testament compare with "faith" in the New Testament? I am afraid the differences have been exaggerated and blown out of proportion. There is a popular myth that has gone around for a long time to this effect:

Old Testament = law and works
New Testament = grace and faith

This overly simplistic formulation has perpetuated the bad habit of treating the Old Testament as the "bad news" compared to the "good news" of the New Testament. But the apostle Paul had no such attitude toward the Old Testament. When he reminded Timothy that *all Scripture* is inspired and useful (now and forevermore), he was talking about the Old Testament (2 Tim 3:16). Keep in mind, too, that Jesus was clear that he did not want to be seen as undermining the Old Testament; rather, he came to fulfill it, to bring it to its climax, to see it valued and maximized to the fullest (Matt 5:17). In the book of Hebrews, in the famous chapter on "faith," the author tries to inspire Christians by appealing to the "faith" of the great patriarchs, matriarchs, and leaders from the Old Testament: Abel, Enoch, Noah, Abraham, Sarah, Isaac, Jacob, Joseph, Moses, Rahab, David, Samuel: "They were commended for their faith" (11:39a). Their faith should be a model for our faith.

Faith Deepened in Jesus

We have taken some time to explain that faith is not new with Jesus and the New Testament. Israel was called to have faith in YHWH. This is obvious from even a cursory reading of the Old Testament. But then what do we make of Paul talking to the Galatians about the coming of "faith"?

> But now that faith has come, we are no longer under a guardian [which is the law]. (3:25 NET; see also 3:23)

In the context of Galatians 3:1–4:7, Paul was clearly talking about the coming of *Jesus*. So why use the word "faith" (*pistis*) here? Paul sometimes used "faith" (*pistis*) as a shorthand way of talking about a personal, covenantal relationship with God. The fact of the relationship was not new, but the *nature* of the relationship had changed with the coming of Jesus. If, formerly, the law had been the primary *means* by which Israel had faith in God and trusted him, something new came in the first century—the Messiah. Before, Torah was the means by which Israel trusted and obeyed God, now it would be through *Jesus*. In a way, Jesus became a new Torah, a new Law, hence Paul's reference to the "law of Christ" (Gal 6:2). This does not mean that Christ brought some new set of rules but rather expresses that he embodies the living link between God and his people and shows them the way to live lives pleasing to God in his own self, especially as demonstrated by his love. Now, this was not meant to cancel out the faith of Israel but rather to deepen it. We find a helpful reflection of this in the Gospel of John: "The law was given through Moses; grace and truth came through Jesus Christ" (John 1:17). John was comparing law and grace/truth, but not to treat one as bad (law) and the other as good (grace). Rather, the law was "good news" for God's people, but the new way of relating to God in Jesus was even greater (see Matt 12:6).

Faith Is Christ Alive in Me

We would be mistaken to believe that "faith" for Paul was simply about believing doctrines and singing hymns, even hymns to Christ. Faith begins with *death*. Not just any kind of death, but more specifically *crucifixion*: "I have been crucified with Christ and I no longer live, but Christ lives in me. The life I now live in the body, I live by faith in the Son of God, who loved me and gave himself for me" (Gal 2:20 NIV). Christian faith is not just gaining (e.g., life, love, Jesus), but also losing—losing one's own life (Luke 9:24; 17:33). Later, in Galatians, Paul describes this self-death as being crucified to the world (Gal 6:14). The "I" who no longer lives is the "I" corrupted by sin (Gal 5:24). To purge that "I" is a great blessing, but you also lose the "I" who accrues power and status to bring self-importance, and that is hard. Your identity becomes absorbed into the resurrection life of Christ, but forever your "faith" will mean you are dependent on the life and name of Jesus Christ.

Think of it this way—my kids (ages fifteen and under) do not have travel IDs. When we fly domestically, their legal identity is connected to mine. Their job in the airport is to stick close to me, because legally they have no recognized identity apart from me. My personal ID includes them, because legally they belong to me. So it is for those who surrender their "I" to become one with Christ by faith. "Faith" means living in a state of dependence on Jesus for life and identity (see Gal 3:26). To be a part of the "household of faith," as Paul puts it (Gal 6:10), is to stick close to Jesus, because without him we are nothing, without him we are dead to God and alive to sin. But unlike the analogy with my kids, we don't have to worry about "losing" Jesus in the airport. He is always with us; he is *alive* within us and we live by *faith* in him. This faith is not theoretical, nor purely cognitive, nor "religious" in a Sunday morning kind of way. It is like walking around attached to a heart or lung machine. It is a part of life, no matter where we go or what we do—whether we are sleeping, working, eating, or playing. To have faith is to live *by faith*, to live with Jesus alive in me.

A Journeying Faith

Recently I went on a retreat where we went through many experiences designed to help us look within ourselves and also trust others more deeply. One specific exercise required participants to walk a long, unknown path outside at night in the wilderness. I was with two partners, but two of us were blindfolded and the third person led the way. It was disorienting. In the darkness, I clung tightly to our sighted "leader," as we bumbled along an unclear path. I was walking "by faith" on a dark journey, trusting in another person for my own safety. This experience has given me new appreciation for Abraham. Paul devotes a large portion of Galatians 3 to this great forerunner of faith. He modeled journeying faith for believers. Such that Paul called Christians "By-Faithers" (*hoi ek pisteos*). "By-Faithers," or believers, are just like Abraham in that they walk by faith on a journey with God that takes them into new and uncomfortable spaces where their trust will be tested and challenged. But if the greatest aim is seeking to be righteous, to do what is right, Abraham knew that this would be all about walking in faith and trust with the God who leads (Gal 3:6).

The By-Product of Faith Is Love

In Paul's own time, one of the most exercising questions was how Christians should relate to the Old Testament law. Jews, the special people of God, had lived according to Torah for many centuries, and they knew this to be truth in the world and light for the path of walking in God's ways. Part of Paul's gospel message was that this particular role of the law had come to an end (Gal 3:24–25). You can imagine how controversial that idea would have been. In the first century, things like adherence to biblical food laws and circumcision had clearly marked out God's people as holy and consecrated to the Lord. If these things had changed, what did "faith" even look like now? It would take a long walk through all of Paul's letters to provide a complete answer to that tricky question, but suffice it to say here what Paul explains in Galatians 5:6: "In Christ Jesus neither circumcision nor uncircumcision counts for anything; the only thing that counts is faith working through love." To be a By-Faither, to be a believer, to know God through Jesus Christ means to love. Jews, of course, had been taught to love God and others according to the Old Testament, but again this command is cast in a new light and given greater depth once it is modeled by the person of Jesus and inspired by the transforming Spirit at work within believers.

Focal Text 2: Romans

From a thematic standpoint, Romans covers a lot of the same ground as Galatians. It is much longer and does not carry the do-or-die urgency of Galatians, but Romans extensively addresses the Christian posture toward the law and the centrality and essence of faith in Jesus Christ. We will add two pieces of the "faith" conversation from Romans to flesh out further what we saw in Galatians.

Faith Believes the Impossible Is Possible

As Paul explains to the Roman Christians, "faith" is not less than knowing and trusting God in Jesus Christ, but it is more than that: it is a new way of existing in the world. Part of this new way is believing the impossible is possible by God's grace and power. Again, Paul used Abraham to illustrate this. Abraham's body was "as good as dead," and yet God told him new life would come from him and his wife, Sarah (Rom 4:19). Abraham did not waver in this promise, but "he grew strong in his faith as he gave glory to God" (4:20). So, Christians today in Jesus Christ are given boldness to think the unthinkable (the weak are strong), believe the unbelievable (life can come out death), and do the impossible (pronounce forgiveness on the sinner in Jesus's name). Who, in their own strength, is capable of these things?

Faith Becoming Obedience

Paul's sixteen-chapter letter to the Romans is bookended by his affirmation that the goal of the Christian life is the "obedience of faith" (Rom 1:5; 16:26). We might conceive of "faith" as the inside-out transformation that takes place within us as God works gospel power to reshape our lives. But that "faith" is not something to keep inside or hide away. It is meant to grow naturally into obedience manifested as love of God and love of neighbor. Faith is more than just belonging to

God and to the church. A life of faith is a whole new life given to God to be used as a vessel for his redemptive and grace-giving purposes for the world.

Is "faith," then, about works? Yes and no. No, God doesn't use humans just to get work done. He is God; he doesn't "need" our works. (As Luther said, "God does not need your works. . . . You should devote the works of faith to the benefit of your neighbor.")[8] But yes, faith is about working when it is set within the context of covenantal life and ministry within the family of God. We are not meant to be "worker bees" slavishly serving the queen. We are children of God through Jesus Christ, blessed and empowered by the grace of God to carry light and life into the world (Eph 2:8–10).

OTHER NEW TESTAMENT VOICES
Matthew 8:10; 15:28; Mark 5:34; Acts 3:16; 2 Corinthians 5:7; Ephesians 2:8–10; Philippians 3:9–11; Colossians 2:6–7; Hebrews 11:1–39; James 2:14–26; Revelation 14:12

Luke 18:8

Faith Is Persistent

There is much we could add on the subject of "faith" from the Gospels, but here I would just add one point from Luke: faith is persistent. In Luke 18, Jesus tells his followers a parable about a widow who wanted justice from a judge. She was relentless. The judge finally gave in to her demands, not because he agreed with her cause, but because he was exhausted! So, Jesus urged his disciples to cry out for justice to God day and night. Faith is so fixated on God as the meaning to all of life, the gift above all gifts, the solution to all problems, that there is nowhere else to turn and nothing else to do but keep asking, seeking, and knocking. This is a risky way to live and few choose this path,

---

8. Martin Luther, *Sermons on the Gospel of St. John*, *LW* (St. Louis: Concordia, 1955), 25.

so Jesus raises the question: "When the Son of Man comes, will he find faith on earth?" (18:8).

Faith for Today

What Faith Is Not

One of my pastor friends recently taught me a term I hadn't known before: "Chreaster" Christians. This refers to people whom the pastors see only on Christmas and Easter (duh!). Suffice it to say, biblical faith is not a "Chreaster" faith. It is not a Sunday faith either. Faith is not activated only on certain "days" in special moments. Neither is it a checklist of beliefs, doctrines, or spiritual thoughts. In fact, it is dangerous today even to think of "faith" as "religious," because inevitably then we reinforce a sacred/secular divide and split our world into two dimensions, one where we worship God, and another where we do nonreligious things like mow the lawn, eat a snack, pay bills, or go for a run. But in a biblical worldview, all that humans do and experience is part of God's sacred world (see Rom 14:8) and faith is necessary in all places at all times.

What Faith Is

Karl Barth famously wrote a massive study of theology called *Church Dogmatics* (sold today in a 14-volume set!). I haven't read all of his *Dogmatics*, but I *have* read his short version called *Dogmatics in Outline*.[9] I was struck by the profound statement he makes about faith when the believer confesses "I believe."

> I believe in, *credo in*, means that I am not alone. In our glory and in our misery we men are not alone. God comes to meet us and as our Lord and Master He comes to our aid. . . . One way or other, I am in all circumstances in company with Him. . . . Of ourselves we cannot achieve, have not achieved, and shall not achieve a togetherness with Him; that we have not deserved that He should be our God, have no

---

9. Karl Barth, *Dogmatics in Outline* (New York: Harper, 1959).

power of disposal and no rights over Him, but that with unowed kindness, in the freedom of His majesty, He resolved of His own self to be man's God, our God.[10]

Faith, from this perspective, is not a "theology" as a matter of first order. It is a relationship. God is with us and for us in the person of Jesus Christ through the Spirit. God comes to meet us, be with us, and help us. In that sense, "faith" is not something we *do*, and it is not something we *think*, but more properly it is a togetherness we join by God's grace.

Faith as Prayer and Worship

To know that one is not alone with the God who has come near, this ought to inspire prayer and worship. And yet the reality is that many (American) Christians don't pray much. Prayer can seem like an obligation or a ritual we do to please God. But the early Christians viewed prayer as the constant suffusing of life with the acknowledgment of the presence and power of God. Hence, Paul told the Thessalonians to "pray without ceasing" (1 Thess 5:17). He did not mean, by this, endless utterance of words, but rather a greater awareness of the presence and blessing of God in thanksgiving (1 Thess 5:18). Faith and prayer become a way of seeing the work of God in all circumstances and at all times. God is there in the little conversations, on the commute to work, at the grocery store, and in the work cubicle. Grace is given in the cool air, the friendly hug or smile, the bus arriving on time. If God is everywhere and believers know this by faith, then worship belongs everywhere and not just in the pew or at the bedside.

Faith as Foolishness

We began this chapter by questioning Mark Twain's little aphorism, "Faith is believing what you know ain't so." In so many ways this is wrong, because Christians have always affirmed there are good and rational reasons for believing. But there is a way to partly acknowledge Twain's statement, insofar as faith can appear foolish to the simple eye. Just as Paul reminded the Corinthians that the message of the

---

10. Barth, *Dogmatics in Outline*, 25.

cross is utter foolishness and nonsense to unbelievers because it can seem contrary to the values of the culture (1 Cor 1:18), faith sometimes tells us to do things that simply don't add up in the estimation of our neighbors. For example, James notes the propensity to favor the wealthy and elite (we might say the "rich and famous"):

> For if a person with gold rings and in fine clothes comes into your assembly, and if a poor person in dirty clothes also comes in, and if you take notice of the one wearing the fine clothes and say, "Have a seat here, please," while to the one who is poor you say, "Stand there," or, "Sit at my feet," have you not made distinctions among yourselves, and become judges with evil thoughts? (Jas 2:2–4)

James's message here is that the wise choice is to treat everyone equally, which seems foolish according to the world if you want to make the "right" kind of friends. We might do this today in terms of which neighbors we befriend or who we associate with on social media. Our flesh might tell us to rub shoulders with people who could raise our status or inflate our importance. But faith tells us to reach out to the least in society (Matt 25:40). Do we have *that* kind of faith?

When I think of the wisdom of God's foolishness and the gift of foolish faith, my mind turns to the life of the theologian Henri Nouwen. As an academic myself, I have much to admire in Nouwen who taught at such prestigious places as Notre Dame, Yale, and Harvard. But he voluntarily left a distinguished academic career to live amongst and minister to a group of intellectually disabled persons at L'Arche Daybreak Community (near Toronto). While, from an outsider's perspective, someone might say that Nouwen limited his "influence and potential" by leaving academia, Nouwen himself felt he had much to learn from this community. Immediately he was paired with a man named Adam, and Nouwen was responsible for helping Adam with simple daily tasks like dressing and eating. At first this was very challenging for Nouwen, but he eventually became close to Adam and Nouwen developed a freshness in his own faith, learning many new lessons from this new companionship. Nouwen felt a special human bond with Adam; he saw clearly his own brokenness and need, "our poverties touching each other."[11] In faith Nouwen made a "foolish" decision to leave his traditional job and enter a reclusive spiritual community. But for Nouwen, he rediscovered himself there, and found God present in a deeper way: Nouwen discovered there what it meant to live by faith.

Faith as Love

I have probably beat this hammer too many times in this chapter, but permit me one more thump: faith is not something believers do in "sacred spaces" like church. Gathering together for worship and prayer is well and great, and it brings glory to God. But genuine faith is an everywhere-all-the-time thing. As Paul made clear, it comes to life in love and service. Faith means listening to God and doing what pleases him, and so often this means extending love and care to the other. I will give you one example from my life. It was my oldest daughter's first day of school (first grade) and I had the "privilege" of getting her there punctually. I was running on time, which is nice, but just barely. On the drive over to the school, I saw a man pushing his car to the side of the road because it had broken down. My normal instinct is to say to myself (1) "I have somewhere I need to be" and (2) "someone else will surely come along and help." Then I heard a voice in my head say, "Stop and help." (The voice in my head was actually my wife's [not present], who does these kinds of caring things all the time.) So, with a sigh, I pulled my car over. As I was still in a hurry, I jumped out and ran up to the back of this man's car. Without saying a word, I just started pushing and the car picked up a bit of speed and rolled to the side of the road after a few minutes. Without saying hello or goodbye, I got back in my car and drove off to get my daughter to school (we made it on time, BTW).

Now, I probably could have done more (offered my phone, or a ride), but in any case, I stopped to help this man because I believe in God. I believe, as Barth explained above, God came to our aid and came to help us. This was just a small and fleeting act of kindness on my part (almost anyone could have done it, and it took no more than ten minutes), but it was still an act of faith. Faith lives with God, trusts God,

---

11. Henri J. Nouwen, *Adam: God's Beloved* (Maryknoll, NY: Orbis Books, 1997), 80.

listens to God, and acts accordingly, and love is the result. If it does not become love, it is not faith.

Suggested Reading

Karl Barth. *Dogmatics in Outline*. New York: Harper, 1959.

Matthew W. Bates. *Gospel Allegiance: What Faith in Jesus Misses for Salvation in Christ*. Grand Rapids: Brazos, 2019.

———. *Salvation by Allegiance Alone: Rethinking Faith, Works, and the Gospel of Jesus the King*. Grand Rapids: Baker Academic, 2017.

Nijay K. Gupta. *Paul and the Language of Faith*. Grand Rapids: Eerdmans, 2020.

Luke Timothy Johnson. *The Creed: What Christians Believe and Why It Matters*. New York: Doubleday, 2003.

Teresa Morgan. *Roman Faith and Christian Faith:* Pistis *and* Fides *in the Early Roman Empire and Early Churches*. Oxford: Oxford University Press, 2017.

CHAPTER 7

Grace

Changed by God's Favor and
Called to Be Givers

Ephesians

Sometimes I cringe at bad theology in some of the worship songs on Christian radio. But if I turn the dial, I might catch a U2 song, and often I am struck by the profound theological insights from Bono's wandering and wonderous spirituality. One of my favorite U2 songs is "Grace." We Christians see this word all the time, in church names, in liturgies and hymnals, and it can become so familiar to us as religious terminology that it loses its impact as a profound concept at the core of the gospel and the divine-human relation.

Bono cleverly personifies the biblical concept of "grace" in the same style as "Lady Wisdom" of Jewish tradition. For Bono, "grace" is like this beautiful woman who brightens every room and brings life to every person she encounters. She is shockingly generous and forgiving; she doesn't treat people how they deserve to be treated. She treats them better. Bono's song has a psalm-like feel, easily memorized and impossible not to sing along to![1]

---

1. U2, "Grace," from the album *All That You Can't Leave Behind*, produced by Daniel Lanois and Brian Eno (Dublin: Island/Interscope, 2000).

Now and again Bono has been asked to explain the inspiration for his music. It is obvious this one comes from the gospel of Jesus Christ.

[Grace is] my favorite word in the lexicon of the English language. It's a word I'm depending on. The universe operates by Karma, we all know that. For every action there's an equal and opposite reaction. There is some atonement built in: an eye for an eye, a tooth for a tooth. Then enters Grace and turns that upside down. I love it. I'm not talking about people being graceful in their actions but just covering over the cracks. Christ's ministry really was a lot to do with pointing out how everybody is a screw-up in some shape or form, there's no way around it. But then He wants to say, well, I am going to deal with those sins for you. I will take on Myself all the consequences of sin. Even if you're not religious, I think you'd accept that there are consequences to all the mistakes we make. And so Grace enters the picture to say, I'll take the blame, I'll carry the cross. It is a powerful idea. Grace interrupting Karma.[2]

As my colleague Dr. Loren Kerns would say, grace is "evergreen," it will never become old-fashioned or go out of style. I am struck by Bono's claim here, "[Grace is] a word I'm depending on." The reality is "karma" can be cruel. We all need to be "graced" by others and by God. How close is Bono's conception of grace to how this word (in Greek, *charis*) was used in the New Testament by someone like Paul? I would say, *pretty darn close.*

I want to skip over, for now, all the complex and esoteric theological arguments about divine grace, human will, faith, works, and salvation.[3] Sometimes that debate can distract us from the plain and simple nature of God's grace toward humanity in Jesus Christ. If we were to put the matter simply, grace involves *God's generous kindness toward sinners climactically expressed in and through Jesus Christ.*

---

2. Bono, in *U2 by U2* (London: HarperCollins, 2006), 300.

3. For an overview of that discussion, see "Justification by Faith and Judgment according to Works," in Nijay K. Gupta, *A Beginner's Guide to New Testament Studies* (Grand Rapids: Baker, 2020), 145–56.

Old Testament Background

You could say that all thirty-nine books of the Old Testament offer case studies in divine grace, so we will have to be very selective. We could easily point to the exodus as a gracious act of love and kindness on the part of the covenant God. We could identify the many times YHWH preserved his sinful people and held back his punishing hand. But I want to zoom in on just one psalm, Psalm 86, a song of David.

David acknowledges, "I am poor and needy" (v. 1). David was a man plagued and hunted by foes (86:14). They desired to take his life in cold blood. David was both wise and strong, but he knew that this was not enough to preserve his life. He knew that he lived only by the grace of God. He was a great ruler and teacher, but he knew that he had to rely on the God who hears his prayers (86:2–3). His prayers were not prim and proper, but often uttered in wails and cries out of desperation (86:6–7). Recognizing his vulnerability and weakness, he clung to a God he knew to be forgiving, good, loving, merciful, and strong: "For great is your steadfast love toward me; you have delivered my soul from the depths of Sheol"; "you . . . are a God merciful and gracious, slow to anger and abounding in steadfast love and faithfulness" (86:13, 15).

Whenever we are tempted to use words to describe the Old Testament such as "works," "law," "old," archaic," "legalistic," we should read Psalm 86. In it we encounter the same Helper of mortals that we find in 2 Corinthians 8:9, a Lord full of kindness and grace. Grace doesn't cancel out punishment. Grace doesn't undermine justice. Grace doesn't "enable" bad behavior. Grace involves a relationship of loving-kindness where one person favors the other person in their heart and action. As it is written, "If the LORD had not been on our side when people attacked us, they would have swallowed us alive" (Ps 124:2–3 NIV)—another psalm of David, by the way.

Focal Text: Ephesians

You could roll dice and let chance decide which letter of Paul to focus on for the topic of grace—they almost all seem to dwell on this important word *charis*. But if there is a "grace-king" of them all, surely it must be Ephesians. *Charis* is a repeated tone throughout this sonorous epistle. One noticeable feature is the fact that Paul "bookends" the letter with "grace":

> "Grace (*charis*) to you and peace from God our Father and the Lord Jesus Christ" (1:2)
> "Grace (*charis*) be with all who have an undying love for our Lord Jesus Christ" (6:24)

The way *charis* peppers Paul's letters, especially in greetings and liturgy-like moments, probably demonstrates that this became an important term in early Christian vocabulary. It seems to have been a word that could be used as a synonym for "bless/blessing." Be that as it may, Paul simply could not get this word out of his mind as he wrote to the Ephesians.

Praising God's Gracious Character (Ephesians 1:6–7)

Ephesians has sometimes been described as the "epistle of grace." Imagine a front room in a church, where a worshiper can meditate on a beautiful image of Christ or the Trinity before entering the sanctuary. In the early verses of Ephesians, we find the verbal form of such meditative inspiration. God's people were chosen to be loved and cared for by God before the creation of the world, and he decided—even before the beginning—to make them special, holy in his sight (1:4–5). This divine act of redeeming, adopting, and sustaining not only glorifies his human creatures, but also echoes back to himself in honor and praise (1:6). Many powerful lords and great kings over the years have been admired for their might and victories in battle. This one, known by his people as the One Father God, is glorified because of his *grace*, or his love and favor toward others (1:6a). He shares, blesses, and lifts up his people freely and generously through his Son, the one he loves (1:6b).

Paul points to the climactic gifts received from Father and Son: redemption through his blood (i.e., his self-given death), offering the forgiveness of sins (1:7a). If God knew from the beginning—even *before* the beginning—that this sacrifice would be made to claim his people from evil and death once and for all, then the giving of God's Son, Jesus Christ, was not a last-minute plan, but a divine act resonant with God's gracious character—this is who he is.

We can easily contrast God's character to that of the Roman emperor Nero. He was known to be vindictive and vicious; allegedly killing his mother, his first wife, and ordering the deaths of several of his political critics and enemies. The Stoic philosopher Seneca wrote a letter-essay to Nero encouraging clemency, that is, generous restraint:

> I have determined to write a book upon clemency, Nero Caesar, in order that I may as it were serve as a mirror to you, and let you see yourself. . . . It is worth your while to consider and investigate a good conscience from every point of view, and afterwards to cast your eyes upon this enormous mass of mankind—quarrelsome, factious, and passionate as they are. (*On Clemency*, 1.1)

Compare that with what Paul believed about the grace of the God he worshiped. In Romans, Paul extols the richness of God's kindness, long-suffering, and patience, the character traits of One who longs to forgive, not punish, and is willing to wait for their repentance (Rom 2:4).

Grace Undeserved (2:4–10)

If Ephesians 1 offers the panoramic perspective of God's cosmic grace toward his sin-captive creatures, then Ephesians 2 zooms in to focus more specifically on God's love for individual sinners. A text like Eph 2:4–10 is almost like Ezekiel's "Valley of Dry Bones" (Ezek 37:1–14) transposed in Pauline colors and hues. Those who were dead in their sins come to life with Christ because of God's love and mercy (2:4–5). God's people are rescued, redeemed, saved, but not because they are deserving; only because of divine grace (2:5, 8). Ezekiel's vision ends with a human army, standing strong and ready at arms. Impressive, indeed. But Paul trumps this. Christ's people are raised high up into the heavenly realms in Christ Jesus (2:6). Again, this privilege is not based on ruling talent, family name, or contributing wealth; rather, it is to point to "the immeasurable riches of his grace in kindness toward us in Christ Jesus" (2:7).

Grace Calling (3:2–9)

Throughout Ephesians, Paul continues to focus on divine love and grace, rather than human status and desert; but Paul also sees "grace" as more than a gift. He understands it as a calling, an investment from God toward humans participating in his redemption project. Paul referred to his own apostleship as "the commission of God's grace that was given me for you" (3:2; cf. 3:7; Gal 2:9; Rom 12:3). Paul knew he was not fit for this role, especially because he had an ugly history of persecuting the church (Gal 1:23). As John Barclay notes, "God's mercy is not selectively distributed according to any criterion of gender, age, social class, moral achievement or ethnic identity. . . . Neither [Paul's] positive nor his negative tokens of worth could offer an explanation."[4] Yet, he had to be faithful to God's gift, not only of salvation, but of his commission for gospel ministry, namely, "to bring to the Gentiles the news of the boundless riches of Christ" (Eph 3:8). Grace is not permission to do anything one wants without consequence. It is a generous act of God to rescue and redeem mortals. But there is more. Those mortals are then called to a new family and a new life. Grace is a gift *and* a responsibility.

Grace Together (4:1–7)

The fourth chapter of Ephesians gives some attention to the unifying dynamics of divine grace. God's grace called believers together to exercise their *gifts* for the benefit of the whole: "Each of us was given grace according to the measure of Christ's gift" (4:7). Paul affirms that these gifts are not to be used for self-promotion or personal gain. They are meant to support the one people.

> There is one body and one Spirit, just as you were called to the one hope of your calling, one Lord, one faith, one baptism, one God and Father of all, who is above all and through all and in all. (4:4–6)

The bottom line here is that insofar as God is kind and giving, and insofar as he not only saves but also calls to serve with special gifts,

---

4. John M. G. Barclay, "Pure Grace? Paul's Distinctive Jewish Theology of Gift," *Studia Theologica* 68.1 (2014): 4–20, at 11; online: http://dro.dur.ac.uk/12667/1/12667.pdf.

so believers ought to "lead a life worthy of [their] calling" (4:1) for the welfare of the whole. This grace is something they equally share in *together*. Chapter 4 ends with the notion that believers are not only those who *receive* grace, but they are also called to *give* grace: "Let no evil talk come out of your mouths, but only what is useful for building up, as there is need, so that your words may give grace to those who hear" (4:29). Just a bit later Paul exhorts the Ephesians to be filled with kindness, compassion, and forgiveness (4:32)—in other words, grace.

OTHER NEW TESTAMENT VOICES

Luke 1:30; John 1:14–18; Romans 5:15–21; 1 Corinthians 15:10; Ephesians 2:5–8; 1 Timothy 1:14; Titus 2:11; Hebrews 4:16; James 4:6; 1 Peter 4:10

---

2 Corinthians 8:9

Grace Is Costly

Ephesians is especially good at highlighting how God's grace is grand and beautiful. But I find that 2 Corinthians emphasizes how grace in the way of Jesus is *costly*. Amid an argument for gentile churches contributing to a benevolence ministry for poor churches in Judea, Paul describes "the grace of our Lord Jesus Christ" as a master example for all believers to imitate: "Though he was rich, yet for your sake he became poor, so that you through his poverty might become rich" (2 Cor 8:9 NIV). This is a stunning image of grace. What kind of person would do this?

Keep in mind, in the ancient world—a sociological and economic environment that promoted competition and rivalry (not grace)—it would have been a remarkable happenstance for an elite, a lord (*kyrios*), to spend himself into poverty in order to make someone *else* rich. Notice the almost reckless extravagance of this exchange: the *kyrios* doesn't just hand out a dole of supplies or money (beneficent people did this all the time—they still do), but he wastes himself away into financial oblivion. And he does so, not just to lift the poor out of poverty but to catapult them into news-making wealth. This once-poor other is spoiled with the best of everything and far too much to use. From an economic standpoint this *kyrios* is a damn fool. The world calls this "irresponsible." The gospel calls this "grace."

Grace for Today

Do We Owe Anything to the God of Grace?

John Barclay argues that we must not assume today that the Bible's emphasis on divine grace involves "no strings attached." Bonhoeffer called this "cheap grace."[5] Rather, God showed this amazing grace in order to "create a bond between the divine and the human."[6] God giving gifts to mortals lavishly does not automatically mean he has no expectations. God is not a "disinterested" giver; he is *very* interested! God "invites a personal, enduring and reciprocal relationship—an ethos very often signalled by the use of the term *charis* [grace]."[7] Barclay refers to the Christ-gift as "unconditioned" (requiring no prior condition), but "it does not thereby escape the bonds of reciprocity and rise to the modern Derridean ideal gift without hope or expectation of return."[8] Put simply, believers "owe" their lives and worship to God, not because it pays God back, but because of that new life found in relationship with God. This is implied throughout Paul's letters, as in Romans 12:1 (NIV), "Offer your bodies as a living sacrifice, holy and pleasing to God." Or 1 Corinthians 6:20, "For you were bought with a price; therefore glorify God in your body."

This reminds me of Cyprian's reflections on what it means to pray for God's will to be done, as prescribed in the Lord's Prayer (Matt 6:9–13). Cyprian, a third-century theologian, imagines Christians

---

5. Dietrich Bonhoeffer, *The Cost of Discipleship* (New York: Simon & Schuster, 1995), see esp. 44–68.

6. John M. G. Barclay, "Did Paul Believe in the One-Way Gift?" *Proceedings of the Irish Biblical Association* 39 (2016): 30–44, at 36–37.

7. Barclay, "Did Paul Believe in the One-Way Gift?," 37.

8. Barclay, "Did Paul Believe in the One-Way Gift?," 37.

in every way imitating Christ, who perfectly carried out the divine will. Believers, Cyprian explains, must be filled with humility, faith, truth, justice, mercy, and peace as well as be God-loving and fully committed to Christ, "preferring nothing whatsoever to Christ because he preferred nothing to ourselves, clinging inseparably to his love, standing by his cross with courage and faith and, when his name and honor are contested, being a confessor by constancy in the crown by patience under sentence to death."[9] Loving God, "preferring nothing whatsoever" to Christ, is not a "salvation-earning" work. It is the most natural, faithful, and fitting response to the incredible love of God in Jesus Christ.

Becoming Grace Givers

If there is one clear and enduring message of the Bible, it is that God's character is to pour out love and grace on the undeserving. Israel experienced this, especially in God's rescuing of his people from slavery in Egypt. Saint Paul knew this all too well, announcing to his protégé Timothy this "trustworthy saying": "Christ Jesus came into the world to save sinners—of whom I am the foremost. But for that very reason I received mercy, so that in me, as the foremost, Jesus Christ might display the utmost patience, making me an example to those who would come to believe in him for eternal life" (1 Tim 1:15–16). In turn, Paul lived a life of grace-giving. I am reminded of the episode in *Les Misérables* where Jean Valjean, an ex-convict, finds a bed to rest in for the night at the home of Bishop Bienvenu. In the middle of the night, Valjean quietly steals Bienvenu's expensive silver and runs off. The police capture Valjean and return to Bienvenu. Beinvenu lies and says that he gave the silver to Valjean as a gift, and plays it up by saying he forgot to take the silver candlesticks. After the police leave without Valjean, Bienvenu warns him about the power of grace:

> Forget not, never forget that you have promised me to use this silver
> to become an honest man. . . . Jean Valjean, my brother: you belong

---

9. A. Stewart-Sykes, trans., *Tertullian, Cyprian, and Origen: On the Lord's Prayer* (New York: St. Vladimir's Seminary Press, 2004), 75–76.

no longer to evil, but to good. It is your soul that I am buying for you. I withdraw it from dark thoughts and from the spirit of perdition, and I give it to God![10]

This is such a poignant example of amazing grace, grace that gives and spoils, grace that changes and challenges, and grace that creates a powerful force for good in the world.

Amish Grace[11]

On the morning of October 2, 2006, Charles Roberts killed five young girls in a schoolroom at West Nickel Mines Amish School, and injured several more. As police charged into the building, Roberts killed himself. Roberts left behind a wife, Marie, and three young children of his own. While nothing could bring back those Amish children, the response from the West Nickel Mines Amish community was nothing short of astonishing. Immediately after this tragedy they decided to forgive Charles Roberts. That act alone would be hard enough, and others may never get there in their lifetime. But more than that, they visited the shooter's widow, Marie, to care for her and express their concern for her family. Marie recalls that visit, commenting, "They were concerned about me and concerned about the kids, and wanted us to know that they supported our family." Not much later, when her family went to bury Charles Roberts, the Amish community attended and placed themselves in front of the cameras—even picture-shy as they are—to give Marie's family privacy and dignity. If all that were not enough, they made a financial donation to Marie for her ongoing welfare and that of her family. *Amish grace indeed.*

Turning back one more time to Paul, we can note how Barclay paints a picture of the apostle's theology of grace that looks a lot like this Amish grace. Humans too often ask if the other is deserving of

---

10. Victor Hugo, *Les Misérables* (New York: Dodd, Mead & Company, 1862), 28.
11. The information shared about this event is largely drawn from this news report: Kaitlyn Folmer, Natasha Singh, and Suzan Clarke, "Amish School Shooter's Widow, Marie Monville, Speaks Out," ABC News, September 30, 2013, https://abcnews.go.com/US/amish-school-shooters-widow-marie-monville-remembers-tragedy/story?id=20417790. For a book-length study, see Donald B. Kraybill, Steven M. Nolt, and David Weaver-Zercher, *Amish Grace: How Forgiveness Transcended Tragedy* (Hoboken, NJ: John Wiley, 2010).

"my" help. That is, we have certain standards about the worthiness of the other to receive our help or grace. What is so amazing about God's grace is that it "breaks all sorts of social norms and expectations. The gift of Christ is larger than it should be. It is undeserved forgiveness."[12] How do we imitate this kind of grace today? Barclay points to many everyday examples. Think of someone who sits and chats warmly with a homeless man. Or look at Pope Francis's example of taking time away from his official events to visit prisoners. While these snapshots of modern grace may be culturally risky, they honor the God who humbles himself to care for his creatures.

Suggested Reading

John M. G. Barclay. *Paul and the Gift*. Grand Rapids: Eerdmans, 2016.
———. *Paul and the Power of Grace*. Grand Rapids: Eerdmans, 2020.
Frank Matera. *God's Saving Grace: A Pauline Theology*. Grand Rapids: Eerdmans, 2012.
Miroslav Volf. *Free of Charge: Giving and Forgiving in a Culture Stripped of Grace*. Grand Rapids: Zondervan, 2006.

---

12. Wesley Hill and John M. G. Barclay, "What's So Dangerous about Grace," *Christianity Today*, December 31, 2015, www.christianitytoday.com/ct/2016/january-february/whats -so-dangerous-about-grace.html.

CHAPTER 8

Fellowship

Sharing Life with God and Others

Philippians

I hate fellowship. Okay, sorry, that sounded harsh. What I mean is, I hate *"small talk."* Unfortunately, in most of the churches I have been in in America, that tends to be the way we think about fellowship. *Take two minutes and say hi to the person next to you.* (This is why I volunteer to take the kids to their Sunday School classes.) *Stick around after church for donuts and coffee. It'll be fun!* I gained insight about the American culture of "fellowship" when I was reading an article about how immigrant pastors process their experience of American churches. Guatemalan pastor Wilmer Ramírez recounts his first visit to an American church. The American pastor, announcing a church event, said, "Be sure to come. You'll have a blast!" Ramírez never heard pastors talk like this in Guatemala. He found it bewildering that this pastor was emphasizing the entertainment value of the event and not how one would grow in their faith. "I wondered if 'having a blast' was the most important thing for Christians in the US."[1]

---

1. Marshall Shelley, "What Christians in the US Can Learn from Immigrant Pastors," *Christianity Today*, January 11, 2018, www.christianitytoday.com/pastors/2018/january-web-exclusives/what-christians-in-us-can-learn-from-immigrant-pastors.html.

That is a strong, though accurate, indictment of the American church. And this applies to how we see "fellowship." Based on just a quick Google search for "church fellowship ideas," I immediately found suggestions like "themed dinners," "board game mania," "Wii challenge night," and "treasure hunt." Fellowship has become so "optional" that it is virtually nonexistent for busy Christians today. Or it is about having fun times and creating "bonding moments." We are so far from recognizing, valuing, and practicing *true* Christian fellowship—what the Bible describes—that it is worth taking time to just start with the basics. *What is the New Testament talking about when it uses the word "fellowship"?*

The Greek word we translate into English as "fellowship" is *koinōnia*. It comes from the base word *koinos*, which means "common." Think of a modern gymnasium locker room—that would be considered a *koinos* space because many people enter into this place and share its resources. As a noun, as a "thing," *koinōnia* means commonness, partnership, or (to make up a word) "sharedness." So, for example, *koinōnia* was one way of referring to a marriage contract.[2] This involves two separate people *sharing* one life. I think of Genesis 2, where Adam and Eve became *one flesh*; that is, they still maintained separate personal identities, but their lives intertwined so thoroughly that they lived one life together.

When we talk about "fellowship," then, in these terms, we should not be talking about "fun social gatherings," or "get to know you" events. (That does not mean such activities are inherently evil, but it does mean we need to set these aside when we are talking about Christian fellowship.) The terminology confuses the matter, because *koinōnia* was a common word in Paul's time (pun intended!), but today the word "fellowship" seems like old-timey religious talk today. We would be better off calling it "Christian partnership," "Christian community," or "Christian sharing." None of these sounds exactly like *koinōnia* but they get a lot closer. Paul was very passionate about *koinōnia*. In fact, he assumed it was an essential ingredient of the Christian life. But before we look at the parade of examples of *koinōnia* in Philippians, let us briefly turn to the Old Testament.

---

2. See James Moulton and George Milligan, "*koinōnia*," *The Vocabulary of the Greek Testament* (Peabody, MA: Hendrickson, 1997), 350–51.

Old Testament Background

If we think of "fellowship" as playing bingo in church after the potluck and before the pie contest, then there was nothing like this in ancient Israel (nor in the early church). But if we define "fellowship" as living life together, sharing life in common, this is the essence of Israel's life with God. They might not have called it "fellowship," but if they had heard it defined, they would have said, *Oh yes, that is what our "covenant" is all about.* Covenant is about mutual trust, risky involvement, and all those things that come with turning toward each other and intertwining lives.

We catch so many insightful glimpses into fellowship in the life of Israel, it could fill many books, but I want to just point you to two examples. The first one comes from Exodus where Joshua takes responsibility for leading Israel in their fight against the Amalekites. Moses did not step into the war being waged on the ground, but went up on a hilltop with Aaron and Hur. Scripture tells us whenever Moses held his hands up, Israel became stronger and overpowered the Amalekites. But when Moses felt tired and lowered his hands, Amalek would prevail. (*No pressure, Moses.*) So what did Aaron and Hur do? They saw Moses's weariness as the battle waged on and they looked around for a large rock for him to sit on and rest his legs (17:12a). (That is not quite fellowship yet. That is just a very thoughtful gesture.) Then they stood on each side of him and braced his arms: "so his hands were steady until the sun set" (17:12b). *That* is fellowship. Surely holding Moses's hands up would have been depleting for Aaron and Hur—it was not *no big deal.* But they knew this one task was important, and they *shared* strength to do it. Moses was called to this impossible work, but he was not alone. He had a "fellowship."

A second image: the manna provision. In the wilderness, God rained special bread from heaven that would feed his people. We often think of this as a vertical miracle—God sending food down from heaven, but there was a key social component as well that we often leave out in retellings of this miracle story. There was *just enough* manna for each person to have one portion. If any one person took even a *little* too much, someone else would go hungry. *Why would God send so little manna?* Certainly it was so they would trust him, but it is obvious that it was *also* so they would learn to care for one another as well. The Israelite leaders of a tent would take extra manna to feed small children, the lame, and the elderly. And there was always the temptation to take just a tad bit more, "just in case." But they had to learn the lesson that part of *fellowship*, being part of a sharing community, is not just *giving*, but also making sure not to take more than you need. This was a significant, life-shaping lesson in community care, respect, and, yes, *love* for Israel in the desert.

Let's jump ahead in time to the Second Temple period, the era of Jesus and Paul, and also the era of a Jewish sage called Ben Sira. Ben Sira was a wisdom teacher and many of his aphorisms were collected and respected by Jews. Ben Sira is especially interesting when it comes to talking about "fellowship," because his sayings are in Greek and we can learn much from his use of *koinōnia* (and other related terms). We will look at a few examples before turning to Paul and Philippians.

> There are friends who share your table, but they will not stand by you in time of trouble. (Sir 6:10, modified version of NRSV)

We might say, "Some so-called friends hang out with you for 'fellowship,' but when their commitment to you is tested, they are gone." There is true fellowship, and there is superficial fellowship. And Ben Sira urges us to know the difference.

> Whoever touches pitch gets dirty, and whoever associates with a proud person becomes like him. (Sir 13:1)

This is a pretty simple example, but it makes a profound point. Here "associates" could be translated as "has fellowship with" and imagines the lives of these people touching and intermixing. Put another way, "true fellowship" gets each person "dirty" with the life of the other. When we think about this kind of fellowship in the life of the church, we could say it this way: If you are not "touching" people's lives so closely and intimately that their personal marks can be seen on your life (i.e., "dirt"), and vice versa, then you're not doing fellowship right.

One more example:

> Gain the trust[3] of your neighbor in his poverty, so that you may
> rejoice with him in his prosperity. Stand by him in time of distress,
> so that you may share with him in their inheritance. (Sir 22:23)

Ben Sira is very practical about the value and necessity of sharing life together. Being there for your neighbor can be hard, especially if you need to let go a little bit of your financial security. But Ben Sira is a realist—eventually *you too* will be in need, and that thankful neighbor will remember you. To share with them in their inheritance means being accepted as *family*. What if *we* lived in neighborhoods and communities that treated each other like family, not just with smiles and hugs—though we might need those warm gestures sometimes—but also with money and other forms of tangible support?

Focal Text: Philippians

Paul, a fellow Jew steeped in Jewish tradition, would have resonated with these wise words from Ben Sira. Indeed, Paul and Ben Sira would have agreed that the life destroyed by sin can only be restored to wholeness in community by God's presence and grace. Put another way, we can only truly know genuine fellowship with each other when we are restored to proper fellowship with *God*. For example, Paul commends to the Corinthians this notion: "God is faithful; by him you were called into the fellowship of his Son, Jesus Christ our Lord" (1 Cor 1:9). Again, let me say that I find the English word "fellowship" to be mostly corrupted by modern (mis)use. I might prefer to translate this "by him you were called into a *shared life* with his Son, Jesus Christ our Lord." Sin tears apart and leads us to push each other away; but God stitches together and reconciles. The heart of Christian "fellowship" is the gospel that

---

3. Interestingly, unlike the earlier examples, here you don't find the *koinōnia* word group; but you find *pistis*, which is often translated as "faith" in the New Testament (here translated appropriately as "trust").

draws us in and forms us into one body and life. To flesh this out, we will look especially at life-sharing language in Philippians.

Sharing the Spirit

In Paul's letter to the Philippians, he commends them for many good communal virtues and habits. But he also shows concern that there is some disunity and perhaps even rivalry that threatens to fracture their community. Before trying to solve some of these social problems (see Phil 4:2–3), Paul reminds them of their first joy and love when they received the gospel. They had experienced encouragement in Christ, comfort by God's love, and fellowship of the Spirit, which means something like *a deep and transforming presence of and companionship with God's Spirit* (2:1). They came to share life with God through the Spirit, and it brought unspeakable love and peace.

But what happened to that peace? The answer: life. Life has its ups and downs, and the Philippians were experiencing some downs. This could lead to despair—where is God in the suffering? Paul's answer was not some form of transcendental escapism to "commune with God," but quite the opposite, *sharing in Christ's sufferings.*

Sharing in the Sufferings of Christ

Paul was rotting in prison, so to speak, while he was trying to console and cheer up the Philippians in the midst of *their* discouragement. But he had learned a secret. Suffering does not necessarily mean God has abandoned you. In fact, it can play a role in drawing the believer *closer* to God. To know the God of all power, the one who conquered death, is to know Christ by *sharing in his sufferings and by becoming like him in his death* (Phil 3:10). Paul learned that Christ didn't suffer so we wouldn't have to suffer; no, suffering will continue to be a reality in a broken world waiting for full redemption. But suffering can be *relocated*, as it were, into the safe and secure life of Christ. If we choose to combine our affliction-filled lives with the One who was afflicted for us, we can share his resurrection resources as well.

This becomes not a mystical paradigm of religious spirituality, but a whole way of life; a manner of sharing in the troubled lives of others to share their troubles. In fact, Paul tells the Philippians precisely this when he thanks them for sending him gifts in his imprisonment: "It was kind of you to share my distress" (4:14). We know the Philippian church had recently gone through a time of poverty, so when Paul says they *shared* his needs and troubles, this means they gave up resources at a personal cost.

Sharing One Life

In Philippians 1:27, Paul offers what most scholars consider to be the main idea or central instruction of the letter: "live your life in a manner worthy of the gospel of Christ . . . standing firm in one spirit, striving side by side with one mind for the faith of the gospel." The image Paul conjures up is one of separate people joining together as one "unit" in lockstep. Similarly, in chapter 2, he calls them to be "of the same mind, having the same love, being in full accord and of one mind" (2:2). There is more of a sense of intimacy and communion in this verse in chapter 2. We see this modeled in Paul's friendship and partnership with Timothy. Paul felt confident sending Timothy to minister to them as "another Paul," so to speak, because he had shared Paul's life so deeply (see 2:19–22).

Sharing in Mission

Christians do not just need each other for money and companionship, but also to serve the world together as one body in the work of the gospel. Paul repeatedly thanks and commends the Philippians for their partnership or fellowship with him in his apostolic ministry. They *shared* this work with him from day one (1:5). I am sure Paul has money in mind, but it must have been much more: prayers, messages of encouragement, Philippian emissaries who came and helped him on occasion. And this meant the world to Paul. These Philippian believers were in his heart, showing great love and compassion for him, and cheering him on in his difficult ministry (Phil 1:7).

One might think that Paul had many such supportive churches, but he makes it clear this was not the case. In the early days of his ministry, "no church shared with me in the matter of giving and receiving, except you alone" (4:15). The phrase "giving and receiving" implies *mutuality*, an agreement to pool resources and share some kind of need and share another kind of benefit (lending money and goods a common example). It was a risky venture that was apparently *too* risky for most communities. Each church had their own idea of what true fellowship looked like. Speaking of which, let's consider how Luke expresses Christian fellowship as we look at this language in Acts.

OTHER NEW TESTAMENT VOICES
Matthew 18:20; John 15:12–17; Romans 12:4–5; Galatians 6:2; Ephesians 4:2–6; Colossians 3:14; Hebrews 10:24–25; 1 Peter 4:8–9; 1 John 4:11

Acts 2

Luke's account of the growth of the church in Acts offers a rather breathtaking depiction of Christian fellowship. You might recall that Luke presents a fourfold set of practices of the church: "They devoted themselves to the apostles' teaching and fellowship (*koinōnia*), to the breaking of bread and the prayers" (2:42). But what did Luke mean by "fellowship"? Again, I can assure you he did not have bocce ball on the church lawn in mind. Actually, if you continue reading, Luke clarifies what he means by "fellowship": "Now the whole group of those who believed were of one heart and soul, and no one claimed private ownership of any possessions, but everything they owned was held in common" (4:32; cf. 2:44). I think it would be quite a radical step to try anything like this today, but I am still struck by the words "held in common." Whatever else the church does (worship, teaching, service), Luke makes it clear it is especially a place of *sharing*. Church wasn't a privatized worship experience where spectators could pop in and out for consumption. It was a place of exchange and interchange, giving and receiving, shifting and moving resources to attain that wilderness manna vision where no one had too much or too little. That is the church's miracle, not heavenly bread *per se*, but heavenly sharing (see 2 Cor 8–9).

Fellowship for Today

C. S. Lewis's *The Great Divorce* begins with these rather aloof and grouchy people living in the "grey town" waiting to take a bus ride. I won't spoil the ending, but the main character and narrator, new to this place, is informed that here people don't get along with each other. When he asks why the town is so empty, someone explains that everyone is too "quarrelsome" to live together.

> As soon as anyone arrives he settles in some street. Before he's been there twenty-four hours he quarrels with his neighbour. Before the week is over he's quarrelled so badly that he decides to move. Very likely he finds the next street empty because all the people there have quarrelled with their neighbours—and moved. So he settles in. If by any chance the street is full, he goes further. . . . Finally he'll move right out to the edge of the town.[4]

The narrator asked about people who moved to the grey town long ago—where are they? He received this reply.

> [With a telescope] you can see the lights of the inhabited houses, where those old ones live, millions of miles away. Millions of miles from us and from one another. Every now and then they move further still. That's one of the disappointments. I thought you'd meet interesting historical characters. But you don't: they're too far away.[5]

Lewis's portrayal of the grey town is not some kind of literal depiction of hell, contrary to popular belief. Rather, it represents a place absent of God's grace. Left to our own vices, we humans instinctually fight and separate. That is the power of sin in our lives. The gospel is the message that *God* has come to *us*, and has offered to share his own life with us, and to fill us up with himself. And a key component of that new life with and in him is living life with others. But I am afraid our modern Christian culture looks more like Lewis's nightmare world

---

4. C. S. Lewis, *The Great Divorce* (New York: HarperOne, 2009), 10.
5. Lewis, *Great Divorce*, 11.

than it does the great communion of Philippians or Acts 2. Fellowship is not an optional benefit of faith, but a necessity. It is not entertainment, but a mission of the gospel. Our Christian distance from one another signals our distance from God. If you are like me, you will read Lewis's description and see too many churches and Christians living separate lives. Is there hope? Yes, there is always hope, but sometimes the church has to think anew about such things by looking at examples outside the church.

The "Car Pool" Church

I am at an age and life stage where my kiddos are all in sports, sometimes more than one sport at a time. So, I work during the day, and then my wife and I drive them around in the evening. One of my lifelines is my neighborhood car pool. There is a constant exchange of texts between parents about pickups and locations and drop-offs. It is interesting to me how I can "miss" a Sunday at church, and everything is fine (people hardly even seem to notice). But if my car-pool partner is unavailable, it completely wrecks my life! Or, perhaps to put it the other way around, with my kids' sports car-pool community, we share life in such a way that they live life with my family and I with theirs, and we are all deeply and constantly aware of our desperate need for one another. *What if church was actually like that? Where, instead of saying, "I need a break from church because I am busy," you might say, "I can't wait until Sunday because those people take care of me so well!"* And lest we think "taking care of each other" is primarily "spiritual" or "emotional" or "religious," read Acts 2 again—they *literally* took care of each other. Like my car pool. *Imagine that.*

The "Give-and-Take" Church

When I was in grad school, on campus there was this mysterious little building, more like a shack, lovingly called the "Give-and-Take." Seminaries have a transient population—students are there for a few years of education, and then they move on. So, when moving out time came around, students would donate unwanted belongings to the shack: furniture, books, clothes, kitchen utensils, appliances, etc. And when new people moved in, they could visit the Give-and-Take—and take.

Sometimes we had international students coming with their families, and they would have little money and few belongings. So, the Give-and-Take was a blessing, to say the least. They would probably never even *meet* the people who once owned these belongings (kitchen knives, blankets, sewing machines, small TVs), and yet these people shared lives. In a sense, the Give-and-Take didn't cost anyone anything. But to those in need, it was life-giving. And if we remember Ben Sira's counsel, *giving* is a wise investment in life, because someday we too will be *needy*.

The "Fix-It Fair" Fellowship

In Portland, Oregon, where I live, there is a delightful little annual event called the "Fix-It" fair. It is not a religious event, it is a city-sponsored community service where people come together with their broken items: toaster, microwave, clothing with awkward holes and tears, flat bicycle tires. You can bring one item for a fixer to fix. And who are these fixers? They are volunteers, just people who happen to have a skill in one of these areas. Did I mention this event is free and includes lunch and free childcare? This is all about a community pooling resources and expertise and helping each other out. No one person knows how to do everything, and there are some people who have very little and need lots of help. What if the church had a "Fix-It Fair" mentality of mutuality and reciprocal service and care—rather than just gathering for "worship," and scattering for the rest of life, left to deal with all of our problems alone?

The Christian Virtue of Being "Sharey"

Someone might hear these reflections on fellowship and think: *I should be more generous.* Perhaps, but that is not what fellowship is really about. I fear that when people hear the word "generosity," it sounds like giving what is extra or leftover. Like, "I have an extra cookie, I will be generous and give this to someone else." That is kind, and it is generous, but fellowship is different. Fellowship is this crazy notion that I have *more* when I share with someone else something *I* need.

In 1 Timothy 6:18, Paul instructs his friend to encourage wealthy believers to be "generous," *eumetadotos* (that is, to give away what is extra when their own needs are met). But even more than that, they should be *koinōnikos*, Paul adds in this verse. We don't have an exact word match for this in English (you might notice it is related to *koinōnia*). It is an adjective, so we might make up a new word, "sharey." "Be sharey," Paul tells them. This means not just giving our surplus, but sharing what *you* use, what *you* have. *What would the church look like and act like if it was a "sharey" place?*

Suggested Reading

Robert J. Banks. *Paul's Idea of Community*. Peabody, MA: Hendrickson, 1995.

Dietrich Bonhoeffer. *Life Together and Prayerbook of the Bible*. Minneapolis: Fortress, 1996.

Luke Timothy Johnson. *Sharing Possessions: What Faith Demands*. 2nd ed. Grand Rapids: Eerdmans, 2011.

Scot McKnight. *A Fellowship of Differents: Showing the World God's Design for Life Together*. Grand Rapids: Zondervan, 2014.

CHAPTER 9

Hope

Leaning into God's Redeemed Future

1–2 Thessalonians

My favorite *Star Wars* movie is *Rogue One*.[1] (I know, that's crazy, right?)
If you haven't seen *Rogue One*, this film offers some of the backstory of
the origins of the notorious (original) Death Star, and the attempt by
a group of rebels to find a way to destroy it. The main character, Jyn
Erso, was coerced into the rebel cause and previously claimed not to
have political allegiances. She hesitantly agrees to help and joins forces
with rebel leader Cassian Andor. In one of the early scenes, Erso is
given information about the rebel plan. The plan leaves a lot to chance
and its integrity hangs by a thread. Andor acknowledges that the plan
could fail, but that where there is a chance, there is hope. Erso scoffs
at Andor's use of the word "hope." Andor replies, "Rebellions are built
on hope."

That last statement by Andor becomes a motto of the movie (and
is used again later by Erso when she addresses the rebel alliance leadership): *rebellions are built on hope*. It makes for a great movie line in an

---

1. *Rogue One: A Star Wars Story*, directed by Gareth Edwards (Lucasfilm: Walt Disney
Studios Motion Pictures, 2016).

action/sci-fi movie. But it is also true. When a smaller group within an oppressive regime dares to fight the powers and seek its independence, it requires hope; hope that they can win, hope that luck and fate are on their side, hope that what they lose along the way will be less than what they gain in the end if they triumph. For the oppressed, hope is really *all* they have.

A couple of years ago, I had occasion to read again the *Diary of Anne Frank*. In her period of hiding and isolation, this amazing young teenager lived in a world of dreams and imagination—and hope. Hope became a world unto itself where she could escape; it was her only salvation from the horrors of isolation, fear, and despair.

> Again and again I ask myself, would it not have been better for us all if we had not gone into hiding, and if we were dead now and not going through all this misery, especially as we shouldn't be running our protectors into danger any more. But we all recoil from these thoughts too, for we still love life, we haven't yet forgotten the voice of nature, we still hope, hope about everything. (Friday, May 26, 1944)[2]

The English word "hope" can be used in many different ways. Hope can focus on events or situations ("I hope that my flight won't get cancelled"); hope can dwell on relationships ("we put hope in our new principal, that she will get our school back on track"). Hope can sometimes be about something insignificant ("I hope the coffee shop is open today"); or something *very* important ("I hope he will be okay"). Scripture uses the language of hope to talk about any and all of these kinds of things. Sometimes, the "hope" involves wishes and desires. Herod *hoped* to witness a miracle of Jesus (Luke 23:8). Paul *hoped* to get a chance to see the Roman believers in person (Rom 15:24). These are expressions of wishes for the future, but not much hangs on their outcome. But when we think and talk about a New Testament *theology* of hope, we have in mind weightier uses of this vocabulary, where more indeed is at stake.

---

2. David Barnouw and Gerrold Van Der Stroom, ed., *The Diary of Anne Frank*, The Revised Critical Edition (New York: Doubleday, 2003), 684.

And we know what this is like today. In politics and popular culture we find many interesting, more meaningful uses of "hope" language. One popular motto against breast cancer is "I hope, I fight, I will win." The presidential campaign theme for Barack Obama was "Hope." George Washington Carver (1864–1943) once said, "Where there is no vision, there is no hope," in reference to the dreams of freedom and equality for black people. In these instances, "hope" becomes a matter of life and death.

Likewise, in the New Testament, "hope" is sometimes used to communicate some of the most central theological ideas related to salvation and redemption. Paul talked about the "God of hope" (Rom 15:13). "Hope" was one of the big three master virtues of the Christian life (along with "faith" and "love"; 1 Cor 13:13). In lyrical prose, Ephesians 4:4–6 epitomizes the key unifying themes of Christian faith: one body, one Spirit, one Lord, one baptism, one *hope*. If the Christian hope is not fulfilled and proven to be true in the end, Paul confesses it will have all been for naught (1 Cor 15:19).

Old Testament Background

When I sat down to investigate how the Old Testament uses hope language, I was surprised by what I discovered. I had *assumed* previously that the Bible primarily used "hope" to talk about eschatology, what we think of as final redemption and restoration of God's people and God's world. In that case, I expected "hope" language to appear primarily in the major prophets, as Israel developed a more robust and explicit final eschatology (as we find, for example, in Isaiah, Jeremiah, and Ezekiel). Of course, we do find key eschatological uses of hope language in these prophets, but what was unexpected is that the Old Testament does not portray hope only or primarily as something set upon a distant future time of fulfillment. Israel often engaged in confession of hope in a very "now" kind of way.

This is clear when we look at the many times the psalmists talk about hope. Often, perhaps most of the time, the psalmists talk about hope as covenant trust in God that anticipates and expects God to be near and care for his people. This is not usually portrayed as a "not yet" hope of the distant future, but an "already" hope of the God who attends to the needs of Israel on a day-to-day basis. So, for example, Psalm 38 is a plea for healing from the mouth of the suffering David. He is utterly miserable, inconsolable. But he confesses, "It is for you, O Lord, that I wait [or hope]; it is you, O Lord my God, who will answer" (v. 15). His hope is not in some kind of afterlife redemption but in a here-and-now provision: "Do not forsake me, O Lord; O my God, do not be far from me; make haste to help me!" (vv. 21–22a).

When we look at the Septuagint's use of hope language, we discover that the translator(s) of LXX Psalms chose *elpis/elpizō* ("hope"/ "I hope") to translate a very common Hebrew word for "trust" (*batakh*). What that means is that they identified hope with trust and trust with hope. For example, Psalm 91 is a hymn proclaiming the assurance of divine protection. In verse 2, the psalmist confesses that God is the one whom he trusts (*batakh*). The Septuagint uses the Greek verb *elpizō* to communicate this: "my God, I will *hope* in him." Hope is seen here as trust while leaning into an unknown future, yet relying on a tried and true relationship. In verse 4, where the Hebrew text says, "under his wings you will find refuge," the Septuagint again uses *elpizō*, "under his wings you will find *hope*."

In Isaiah (and a few other places in the major prophets) we start to find a more "not yet" articulation of hope, where Israel looked ahead to a great transformative event that would bring full and final redemption and restoration. A David-like king would arise to bring justice to the nations, and all hopes would be fulfilled (Isa 11:10). There would be salvation and joy for Israel, a people who waited for the Lord to act (25:9). In the Septuagint text of 28:5, the writer imagines that day in this way: "the Lord Sabaoth will be the garland of hope, which is woven in glory."

In the Old Testament, Israel conceived of hope as a forward-looking expression of day-to-day trust in God. We do find a few occasions where this "hope" puts on binoculars and gazes into the far distance to catch glimpses of final glory. But, by and large, Israel's expression and confession of hope expects the covenant God to guide each and every future step and to respond now to each and every plea.

Focal Text: 1 Thessalonians

We know that the believing community in Thessalonica was traumatized by the death of beloved members of their community (1 Thess 4:13). We don't know how they died, but we do know that this struck fear into their hearts. Perhaps they took these deaths not only as tragic losses to their community, but also as bad omens. *What if it was a sign that they had offended their former gods?* Whatever the exact scenario, this rocked their world, and also their faith. Paul wrote a pastoral letter of encouragement to spur them on toward faith, love, and *hope*. Hope can be a powerful motivator (as we saw above with Jyn Erso and the crew of *Rogue One*). Paul reminds these believers that they were famous for their trust in God; they have only to persevere in that same hope (1:3).

When it comes to how they were processing the deaths of their friends, Paul did not discourage them from grieving. Lament and grief are important practices reflected in Scripture (see Lamentations; Psalms 7, 22, 44, 51). But Paul told them not to express their grief like those who have no hope (1 Thess 4:13). What is this "hope" that he talks about? He goes on to explain, "since we believe that Jesus died and rose again, even so, through Jesus, God will bring with him those who have died" (v. 14). Death is not the final word for their lives. Their home is not in the grave. They are gone now, but not forever. The "dead in Christ will rise" (v. 16). Rising from the grave, though, is just step one, that is not the end of it. The raising up of the dead has a goal and direction. They will join together with the heavenly Lord "and so we will be with the Lord forever. Therefore encourage one another with these words" (vv. 17–18). Death gets a solid punch in, but God wins the fight, life triumphs over death. Across Paul's letters we catch glimpses of why this resurrection hope is so foundational to Paul's faith and joy in life.

OTHER NEW TESTAMENT VOICES
Matthew 11:28; Romans 5:3–4; 15:13; Ephesians 1:18; Colossians 1:27; Titus 3:7; Hebrews 6:19; 11:1; Revelation 3:10–11

Romans 8; Phil 3:21;
1 Cor 13:9–12; 1 Peter 1:8–9

Hope in Freedom

In Romans 8, Paul points to the divine promise that, one day, God will "set [creation itself] free from its bondage to decay" (8:21). Resurrection hope is not *just* about living forever; it is about a vibrant freedom that puts in the past all the ugliness of sin and death. The Bible tends to use the word "death" to sum up the fullness of how sin ruins the world. Once death itself is defeated and done away with, new life will feel like a new kind of freedom we didn't even know we were born for.

Hope Includes the Whole Self

Christian hope is not about imagining souls floating around in heaven. Paul had hope in a bodily resurrection and transformation, and he passed this on to his churches: He "will transform these humble bodies of ours into the likeness of his glorious body by means of that power by which he is able to subject all things to himself" (Phil 3:21 NET). Many people don't understand that Christianity is a very worldly, fleshly religion, in the sense that eternity involves bodies, *transformed bodies*, but bodies nonetheless. We don't have to wonder what resurrection life will be like. It is an embodied life, freed from the cancer of sin and the threat of death.

Hope Anticipates a More Perfect Union with Christ

Christian hope recognizes that in this world, right now, we cling to God's promises, and we trust him even though we can see only little pieces of the bigger picture. Knowing God now is the essence of the gospel, but even that knowing has its limits. Paul told the Corinthians that we see God and true reality as if looking into a mirror at dusk, but one grand day we will see clearly and perfectly; we will know him more fully, our faith and hope will turn to true knowledge (see 1 Cor 13:9–12). First Peter presents a similar understanding of anticipating a deeper communion with Christ: "Although you have not seen him, you love him; and even though you do not see him now, you believe in him and rejoice with an indescribable and glorious joy, for you are receiving the outcome of your faith, the salvation of your souls[3]" (1 Peter 1:8–9).

Pondering the blessed future is quite a delight, but all too often the real world jolts us from those dreams. And this was a challenge, no doubt, for the Thessalonian believers, who were facing rejection from their neighbors and fears about losing more members of their community. But Paul challenged them not to shrink from their problems and fears. Rather, they ought to face them head-on, like intrepid soldiers marching into battle, warriors of the light. I can almost hear the call to arms now:

> **Paul:** *Who are we?*
> **Thessalonians:** *Soldiers of Daylight!*
> **Paul:** *What is our shield?*
> **Thessalonians:** *Faith!*
> **Paul:** *What is our armor?*
> **Thessalonians:** *Love!*
> **Paul:** *What is our helmet?*
> **Thessalonians:** *Hope!*
> **Paul:** *What are we promised?*
> **Thessalonians:** *Salvation!*
> **Paul:** *Attack the darkness!*[4]

Sounds violent, but this is precisely Paul's strategy for spurring on faith, hope, and love for a beleaguered community. There were no better models of courage and resilience in the ancient world than warriors and soldiers. Hope was a Christian weapon of war against despair. Rebellions against fear, doubt, sin, and death are built on the hope of God's promised victory, his unyielding attack against evil that will swiftly destroy any and all enemies with a single blow (2 Thess 2:8).

---

3. When Peter uses the word "souls" here, he does not mean bodiless spirits; Jews could use the Greek word *psychē* (soul) in reference to the person.

4. See 1 Thess 5:7–9.

Hope for Today

Exercising Hope

It is one thing to sing or confess, "God is my hope." But what does it actually *look* like in daily life? How do you *practice* hope? How do you *grow* in hope? First, we have to stop thinking of hope as vague wishes about an ethereal future in heaven. Paul would not have condoned Christians sitting on their hands, living in a fantasy where they dreamt about utopian bliss. Hope requires imagination, but that heavenly imagination, then, is meant to have a direct impact on our present lives. In 1 Thessalonians, Paul transports that beleaguered church into the eschatological future where God finally vanquishes evil and the dead rise to glory. Then Paul brings them back into the here and now to tell them to be brave, living in hope and knowing that God will accomplish all these things. The future is meant to teach them the truth, so that they will live with faith and hope, empowered by that secret wisdom.

With this perspective in mind, it is helpful to think of hope not so much as a desire to experience but as a muscle to exercise. Put another way, the mature lean on hope, trusting in Jesus Christ; the alternative is to shrink from difficulties and live in hesitation or apathy. Paul addresses this in Romans 5:1–5 in relation to the obstacle of suffering. Paul argues that, for the Christian, suffering should not be an occasion for despair, but for hope. In fact, Paul argues that believers should count difficulties a *blessing*! Not because suffering is inherently good—God is no masochist—but because it affords believers an opportunity to grow in their faith and hope. Paul says that suffering *can* cultivate within us endurance or perseverance—we can begin to acclimate ourselves to it and adjust. We can build resistance to difficulties, to "weather the storm." Then, endurance can become "proven character," strength and resilience tested by many hard experiences. Paul could have ended there, with "proven character," but he actually ends the list with "hope": character can become hope (5:4–5). This is not just any kind of hope. This is hard-won hope, acquired by having pushed through the vain wishes for a perfect and pleasant life here and now into a fully formed dedication to God's promised kingdom.

Let us reflect on this kind of hope in a parable. Three men were diagnosed with the same leg infection and the doctor told them, "The infection cannot be cured. We need to amputate the leg. With hard work and determination, you will walk again with a prosthetic leg. The surgeon can perform the amputation procedure in a month. Prepare yourself for a difficult transition."

Each patient reacted to this news in a different way. The first patient was horrified by the diagnosis and chose to ignore the problem, "hoping" it would go away. He kept delaying the surgery out of fear, and died from the infection. His hope was vain hope.

The second patient was also horrified by the diagnosis and killed himself the next day. He did not believe there was a life worth living after the planned surgery. This man had no hope at all.

The third patient was troubled by the diagnosis, naturally. But he faced the reality of the infection with sobriety and trusted the doctor, who was also his close friend. So, he established a program of exercising his arms, torso, and healthy leg every day, in preparation for life after the surgery. This third man lived in true hope, the kind of hope Paul talked about, not wishy-washy hope, but hope fully invested in a future promised but not yet realized.

So, how do believers today actually live in Christian hope?

Hope as Deposit and Dance

The Christian must cling to two kinds of hope in this life. One kind of hope is the promise of a fully redeemed future. In Colossians, Paul talks about how faith and love today are fueled by a hope "laid up for you in heaven" (Col 1:5). First Peter points to this same hope as an inheritance (1 Pet 1:4). In the twenty-first century, we often think of an inheritance as *money*. But in the ancient world, economic value was placed in property (e.g., a house) and possessions (e.g., heirlooms, furniture, clothes). Christian hope is oriented toward a new home, a place of belonging and rest. The believer takes comfort now in the work God is doing to prepare a perfect, new-creation community devoid of sin, evil, darkness, pain, and death. But in the meantime, the work of the people is to serve well the Father in his absence, until he returns. The inheritance is safe and secure; the job now is to live with the peace of that hope and to obey the mission of bearing God's image on earth.

Hope is not only like the promise of an inheritance, but also like a dance. I don't dance often (or well!), but I know that when two people dance together, it requires faith and hope. You place your trust in the other person as a dance "partner." You synchronize your bodies and there is a constant feedback loop of responding to each other's movements. Faith involves trusting the other person and tuning into their body; hope is the keenly attentive anticipation of each next move of your partner. In the Christian life, this kind of "dancing" hope is not the patient, waiting hope of the final inheritance, but the daily energetic hope of a relationship dance with Jesus Christ: prayers whispered throughout the day, little risks of faith that expectantly anticipate the Spirit's work, simple trust that believes God will place steady ground under the foot taking each next step.

Embracing Anger and Joy

Hope should make us angry. If we knew the beautiful peace of God's redeemed kingdom, we would be angry about the war and injustice that are rampant today. If we knew the freedom and joy of God's redeemed kingdom, we would be angry about all the hatred, enslavement, and misery that plagues our societies. If we knew the abundance and generosity that we will experience in God's redeemed kingdom, we would be outraged over the unnecessary poverty that crushes our communities. Anger should be a natural response to the state of a world devastated by our sin. And that anger should lead to action on behalf of the marginalized, the unfairly imprisoned, the war-torn, and the economically abused. Are we angry enough because of our hope?

At the same time—paradoxically—we ought to be filled with deep gladness, just as Paul says: "Rejoice in hope" (Rom 12:12). Whatever challenges, problems, or obstacles we are facing, they are relatively insignificant in view of the peace and satisfaction of "eternal glory" for which we long and wait. So, "we fix our eyes not on what is seen, but on what is unseen, since what is seen is temporary, but what is unseen is eternal" (2 Cor 4:17–18 NIV). To sing, "It is well / with my soul," as the old hymn testifies, is not to deny or bottle up the trouble and trauma of today. Rather, when we enter the pure glory of God's good end, the suffering we have experienced will seem to have lasted just a "little while," as 1 Peter reminds us (1 Peter 5:10).

Live in the Future—Now

Let's say you knew that you were going to move out of state *tomorrow* and start a new job next month. If you were in a sassy mood, you might go into your workplace and tell off your mean boss. None of the changes would have actually happened yet; you may have signed paperwork, but the new job would still lie in the future. But you have confidence in these changes, so you live now with that future expectation. If you weren't so sure about that other job, maybe you *wouldn't* tell off your boss. But you are so sure of that future, you act now as if all those changes are certain. So, if the Bible tells us what is to come, how are we compelled to live *now*? With Christian hope, believers are called to live boldly and bravely now, already knowing the defeat of sin, death, and evil.

Suggested Reading

Constantine Campbell. *Paul and the Hope of Glory: An Exegetical and Theological Study*. Grand Rapids: Zondervan, 2020.

Paula Gooder. *Heaven*. Eugene, OR: Cascade, 2011.

Nijay K. Gupta. *1–2 Thessalonians*. New Covenant Commentary Series. Eugene, OR: Cascade, 2016.

N. T. Wright. *Surprised by Hope: Rethinking Heaven, the Resurrection, and the Mission of the Church*. New York: HarperOne, 2007.

CHAPTER 10

Salvation

Rescued, Reconciled,
and Established for Flourishing

1–2 Timothy, Titus

Are you saved? When I heard this in sermons in my youth, it was a given that this question was about accepting Jesus as Savior and escaping the fires of hell. Perhaps the question included the notion of going to heaven after you die, but no one ever taught us what happened in heaven and why that would be a good thing—except that it wasn't eternal torment. The preachers I remember were passionate about "saving souls," but they never quite got into the details of what we were being saved *from* exactly or what we were being saved *for*. Popular Christianity tends to paint a one-dimensional, colorless picture of salvation. Something like souls floating blissfully in the clouds. The "other-worldliness" of these images made it seem like "salvation" was about escaping earthly life for a whole other existence we can't even fathom. But that is quite *unlike* how the New Testament writers talked about "salvation." They used everyday language of rescue, relationship, and renewal to describe being saved, including images of being washed clean, being set free, and being born into new life. Even the English term "salvation" may be too overly "Christianized" today to do its work as a suitable representation of rescue and redemption in Scripture. Indeed, "rescue" is a more than suitable English translation of the Greek word *sōteria*, a common noun for salvation in the Greek Bible. We all know what it is like to have a tow truck come and "rescue" you. One time I was stuck in a bathroom stall (with a bad lock) and my wife had to "rescue" me.

I recently came across a breathtaking story that makes for a striking parallel to the dramatic and holistic kind of "rescue" or "saving" that led the New Testament writers to use such language. The story takes place in 1965–1966 when a group of six boys (ages 13–16) ran away from their homeland of Tonga.[1] They stole a boat and headed out hastily in search of Fiji (some five hundred miles away). They took a sack of food and a small gas burner, but no map or compass. Due to their amateur sailing skills and the unfriendly seas, they were lost, adrift for eight days, until they finally spotted land. They ended up on the deserted and infertile island of Ata. These Tongan boys were stranded there for *fifteen months*—one of them broke his leg during their time on Ata. In the two summers they were living there, it hardly rained at all, so they resorted to drinking bird blood to quench their thirst.

Their rescue finally came through Australian Captain Peter Warner, who happened upon them as he was traveling for work. Most stories of dramatic rescues tend to stop there, and the reader is left wondering, *What happened to these boys? Were they okay? Did they live happy, healthy, and fulfilled lives? Did they stay friends?* In this case, we know quite a bit of their story, and it is not all good news. Immediately after Warner delivered them back home, they were arrested for stealing the boat they had "borrowed." Warner took pity on them and paid the boat owner $200 to get the kids off the hook. Furthermore, Warner decided to quit his job in Sydney and stay in Tonga long-term. He started a fishing business there and hired the shipwrecked boys as his crew. Warner mentored and stayed friends with some of them for the rest of his life. One of the boys said, after several decades of friendship, "He [Warner] is like a father to me."[2]

---

1. I draw primarily from Rutger Bregman's account of the situation in "The Real Lord of the Flies: What Happened When Six Boys Were Shipwrecked for 15 Months," *The Guardian*, May 9, 2020, www.theguardian.com/books/2020/may/09/the-real-lord-of-the-flies-what-happened-when-six-boys-were-shipwrecked-for-15-months.

2. Kate Lyons, "The 'Real Lord of the Flies': A Survivor's Story of Shipwreck and

What I find remarkable about this story is not just the work Warner put into "rescuing" the Tongans from unforgiving Ata, but also his compassion, perseverance, and concern for them in the long term. This captures poignantly the difference between a plastic, "get-out-of-hell-free" type of salvation message of Christianity, and a deeper, more relational, dynamic vision of "rescue" that is characteristic of the New Testament.

Our focal point for the New Testament's vision of "salvation" will be Paul's letters to Timothy (1–2 Timothy) and Titus. These short epistles noticeably repeat saving and rescue language throughout, so much so that it is a recognized motif. But before we get to this Pauline correspondence, we need to paint a picture of what "salvation" meant in Jewish religious literature before the time of Jesus.

Old Testament Background

The most vivid portrayal of "salvation" for Israel in the Old Testament is that of the exodus, which we might better call "the Rescue" or "the Redemption." This one big event became a master image for God's life with his people, proving the lengths he would go to to keep his covenant promises to Abraham, Isaac, and Jacob.[3] The people of God long remembered that "the LORD saved Israel that day from the Egyptians; and Israel saw the Egyptians dead on the seashore" (Exod 14:30; cf. 15:2). Throughout the rest of the Old Testament, the Lord is known as the one who brought his people out of Egypt and into a special land (Deut 5:6; Ps 81:10; Amos 2:10; Mic 6:4).

We will return in a moment to the comprehensive significance of this event when it comes to Israel's ongoing experience and expression of redemption from God. Truth be told, though, the vast majority of occurrences of "salvation" language in the Old Testament relate to physical protection and deliverance, usually in the context of battle and political skirmishes (e.g., 1 Sam 7:8). A common type of prayer we

---

Salvation," *The Guardian*, May 13, 2020, www.theguardian.com/world/2020/may/13/the-real
-lord-of-the-flies-mano-totau-survivor-story-shipwreck-tonga-boys-ata-island-peter-warner.

3. See Bryan D. Estelle, *Echoes of Exodus: Tracing a Biblical Motif* (Downers Grove, IL: IVP Academic, 2018); L. Michael Morales, *Exodus Old and New: A Biblical Theology of Redemption* (Downers Grove, IL: IVP Academic, 2020).

find in the Old Testament goes something like this: "Save us, O God of our salvation, and gather and rescue us from among the nations" (1 Chron 16:35). I particularly like David's remembrance of his shepherding youth when God continually preserved him "from the paw of the lion and from the paw of the bear" (1 Sam 17:37). Israel recognized that their fragile lives were in the hands of God; he is the only one who preserves life, thus he is their shield, rock, and fortress (Psalm 62).

At times, though, we see Israel seeking "salvation" (i.e., forgiveness) from their sins. Put another way, sometimes the "rescuing" wasn't from a human foe or hostile nation. Rather, Israel needed rescuing from themselves, from their own sinfulness, and also from the divine wrath and judgment they deserved as covenant breakers. Famously, Psalm 51 voices the penitent heart that knows its own wicked wanderings (51:1–4). "Purge me with hyssop and I shall be clean; wash me, and I shall be whiter than snow . . ." (51:7). The psalmist fears judgment, being driven out from God. He enjoins the Lord with humility and hope, "Restore to me the joy of your salvation and sustain in me a willing spirit" (51:10–12).

As time went on, Israel came to anticipate a final day of judgment, a great assize where God would make all things right. That would involve punishing and destroying God's enemies; it would also include bringing Israel to judgment; thus, it was a day of sober expectation. But because of God's enduring faithfulness (such as with the exodus), Israel could be confident in their salvation (Ezek 36:29; Zech 9:16; Joel 2:30–32).

It is crucial to recognize that "salvation" in the Old Testament had nothing to do with avoiding "hell." Yes, the prophets proclaimed the day of the Lord as a moment of divine judgment, but Israel's "salvation" imagination was shaped by covenant. That is, to be "saved" by God was to live in peace with God and harmony with others. In that sense, "salvation" was not a one-and-done event; it was the beginning of the way life should be.

The Greco-Roman World

Greeks and Romans didn't really have anything like a "day of the Lord" in their religious encyclopedia. Their sense of "salvation" was wrapped up in their understanding that the gods lived in a reciprocal (though unequal) relationship with mortals.[4] Humans paid respect and homage to the gods, and in turn they blessed and protected them. Unsurprisingly, Zeus was sometimes called "savior and liberator."[5] Apollo, as a patron of medicine and prophecy, could also be invoked with the title "savior."[6] This also holds true for Asklepios, god of healing, as well as—no surprise here—the goddess Fortuna (how often is one "bailed out" by luck?).[7]

What did "salvation" mean, though, when a mortal sent prayers toward Olympus? We learn from one inscription this insightful supplication: "May Zeus Savior receive this account favorably and grant in return the benefits of health, safety, peace, and security on land and on sea."[8] "Salvation" is understood here as a "total package" of protection and well-being.

In the age of the Roman emperors, we see "savior" language applied liberally to these sovereigns. Julius Caesar was publicly hailed "savior and benefactor."[9] Most notably, Caesar Augustus was widely celebrated as "savior" of the imperial inhabitants. Roman soldier and senator Velleius Paterculus credited Augustus with bestowing the best riches and good fortune on the Roman people, equal to the patronage of the gods.[10] One famous inscription pronounced Augustus "savior" "who will cause war to cease and will order all things"—wow, that's a lot of pressure for one man![11] Again, "salvation," whether from *deus* (god) or *dominus* (lord), was viewed as protective guardianship, sheltering the vulnerable from harm, and also promoting their welfare and increasing their "quality of life." Now, whether or not gods and rulers *actually* accomplished these things is a whole other matter, but the idea

---

4. See Plato, *Laws* 10.903 b.

5. Pindar, *Odes* 5.17; Aristophanes, *Thesmophoriazusae* 1009.

6. Aeschylus, *Agamemnon* 512.

7. Respectively, *Inscriptiones Graecae* 4.718 and Aeschylus, *Agamemnon* 664.

8. *Lindos: Fouilles et recherches, 1902–1914*, vol. 2, *Inscriptions*, ed. C. Blinkenberg and K. Kinch (Berlin: de Gruyter, 1941).

9. *Inscriptiones Graecae* 8.1835; 12.5, 556; "benefactor" here means someone of power who uses their position and resources to help someone of lesser means.

10. Velleius Paterculus, *Roman History* 2.89.

11. The Priene Calendar Inscription; see W. Dittenberger, ed., *Orientis Graeci Inscriptiones Selectae*, 2 vols. (Leipzig: S. Hirzel, 1903–1905), 2:48–60 (= *OGIS* 458); see also *Sammelbuch griechischer Urkaunden aus Aegypten* 8897.1; Philo, *Embassy* 148–49.

of "saving" or "rescuing" in the Greco-Roman world was viewed as a guardianship relationship meant to secure protection and promote flourishing.

Focal Text: 1–2 Timothy, Titus[12]

Paul could have been dubbed the "Apostle of Salvation," because of the frequency of this language in his letters overall, but the Greek language of salvation (*sōteria* and related terms) has a noticeably high concentration in the Pastoral Epistles (1–2 Timothy, Titus).[13] One of the key descriptors for God and Jesus is the word "Savior" (*sōter*). The way Paul uses this language in these letters is quite grandiose, almost mimicking the style of a public honorific inscription (like the Priene inscription noted above):

> First of all, then, I urge that supplications, prayers, intercessions, and thanksgivings be made for everyone, for kings and all who are in high positions, so that we may lead a quiet and peaceable life in all godliness and dignity. **This is right and is acceptable in the sight of God our Savior**, who desires everyone to be saved and to come to the knowledge of the truth. For
>
> > there is one God;
> > > there is also one mediator between God and humankind,
> > Christ Jesus, himself human,
> > > who gave himself a ransom for all. (1 Tim 2:1–6)

This has the ring of a political public declaration for the welfare of an empire under a gracious lord (*kyrios*), God, reigning through his agent, Jesus the King. A good regent was meant to be gracious, generous, and kind toward his subjects. Not all rulers were, of course,

---

12. For a helpful, detailed examination of salvation language in the Pastoral Epistles, see George Wieland, *The Significance of Salvation: A Study of Salvation Language in the Pastoral Epistles* (Eugene, OR: Wipf & Stock, 2006); note esp. the summaries on 241–42, 265.

13. The *sōteria* word group occurs almost twenty times in these letters (1 Tim 1:1, 15; 2:3, 15; 4:10, 16; 2 Tim 1:9–10; 2:10; 3:15; 4:18; Titus 1:3–4; 2:10–11, 13; 3:4–6).

but this was an ideal, just as Seneca wrote to emperor Nero his advice for the newly crowned emperor, *On Clemency*.

Seneca recognized the limitless power of the emperor as sovereign over the empire, even positioning Nero as a "god upon earth" (*On Clemency* 1.1). In his hands lie the power of life and death. Seneca voices the authority of the imperial seat:

> It rests with me [the emperor] to decide which tribes shall be utterly exterminated, which shall be moved into other lands, which shall receive and which shall be deprived of liberty, what kings shall be reduced to slavery and whose heads shall be crowned, what cities shall be destroyed and what new ones shall be founded. (*On Clemency* 1.1)

So, with such glory resting on his crown, it is all the more urgent that he be patient and kind.

> In this position of enormous power I am not tempted to punish men unjustly by anger, by youthful impulse, by the recklessness and insolence of men, which often overcomes the patience even of the best regulated minds, not even that terrible vanity, so common among great sovereigns, of displaying my power by inspiring terror. My sword is sheathed, nay, fixed in its sheath: I am sparing of the blood even of the lowest of my subjects: a man who has nothing else to recommend him, will nevertheless find favour in my eyes because he is a man. I keep harshness concealed, but I have clemency always at hand: I watch myself as carefully as though I had to give an account of my actions to those laws which I have brought out of darkness and neglect into the light of day. I have been moved to compassion by the youth of one culprit, and the age of another: I have spared one man because of his great place, another on account of his insignificance: when I could find no reason for showing mercy, I have had mercy upon myself. I am prepared this day, should the gods demand it, to render to them an account of the human race. (*On Clemency* 1.1)

This is quite a touching vision of the soft-hearted regent . . . unfortunately Nero did not seem to be too inspired by Seneca's teaching.

But it does overlap with Paul's conception of the grace of God. Paul extols the "kindness and love of God our Savior" who rescued his people even though they had not been perfect citizens. It was purely because of his merciful nature (Titus 3:4–5), whereby he sent "Jesus Christ our Savior" to dispense grace and restoration, giving these sinners hope of eternal life (vv. 6–7). Indeed, "hope" is another keyword in these letters. This does not represent the soul's quiet repose in "heaven." For humans longing for the corrupted world to be redeemed, believers long for "the manifestation of the glory of our great God and Savior, Jesus Christ" (2:13), which is meant to renew creation, not change it into something else entirely. This gracious rescue mission is not intended to preserve one privileged people only but is rather a gift of redemption for *all* people who have faith (Titus 2:11; 1 Tim 4:8–10).

Saved from Sin and Death

What did Paul imagine the Savior's subjects were being saved *from?* There is more than one answer to this question in Paul's writings. First, sinners are in need of saving from their own sins. Paul was readily willing to admit his own culpability: "The saying is sure and worthy of full acceptance, that Christ Jesus came into the world to save sinners—of whom I am the foremost" (1 Tim 1:15). But Paul did not ignore the wider problem of evil and death and their potential impact on believers. Paul confidently claims that "the Lord will rescue me from every evil attack and save me for his heavenly kingdom. To him be the glory forever and ever. Amen" (2 Tim 4:18). The greatest enemy, of course, is death. Christ Jesus "abolished death and brought life and immortality to light" (2 Tim 1:10), but this victory came at a high price. Christ had to sacrifice his own life. Some emperors were known to be generous, but Christ "gave himself" (over to death) to rescue his people (Titus 2:14; cf. 1 Tim 2:6). There is no greater gift, and no other has achieved what Christ has done.[14]

---

14. See Philip Towner, "Pastoral Epistles," *New Dictionary of Biblical Theology*, ed. B. S. Rosner, T. D. Alexander, G. Goldsworthy, and D. A. Carson (Downers Grove, IL: IVP Academic, 2000), 332.

Saved for a New Life and Calling

What are believers saved *for?* Paul did not view "salvation" as an end unto itself, but rather a beginning. He uses the language of "rebirth and renewal by the Holy Spirit" (Titus 3:5), which imagines the exciting "groundbreaking" of a new society. He uses the language of heirship/inheritance, which evokes images of household and home (Titus 3:7). And what do these reborn kingdom citizens *do* with this new life under the Savior? Paul emphasizes redemption for the purpose of action, specifically carrying out a "holy calling" (2 Tim 1:9). Whenever Paul talks about "calling," he means that believers are conscripted into divine service to achieve God's kingdom ends. This is the "holy" part of "holy calling" (2 Tim 1:9). Paul reminds Timothy that he was saved by God's grace for God's purposes. Believers were graciously gifted "life and immortality" (2 Tim 1:10) and are expected to now live up to the standards of this new commonwealth. The "calling" of any good citizen is to contribute to the overall welfare of the community, living in a meaningful relationship of "giving and receiving" (as Paul wrote to the Philippians; see Phil 4:15).

OTHER NEW TESTAMENT VOICES
Luke 1:77; 19:9; Acts 4:12; 7:25; Romans 1:16; 2 Corinthians 7:10; Philippians 1:28; Hebrews 5:9; 1 Peter 1:5; Revelation 7:10; 12:10; 19:1

Acts 5:31

Who Needs a Prince?

In Acts 5, we read about a speech given by Peter (and the other apostles) to the Sanhedrin leaders, in response to their threats to silence them: "We must obey God rather than human beings! The God of our ancestors raised Jesus from the dead—whom you killed by hanging him on a cross. God exalted him to his own right hand as Prince and Savior that he might bring Israel to repentance and forgive their sins.

We are witnesses of these things, and so is the Holy Spirit, whom God has given to those who obey him" (Acts 5:29–32 NIV).

There are so many interesting things we could try to unpack about this text, but my interest was especially piqued by Peter's description of Jesus as "Savior" and "Prince." Christians today are familiar and comfortable with the idea of Jesus as Savior, but imagine if a preacher said—"Who's ready to accept Jesus Christ as their Prince today?" Well, "prince," truth be told, might not be the best translation of the Greek word *archēgos* here. A clearer description would be "ruler." In any case, Peter was making the point that Jesus's work as "Savior" is connected to his power and authority as "Ruler" at the right hand of God. We tend to associate "salvation" with an event and place: we are saved from our sins; now we can go to heaven. But Acts 5:29–32 makes it clear that Jesus's ministry of salvation goes beyond one event to his ruling over God's people, especially calling them to repent from following the way of the sinful world and to follow his true way.[15] And Peter goes on to talk about God's people as those who repent *and* obey. Being "saved," it would seem, is about far more than being rescued. The "saved" need leadership, a tutor and guide to help them flourish. This requires self-reflection, self-discipline, repentance, and obedience.

Salvation for Today

Choir Saved Me

Throughout grade school, I struggled on and off with loneliness and mild depression. I was a brown kid with a weird name in a rural white community in Ohio. I was aimless and unmotivated. But choir saved me. (I became a Christian later on, obviously that was "salvation" on a much grander scale.) Mr. Fleming assembled a motley crew of kids and gave us a safe community. He believed in us, but he also challenged and pushed us. He entered us into choir competitions and set a high

---

15. See the discussion of forgiveness and repentance in chapter 3 [Luke-Acts] of this book.

standard for excellence. We practiced during school, but we gladly also practiced after school when events and competitions were coming up. Mr. Fleming inspired us; he gave us direction; he taught us how to breathe, how to work together, and how to fail gracefully if necessary. We were proud "choir dorks," because we had each other.

Now, I am not saying that religion is just another club with a mission. My Christian faith means far more to me now than any club did then. But I fear that too many churches have a frail vision of "salvation" and its power to create, redeem, and shape. Imagine if the church was a place where people found meaningful belonging. And a safe context for processing their past. And for truly coming to know themselves. And being challenged to "grow up" through repentance and self-discipline. And to participate in a mission together for the good of the world.

Salvation Is the Beginning

Jesus saved us from our sins—the end. That feels like the way a lot of evangelistic sermons go. But from all that we have discussed above in Scripture, it should be clear by now that "salvation" is not just an end, it is also a beginning. In the early fall of 2020, I broke my left foot, my first bone break ever. It was awful. Thankfully, the recovery time ("non-weight-bearing") was relatively short, only a few weeks. So, in a sense, within about a month, my bone had healed. But that was not the end of it. I had to learn how to walk again, in a sense. As you probably know, you don't just start running the minute you take off "the boot." You slowly add weight and increase range of motion. All the little foot muscles have become weak from nonuse, so you have to stretch and strengthen them. Then you walk more and more until you can run. (Warning: I give theological advice, so don't take my routine as medical advice!) What if we conceived of our own salvation not as an end, but as a beginning? I think of Dietrich Bonhoeffer's memorable message to fellow prison inmate Payne Best on the occasion of Bonhoeffer's execution: "This is the end—for me the beginning of life."[16]

---

16. See Eberhard Bethge, *Dietrich Bonhoeffer*, English Translation (Minneapolis: Fortress, 2000), 927.

Suggested Reading

James Beilby and Paul R. Eddy, ed. *The Nature of the Atonement.* Downers Grove, IL: IVP Academic, 2006.

Jeannine K. Brown, Carla M. Dahl, and Wyndy Corbin Reuschling. *Becoming Whole and Holy: An Integrative Conversation about Christian Formation.* Grand Rapids: Baker Academic, 2011.

Joel B. Green. *Why Salvation?* Nashville: Abingdon, 2014.

Charles Talbert and Jason A. Whitlark. *Getting "Saved": The Whole Story of Salvation in the New Testament.* Grand Rapids: Eerdmans, 2011.

Jan G. van der Watt, ed. *Salvation in the New Testament: Perspectives on Soteriology.* Leiden: Brill, 2008.

George Wieland. *The Significance of Salvation: A Study of Salvation Language in the Pastoral Epistles.* Eugene, OR: Wipf & Stock, 2006.

CHAPTER 11

Peace

Wholeness, Goodness, and Harmony in Christ Jesus

Hebrews

Imagine a world of shalom—God's wholeness, God's intention—where some say nothing is missing, and nothing is broken.

—JOSÉ HUMPHREYS[1]

In the summer of 2016, *Hamilton: The Musical* creator and star Lin-Manuel Miranda tweeted the following: "Everyone will sit under their own vine & under their own fig tree, & no one will make them afraid, for the Lord Almighty has spoken. Micah 4:4." A minute later he followed this up with another tweet: "I'm not particularly religious, but the notion of a world where everyone feels safe is calling me right now." On two earlier occasions, he tweeted the same Bible verse without comment. If you are one of the few mortals who hasn't watched *Hamilton*,

---

1. José Humphreys and Adam Gustine, "An Ecclesiology of Shalom," *The Covenant Quarterly* 77.1 (2019): 36–52, at 36; this quote from Humphreys was inspired by the work of John M. Perkins. See Perkins's vision here: https://ccda.org/about/.

it might help to know that this verse is recited almost verbatim in one of the show's songs, "One Last Time," voiced by the character George Washington. (Apparently, the historical George Washington was, indeed, especially fond of this biblical verse and quoted it often in his personal letters.[2])

What was it in Micah 4:4 that was especially attractive to Lin-Manuel? It was the biblical vision of peace, of a redeemed world where every single person has equal access to basic human rights, their needs are met, and they are free to sit under their own proverbial "vine and fig tree." Sometimes we mistakenly assume that peace is the absence of something—war, hostility, tension; but there is a broader conception in the Bible that is ultimately what God's sin-frustrated creation is longing for—wholeness and harmony, what we might call "formative peace."

Old Testament Background

We could look at Micah to consider the biblical vision of peace, but it is wise to begin at the beginning, Genesis 1–2. Ancient origin stories like the Babylonian myth known as the Enuma Elish or the Mesopotamian Epic of Gilgamesh narrate the beginnings of human life fraught with war, bloodshed, and chaos. It is like waking up from sleep, not naturally with the sunrise, but to an ear-pounding fire alarm. "Peace," to say the least, would not be the right word to describe how these cultures looked at the world (even if, of course, they too wanted to see wars end and their economies thrive).

In stark contrast, Genesis begins with the singular work of God freely painting the earth, sun, and stars into being, and recognizing this work as "good." In Genesis 2, we witness unity and harmony between God and the two first mortals, that is until lies, suspicions, and accusations begin to undo God's work of weaving creation together. The most obvious initial evidence of "anti-peace" comes with Cain's slaying of Abel, needless bloodshed forming a sibling rift that could never be mended. This chaos caused by sin had a snowball effect, which grew

---

2. George Tsakiridis, "Vine and Fig Tree," George Washington's Mount Vernon, www .mountvernon.org/library/digitalhistory/digital-encyclopedia/article/vine-and-fig-tree/.

in intensity through Genesis 7. The Abrahamic call narrative (Genesis 12) signals the beginning of hope: God assembling a people who would bring peace to a tumultuous world.

Fast-forward to God's covenant making with Israel, and we see a clear message from God that he will bless this people and shape them into a microcosm of divine peace and harmony. If they follow his words and ways, their land will be fertile and healthy, empty bellies will be full, and "you . . . shall live securely in your land" (Lev 26:5). The Lord promised to give them peace in their land where they could rest without fear or need (26:6). No swords, no dangerous beasts, their children would be many, and God himself would dwell among them (26:7–13). (It sounds a lot like Eden, doesn't it?)

Over many years of ancient Israel's life, that covenant dream was never fully realized. By the time of the Babylonian exile, Israel had all but lost hope. Nevertheless, many of their prophets continued to cast a glorious vision of hope and peace. Isaiah offers one such vision in Isaiah 55. The prophet broadcasts the divine invocation:

> Come, all you who are thirsty,
> > come to the waters;
> and you who have no money,
> > come, buy and eat!
> Come, buy wine and milk
> > without money and without cost. (Isa 55:1 NIV)

Israel is reminded of their special status as God's treasured possession. They are his holy people. Their peace and prosperity are directly related to their relationship with him. In order to find the good life they had been seeking, they must seek the Lord while he can be found, repent and turn to the Lord (55:6–8). This is the only path to *shalomic* life.

> You will go out in joy
> > and be led forth in peace;
> the mountains and hills
> > will burst into song before you,

and all the trees of the field
　　will clap their hands.
Instead of the thornbush will grow the juniper,
　　and instead of briers the myrtle will grow.
This will be for the LORD's renown,
　　for an everlasting sign,
　　that will endure forever. (Isa 55:12–13 NIV)

How will this peace come about? Forty some chapters earlier the prophet focused Israel's hope on a new king, a special ruler who would lead Israel into this beatific vision: "For to us a child is born, to us a son is given, and the government will be on his shoulders. And he will be called Wonderful Counselor, Mighty God, Everlasting Father, Prince of Peace" (Isa 9:6). Many rulers of the world—and regents of Israel— claimed to bring "peace," but usually at the price of war, bloodshed, and wretched loss. *What kind of new king could bring lasting peace without these things?*

Greco-Roman World

In this book, we've already referenced the Star Wars saga, so for some balance let's turn to the Marvel Universe. The first *Avengers* movie (2012) features the appearance of the trickster god Loki of Asgard, invading earth in order to conquer the humans. When Loki first meets human earth-protector Nick Fury, they have a tense exchange. Loki introduces himself as a new ruler coming to bring "freedom" to earth. Fury questions Loki's motives and suspects that he has come to do harm. Loki offers the world peace. Fury, always the wise skeptic, responds: "You say peace. I kinda think you mean the other thing."

Almost transparently, this scene is drawing from colonial ideology, the notion that empires bring "peace" through violent conquest.[3] And the most famous example of this from the ancient world was Rome.

---

3. See Adrian Goldsworthy, *Pax Romana: War, Peace and Conquest in the Roman World* (New Haven: Yale University Press, 2016).

By the time of Caesar Augustus, the emperor had not only expanded and protected Rome's borders, but also "extinguished the flames of civil war" (*Res Gestae Divi Augusti* 1.34). The senate honored Augustus with the *ara pacis Augusti*, the altar of Augustan peace. Augustus continued to expand Roman "peace" through conquest, taking control of the whole Iberian Peninsula and the Alps by force. At the heart of Rome's celebrations of "peace" was the Temple of Mars Ultor, the "Avenger God of War." On several styles of imperial coinage throughout the first century CE, we find the image of the emperor on one side, and on the other the personified attribute PAX (peace) depicted as a woman holding a scepter (power) and an olive branch (peace).[4] As any inhabitant of the Roman Empire was keenly aware, though, this "peace" they experienced came at a cost. Conquered foreigners were taken as slaves. Rome reinforced a heavily stratified society with a few haves and a whole lot of have-nots, not least evident in extreme taxation for most, and luxurious civic benefits only for the elite of cities that adopted "Romanization." Anyone who questioned or challenged Roman order was punished; insurrectionists, like Jesus, were executed precisely because they dared to disturb "the peace."[5] While inhabitants in the Roman empire did not have to fear war from outsiders coming to their city borders, would they have experienced a life of "peace"? Surely not. *There must be a hope of a life greater than that offered by the Caesars*, some would have wondered.

Focal Text: Hebrews

The language and themes of peace are all over the New Testament (not least in places like the Sermon on the Mount and Ephesians's emphasis on Christ as "our peace"; Eph 2:14), but I have found Hebrews to be a text able to capture a powerful testimony of divine peace in Jesus Christ for the wholeness of the world.

---

4. See Jeffrey Weima, "'Peace and Security' (1 Thess 5.3): Prophetic Warning or Political Propaganda," *NTS* 58 (2012): 331–59, especially 335–36.

5. See Marianne Blickenstaff, "Pax Romana," *New Interpreter's Dictionary of the Bible*, ed. Katharine D. Sakenfeld, 5 vols. (Nashville: Abingdon, 2006–2009), 4:421.

Peace with God through Jesus Christ

I would like to make the case to you that peace is a crucial theme in the book of Hebrews, even though the Greek word "peace" (*eirēne*) only appears a few times (7:2; 12:11, 14; 13:20). Hebrews is all about the supremacy of Jesus Christ as the mediator *par excellence* between God and humanity. He is both the great sacrifice that makes peace, and the priestly go-between that brings the covenantal parties together. Through his life, death, and new life, he makes harmonious what sin made cacophonic. This is expressed clearly in Heb 2:11–12 when the writer says that God has made sinners holy and welcomed them into his family through Jesus who calls us "brothers and sisters."

Jesus the Peacemaking Mediator of a New Covenant

Not only is Jesus repeatedly identified as the center of the salvific project of reconciliation between God and mortals, he is called "mediator of a new covenant," the biblical language of peacemaking and peacekeeping (Heb 8:6; 9:15; 12:24a). How did Jesus achieve this peace? In the Old Testament, it was clear that Israel kept the peace with God through sacrifice and repentance, a life changed and a penalty paid by the mercy of God. Hebrews presents Jesus as this process all wrapped in one person; Jesus the great sacrifice, whose sprinkled blood sent a powerful message to God (12:24). By God's own grace, Christ's self-sacrifice quelled the hostility caused by sin, as Jesus "taste[d] death for everyone" (2:9).

Hebrews expresses that Jesus's peacemaking death was not simply a sacrificial act to appease an angry God. The true enemy of this story is not found in ruined sinners or a hostile God, but in the devil who once held humanity in bondage. His chains have now been broken by the power of Christ, specifically by his death (2:14). Little did the devil know when Jesus willingly sacrificed himself (7:27) that he had hidden within him the power of an indestructible life (7:16).

The Bible never fully explains the logic of what a material sacrifice really accomplishes in making peace with God. Jews and Christians knew that God doesn't need food, nor does the death of an animal satisfy the problem of sin in the end. The covenantal sacrificial system was a gracious means whereby God accepted sacrifice made by a penitent sinner as a gift.[6] Hebrews affirms the biblical truth that "without the shedding of blood there is no forgiveness" (9:22), but also Hebrews teaches that material animal sacrifice has a temporary and limited cleansing and pacifying effect (9:12–14): "It is impossible for the blood of bulls and goats to take away sins" (10:4). Only the perfect offering of Christ and his blood could cleanse our consciences and turn us to truly serving the living God (9:14).

Jesus the High Priest

Hebrews gives some space to portraying Jesus as a peacemaking sacrifice, but the more carefully constructed image is that of Jesus as the greatest high priest (4:14; 5:10). Hebrews explains that Jewish priests in general had the privilege of approaching God, and the high priest all the more (5:1; 6:20). They represented Israel by offering gifts and sacrifices for sin on behalf of the people (5:1; 9:6–10, 25). They served as intercessors, bringing the two parties of God and Israel together as one (7:25; cf. 7:19; 10:22). But in Jesus Christ, both unblemished sacrifice and perfect high priest, believers can know God more fully, entering the place where God is "by the new and living way that he opened for us through the curtain (that is, through his flesh), and since we have a great priest over the house of God, let us approach with a true heart in full assurance of faith, with our hearts sprinkled clean from an evil conscience and our bodies washed with pure water" (10:20–22).

Repeatedly Hebrews points back to the prototypical priestly figure of Melchizedek (Heb 5:6–10; 6:20; 7:1, 10–11, 15, 17). He is described as the king of Salem and priest of God who met and blessed the patriarch Abraham (7:1). Hebrews explains that the name Melchizedek means "king of peace," a prefiguration of the Son of God who also plays the role of peacemaker. Repeatedly, we are reminded that Melchizedek blessed Abraham (7:6–7). Again, in the biblical conception, "peace" is not only about the absence of something, like hostility or war, but also the promotion of a gracious disposition between estranged parties. True peace knits together to create a stronger whole. Jesus was able to

---

6. See Mark J. Boda, *A Severe Mercy: Sin and Its Remedy in the Old Testament* (Winona Lake, IN: Eisenbrauns, 2009).

accomplish these things as priest and sacrifice because he conquered the power of sin and ratified a new covenant where the divine law will be written on the hearts and minds of believers (10:16).

A "Peaced" People Who Suffer

Hebrews extols the many divine benefits bestowed on sinful mortals, graciously given through Jesus Christ. Not the least of these is peace with God. This peace is a permanent possession through a new covenant; it richly blesses the people of God. In that sense, this holy people become a "peaced" people, imprinted by the grace of God, given a special kind of wholeness and reassured of the promise of rest. But Hebrews makes it clear that this peace does not preclude suffering or persecution. It is not that God is too weak to end suffering. Hebrews, like many other biblical texts, valorizes suffering as a form of *paideia*, learning how to live well.[7] Paradoxically, Christ himself was made complete through what he suffered (2:10; 5:8). Perhaps this means he could identify more directly with human suffering (2:18).

Hebrews recognizes the intense persecution the readers faced for their faith. They are commended for their perseverance and resilience. Having the peace of God does not mean life is easy. Rather, there can be joy and blessing in the midst of weakness and rejection. A student is not greater than their teacher. If Jesus was shamed and rejected, so will his people endure such things. Hebrews explains that Jesus died *outside* the city gate, signifying marginalization. His followers, then, are called to "go to him outside the camp and bear the abuse he endured" (13:13). But if they stay the course, they will inherit a great reward (10:35). The peace of God empowers ongoing faith in difficulty: "We are not among those who shrink back and so are lost, but among those who have faith and so are saved" (10:39).

This is where the famous "warning passages" come in.[8] Perhaps the author of Hebrews knew or sensed that his readers were losing steam, struggling to press on. But they are warned that stepping off the path only leads you down a worse road (2:1; 3:16–19). Christian faith is a

---

7. See Charles Talbert, *Learning through Suffering: The Educational Value of Suffering in the New Testament and Its Milieu* (Collegeville, MN: Liturgical Press, 1991).

8. Heb 2:1–4; 3:7–4:13; 5:11–6:12; 10:19–39; 12:14–29.

hard journey; there is peace and blessing, but there is also suffering and resistance. But Christ leads the way.

A Peace-Waging People

I learned a new term this year: peace-waging. This is meant to be a play on the language of war-waging. Sometimes, peace can seem like *not* doing anything. But those who seriously advocate for peace, wholeness, harmony, and unity are fighting a serious war against sin, hatred, and chaos. Hebrews depicts a "peaced" people as those who carry out the work and war of waging peace. Just as we say "hurt people hurt people," we can also say "blessed people bless people" and "peaced people peace people." Believers are enjoined in Hebrews to spur each other on to carry out deeds of love and goodness (10:24; cf. 13:1). They should bless strangers with hospitality (13:2). They should visit and support prisoners (13:3). Their "sacrifices" to a peacemaking God are to do good and to learn to share with others (13:16). The final wish-prayer sums up well the peace vision of the gospel of the peacemaking God.

> Now may the God of peace, who brought back from the dead our Lord Jesus, the great shepherd of the sheep, by the blood of the eternal covenant, make you complete in everything good so that you may do his will, working among us that which is pleasing in his sight, through Jesus Christ, to whom be the glory forever and ever. Amen. (13:20–21)

OTHER NEW TESTAMENT VOICES
Matthew 5:9; 11:28–30; Romans 5:1–2; 8:6; 12:17–18; 2 Corinthians 13:11; Galatians 5:22–23; Philippians 4:6–7; James 3:18; 2 John 1:3

The Gospel of John

Peace, as we have seen, is a multifaceted concept in the Bible. Sometimes it refers to a personal disposition and mode, contentment and reassurance before God and in the world. At other times, it appears more as a social reality—a lack of hostility toward others and a sentiment of goodwill and blessing. Surely these are related theologically, but not every text explicitly connects them. But an explicit connection between personal peace and the peace-mission of the gospel *is* made in the Gospel of John. In the Farewell Discourse (John 14–16), Jesus reassured his disciples that when he departed from them, they would not be left on their own. Though it may have been hard for them to understand why Jesus was going away, they would have the presence and help of the Advocate, the Holy Spirit. Jesus pronounced peace on them, in advance of his departure: "Peace I leave with you; my peace I give you. I do not give to you as the world gives. Do not let your hearts be troubled and do not let them be afraid" (14:27). This Jesus-peace was not just some kind of inner tranquility, but also courage and confidence, faith to endure inevitable hardship and suffering. They had the Spirit to envelope them in Jesus's divine peace. As Gail O'Day explains, "The peace of Jesus is the all-embracing sphere of his life, his love."[9] Again, in the Farewell Discourse, Jesus reminded them that his teaching was intended to put them at ease, to bring them peace. Their faith and confidence were to be put in the power of Jesus himself: "I have conquered the world" (John 16:33). And yet they had to witness Jesus's own death. *Surely*, they must have thought in that moment in front of the cross, *Jesus overestimated his power.*

But as the story goes, Jesus appeared in the room where they were hiding after his death, and spoke those familiar words, "Peace be with you" (20:19). (Clearly they had lost the "peace" Jesus had given them beforehand, so he gave it to them again!) And it is repeated again just before Jesus commissioned them: "Peace be with you! As the Father has sent me, I am sending you" (20:21 NIV). They receive the blessing of the Holy Spirit to carry out the gospel mission, but in order to do so, they must have Jesus's own peace. The fact of the resurrection means that Jesus gives peace to them by giving them *himself*. All of this can be connected to Jesus's discourse about the vine and the branches. The branches find life and prosperity—peace—by living fully in the vine

---

9. Gail R. O'Day, "The Gospel of John," *New Interpreter's Bible* 9 (Nashville: Abingdon, 1995), 751.

(15:1–2). Even in the worst of times, when these branches are bent and splintered, they find their life and power in the vine.

It is fascinating to me that "peace" is not considered an end in and of itself in John; it is not a final state of being that restores an Edenic existence, at least not right away. It is a *resource* at the disposal of God's people to protect their hearts and souls as they venture out into the dangerous world with the mission of the gospel. It is a gift, from Jesus himself, empowered and guided by the Spirit, to keep believers "safe and sound," not as a means of repelling suffering, but in order to endure it. And what exactly is the substance of this "peace"? It is the firm conviction of a divine truth which is straightforwardly expressed in a sister text, 1 John: "Little children, you are from God, and have conquered [the enemies of God]; for the one who is in you is greater than the one who is in the world" (1 John 4:4).

Peace for Today

The Troubled Prophet and the Tranquil Priest

As I write in 2021, these last few years in the United States of America have been some of the most tumultuous ones of my life, due to the many struggles that have impacted our nation: racial turmoil, destructive natural disasters, the coronavirus pandemic, a toxic political climate, not to mention ongoing economic issues. I have sat and watched Christian leaders pontificate on social media about what believers should do. On the one side, you have what we might call the "tranquil priest" who says, "Jesus is in control, chill out, pray, and relax, all will be well." On the other side, you have the "troubled prophet" who cries, "Don't just sit there, get in the fight, make change, get angry, make some trouble!" So which voice points us to the truth? Can they both be right?

According to texts like Hebrews and John, the Christian existence itself is a mysterious double life of peace and trouble. There are several reasons for this. First, you have the fact that Christ came, dealt the devil and death their fatal wounds, but they still wreak havoc as sore losers. So the work of new creation hasn't eclipsed all the problems of the old creation. Secondly, Christians aren't called to eternal repose in this life; they are called to difficult mission and ministry for the sake of the gospel. Thirdly, Christian faith is not an end in itself but is a beginning, a new birth, as it were. And the work of being born and becoming whole is a difficult process involving "growing pains." Or we might use the image of being "out of shape" and needing to conform to the shape of Christ, a molding process that can be painful.

So perhaps it is wrong to think about the Christian life as *either* the tranquil priest *or* the troubled prophet. It seems we need to embody both of them. When the boat of life is *really* rocking, we ought to cling to the God of peace who sent Christ and the Spirit to buoy us. *It is well with my soul.* At the *same* time, we must heed the call to stand up in the boat, put on our binoculars and find out *what* is rocking the boat. We have a God-given responsibility to make the seas and the boat a safer place for others. That requires us to roll up our sleeves and do something about the problem.

In the end, Christian peace is not a place to rest. It is more like a protective layer around our hearts and souls that enables us to face the many difficulties and challenges of life with resilience and fortitude.

A Peace Theology for Social Media

Social media is not the single cause for the noise and hostile division in our world today, but we all know the role it plays in amplifying negativity and setting up echo chambers of our own favorite ideas and things.[10] The solution is not deleting all your apps and closing all your accounts; that's an extreme, perhaps even ascetic, solution. But given the digital and global world of communication we now live in, I think it beneficial to consider having a theology of social media, more specifically a "Peace Theology for Social Media." What is your goal when using social media? For some, it is purely entertainment, talking about sports and movies, or catching up with friends. For others, it is focused on business, advertising and promoting services and products or engaging with customers. Some want to talk politics. Some are interested in

---

10. Here is one reputable study: Brooke Auxier, "64% of Americans Say Social Media Have a Mostly Negative Effect on the Way things Are Going in the U.S. Today," Pew Research Center, October 15, 2020, www.pewresearch.org/fact-tank/2020/10/15/64-of-americans-say-social-media-have-a-mostly-negative-effect-on-the-way-things-are-going-in-the-u-s-today/.

history or literature. (And then there is #WeirdChristianTwitter.) But have you considered *how* you engage with social media, not the apps specifically, but the spirit of the enterprise itself?

I propose that Christians should have a commitment to sowing peace and blessing in any and all forms of social engagement, including and even especially on social media. Christians are still "Christian" on our phones and laptops. We are still humans interfacing with other humans. The easiest thing to do is to like someone's sarcastic, cynical, or mocking comment about a person, ideology, or value. It's fun and it feels good. I know the feeling. But what I am challenged by is Hebrews's winsome spirit of peace and unity, especially as advocated in its final chapter (13:1–25).

Love One Another as Brothers and Sisters (13:1)

Is social media a place where we can and should show love, even to our enemies? We know the answer to this question, but I rarely think about this when I open apps on my phone and start scrolling and typing. It can be assumed that in the worldview of Hebrews, "brothers and sisters" are those people whom we care about the most. Hebrews calls readers to love others, really to love *all*, as brothers and sisters. Several years ago, I made a mocking comment toward a public figure on social media. An acquaintance of mine, some seven thousand miles away, privately messaged me and convinced me that my comment was out of line. You know what? He was right. I apologized and removed the comment. I wasn't loving my brother. I gave myself permission to be a jerk on social media because "that is the style of discourse," but that was an excuse that Hebrews would not entertain.

Attend to the Outsider (13:2)

Hebrews is insistent that Christians care for the stranger, the outsider. This could mean that on social media we think about attending to marginalized voices. Are we bringing *everyone* into important conversations? When we let social media construct echo chambers of our own favorite ideas and people, it is a lot like locking your house. *Would you let a stranger in?*

I make it a point to follow different kinds of people on social media, even people I disagree with. And every now and again I even "like" one of their posts or comments, even if I agree with it only slightly. That is because I don't want to draw these clear lines of "us vs. them," divisions that lead to self-superiority and judgmentalism.

Practice Empathy (13:3)

Hebrews talks about caring for the prisoner as if you yourself are a prisoner together with them. Essentially, Hebrews calls for empathy, putting ourselves in the shoes of others who are unlike us. Social media, to be frank, does not encourage empathy when it comes to theological, moral, or ideological differences. We have so many other options: mute, unfollow, block. But a fundamental principle of Christian peace-waging is respecting the humanity of the other and trying, as hard as that is sometimes, to see the issue from their perspective. Empathy does *not* mean we have to adopt the view of the other, it doesn't mean we even have to *like* the view of the other, but it does mean we have to humanize (and not demonize) the other.

Imitate the Best (13:7)

Hebrews goes on to talk about imitating the good faith of trusted leaders. This is wise advice for all of life, of course, but all the more for social media. When we look around at various influencers, culture shapers, and thought leaders, we can get a sense for those people whom we gravitate toward and even imitate in tone and spirit. Hebrews would encourage us to "imitate the best." The best are shaping the world with words to make it a better place. And all good leaders can be weighed by their lifestyle and as Hebrews puts it, "the outcome of their way of life" (13:7).

Check Your Facts (13:9)

As I thought about whether Hebrews 13 is relevant to our use of social media today, I almost fell off my chair when I read 13:9: "Do not be carried away by all kinds of strange teachings." Need I say more? Check your facts, people.

Do Good (13:16)

The big message of peace-waging, whether it takes place in year 50 or 2022, is pretty simple: "Do good and . . . share with others" (13:16 NIV). It's a really simple idea, but our lesser angels seem to take control when we log on to our social media apps. Sometimes we make peace too big of an endeavor, something that people make in a War Room or a UN meeting. But the kind of peace that Hebrews invites regular, everyday people to make is as simple as speaking carefully and graciously at all times, treating our enemies as brothers and sisters, and modeling the goodness we want to receive from others. If we can manage to do this even sometimes on social media, "with such sacrifices God is pleased."

Suggested Reading

Mark J. Boda. *A Severe Mercy: Sin and Its Remedy in the Old Testament.* Winona Lake, IN: Eisenbrauns, 2009.

Michael J. Gorman. *Becoming the Gospel: Paul, Participation, and Mission.* Grand Rapids: Eerdmans, 2015.

Willard M. Swartley. *Covenant of Peace: The Missing Peace in New Testament Theology and Ethics.* Grand Rapids: Eerdmans, 2006.

CHAPTER 12

Religion

Revering God by Loving Neighbor

James

In 2012, a video went viral on YouTube, the Spoken Word poem "Why I Hate Religion, But Love Jesus," by Jeff Bethke.[1] The four-minute video reached six million views within a week, more than double by a month's time. Later on, Bethke explained that his purpose was to draw a sharp distinction between Jesus and false religion, but the simple wording used in the title and throughout the video made Jesus appear to be the enemy of "religion." Here is a selection of some of the statements Bethke makes about religion:

> What if I told you Jesus came to abolish religion? . . .
> If religion is so great, why has it started so many wars? . . .
> Because the problem with religion is it never gets to the core,
> It's just behavior modification, like a long list of chores. . . .
> One is the work of God, one is a man-made invention,
> one is a cure, and one is the infection.

---

1. Jefferson Bethke, "Why I Hate Religion, But Love Jesus || Spoken Word," YouTube, January 10, 2012, www.youtube.com/watch?v=1IAhDGYlpqY.

Because Religion says do, Jesus says done.
Religion says slave, Jesus says son,
Religion puts you in shackles, but Jesus sets you free.
Religion makes you blind, but Jesus lets you see.

As you can imagine, there were *many* reactions to Bethke's statement, some more approving and others sharply critical. One of the more insightful critical responses came as a recorded Spoken Word poem by a Catholic priest, "Father Pontifex" ("Why I Love Religion, and Love Jesus"). Pontifex makes a number of direct counterclaims, from a Catholic perspective, to Bethke's statements. Here is a selection from Pontifex's piece:

What if I told you that Jesus loves religion,
And that by his coming as man he brought his religion
          to fruition. . . .
See His religion is the largest worldwide source of relief,
For the poor, the hungry, the sick and repentant thief. . . .
We all detest hypocrisy, and empty show is just the worst,
But blaming religion for contradiction
Is like staring at death, and blaming the hearse. . . .
So as for religion I love it, I have one because Jesus rose from
          the dead and won,
I believe when Jesus said IT IS FINISHED, His religion had
          just begun.[2]

A starker contrast of views on Jesus and religion is hard to find. What is "religion" and do Jesus and Christianity reject it or support it? This is a difficult question to answer because (1) there are different connotations to the meaning of the word in *modern* usage (as the engagement between Bethke and Pontifex demonstrates) and (2) the word "religion" doesn't occur very often in the Bible. As for the second point, that is not because religion is not an important concept in

---

2. Full transcripts for both Bethke and Pontifex can be found in "Why I Love Religion and Love Jesus," Young Catholic Crusaders, March 6, 2012, http://young-catholics.blogspot.com/2012/03/why-i-love-religion-and-love-jesus.html.

Scripture—quite the opposite. But it is one of those things that is *so* pervasive that it is taken for granted. Nevertheless, it is a *concept* worthy of study, especially for us moderns who live in a secular age, and there is one text in the New Testament in particular, the letter of James, that gives more focused attention to the Greek word *thrēskeia*, "religion." According to James, religion is good and necessary, and you might even be a bit surprised about what James argues is the essence of religion. But first things first, what *is* religion?

Old Testament Background and Greco-Roman Context

There is a little cartoon that provides insight into how we view religion and especially Christianity today. A man goes into a bookstore and asks where he can find a Bible. The bookstore associate checks his computer inventory and matter-of-factly replies, "The Bible . . . that would be under self-help."[3] To many today, "religion" is a personal choice and serves some sort of existential purpose of bringing inner peace and fulfillment. Now, there is nothing wrong with pursuing inner peace—the Bible *does* address this—but it would be far off the mark to imagine that ancient people thought of religion in this way. Religion, for almost all ancient people, was an obligation and had very little to do with personal choice or the leisurely pursuit of inner peace. The Romans described religion as *pax deorum*, the maintenance of a peaceful coexistence with the gods, recognizing their superior power and honoring them with sacrifices, prayers, and gifts (Cicero *On the Nature of the Gods* 1.116; 2.8). This was, more or less, how it worked for other people groups, whether they were Egyptians, Assyrians, or Greeks. The gods are divine rulers, and mortals owe them thanks, respect, and obedience.

Jews, in this regard, were both similar to and different from other groups when it came to religion. Yes, they believed their one God was their true and highest ruler (see Pss 47; 145). They made sacrifices to their God and offered prayers of thanksgiving. But there was a very

---

3. Cartoon by Peter Steiner, *New Yorker*, July 6, 1998, p. 33.

specific framework and orientation of their religion: covenant. Just as a lesser nation might attach itself to a great nation through a special reciprocal treaty, so God made a pact with Israel. And this covenant comprehensively guided Israel's religious perspective and practices.[4]

How do you sum up the nature of the Jewish religion, especially since the Old Testament (Hebrew Bible) is so long—much longer than most ancient sacred texts? One important place to look is somewhat obvious, but perhaps it's obvious for a reason: the Ten Commandments (Exod 20:2–21). YHWH first reminds his people that he rescued them from slavery in Egypt to live a free life in worship and service to him (v. 2). The first few commandments establish boundaries for properly honoring God: Israel should have no idols (vv. 3–6), respect God's name (v. 7), and observe a holy day each week, which is dedicated to God and free from work (vv. 8–11). The second half or section of the Ten Commandments sets up expectations for communal life: respect for parents (v. 12), respect for life (v. 13), respect for marriage (v. 14), respect for property (v. 15), respect for the truth (v. 16), and respect for the belongings and relationships of one's neighbors (v. 17).

One way that the Old Testament distinguished itself from the religious conceptions and practices of other contemporary peoples was in its use of love language. Outside of Judaism and Christianity, it was uncommon to find sacred texts talking about (nonsexual) love between mortals and the divine. But Jews, by the time of Jesus, were known to have regularly prayed the Shema, the special prayer found in Deuteronomy 6:4–5 (NIV): "Hear, O Israel: The LORD our God, the LORD is one. Love the LORD your God with all your heart and with all your soul and with all your strength." In many ways, the Jewish religion could be summed up here as a commitment to love and respect God, and as we have seen with the Ten Commandments, this should also include loving and respecting one's neighbor. As a religious handbook, any ancient person would have expected the Jewish sacred texts to include information about sacrifices, proper use of temples, and establishing a

---

4. See Patrick Miller, *The Religion of Ancient Israel* (Minneapolis: Fortress, 2007); also Walter Brueggemann, *Worship in Ancient Israel* (Nashville: Abingdon, 2005); Aaron Chalmers, *Exploring the Religion of Ancient Israel: Prophet, Priest, Sage, and People* (Downers Grove, IL: IVP Academic, 2012).

proper priesthood. The Old Testament, of course, includes all these, but it offers so much more in terms of creating a harmonious covenantal community with a mission to combat sin and bring light and life to the world. When I read the Old Testament, this seems to me quite dissonant with both of Bethke's criticisms of "religion" as a man-made fabrication and a list of chores. Religion, in Jewish experience, is a dynamic relationship with God tied to all areas of life, aiming to radiate harmony and life to a sin-wrecked world.

Focal Text: James

When I first heard Bethke's "Why I Hate Religion, But Love Jesus," I immediately thought, "This would make no sense to James." James wrote about religion positively (we will return to the key statement in James 1:27 in a moment), but he *could* differentiate between genuine religion and hypocritical or compartmentalized religion. We will explore James's understanding of true and godly religion.

The five chapters of the letter of James contain a series of topics including attitudes toward suffering, the problem of favoritism or bias, issues of wealth and poverty, and the dangers of negative speech against others. It can seem like these topics are thrown together into a "New Testament Proverbs" grab bag when we read this text, but almost all the ideas seem to relate in one way or another to James 1:22–27 and 2:14–24. The first of these sections is about the appropriate human response to divine revelation, the word of God (1:22). James instructs his readers not only to listen to the word (like I half-listen to the news on the radio while I unload the dishwasher in the morning); they must soak themselves in it and then perform it. James is all about practical religion or practiced piety. He scoffs at the hypocrites who pretend to be "religious" by practicing certain rituals and activities, but then treat their neighbors with malice or disrespect.

In 2:14–24, James explores this phenomenon in reference to "faith" and "works." James appears to know of a version of Christianity that can *look* spiritual and put on a good show; it can "talk the talk," but doesn't actually "walk the walk" (see 2:14). It's like when we tell a hurting friend,

"I'll pray for you," but then we don't *actually* bother to do something tangible to improve their situation (see James 2:15–16). James believes that self-centered religion is empty and vapid, like an idol. Religion isn't self-help; it is God helping us and pouring himself into us so that we will honor him back by serving and loving others—true religion helps others!

Let's return now to James's use of the language of "religion" and "religious" in James 1:26–27. Traditionally, the Greek terms *thrēskos* and *thrēskeia* referred to a group's mechanisms for respecting and honoring the gods.[5] In most cases this pointed to material sacrifices, prayers, and gifts for the gods. But here James was extending its meaning far beyond the temple and altar. Just as the Old Testament expected love of God and love of neighbor in all places and ways, so James too was painting a picture of a comprehensive life ethic and religious perspective that was holistic and authentic (1:26). In 1:27 he explains that the purest form of religion (*thrēskeia*) is care for orphans and widows and generosity over and against worldliness.[6]

On the basis of this notion of true religion as outward-facing, embodied piety, James tackles numerous social matters, but none more than economics (1:9–10; 2:1–7; 5:1–6). What does religion have to do with money? The answer to this would be obvious if we knew that James is sometimes called the "Amos" of the New Testament. In Amos, the Lord charges Israel with covenantal disobedience and threatens them with judgment (Amos 2:4–5). A major part of this corruption is economic: "They sell the innocent for silver, and the needy for a pair of sandals/They trample on the heads of the poor, as on the dust of the ground, and deny justice to the oppressed" (2:6–7 NIV). While Israel dutifully brings obligatory sacrifices and tithes, their hearts are not turned toward love of neighbor (4:5–6): "You trample on the poor and take from them levies of grain" (5:11). The poor are deprived of justice

---

5. See Ceslas Spicq and James D. Ernest, "*thrēskeia*," *Theological Lexicon of the New Testament* (Peabody, MA: Hendrickson, 1994), 200.

6. Elsa Tamez paraphrases James 1:27 in this way: "Religion pure and untainted before God is visiting and assisting the oppressed groups like widows and orphans and keeping oneself uncontaminated by the world, that is, not following the perverted values of society"; see Elsa Tamez, *The Scandalous Message of James: Faith without Works Is Dead* (New York: Crossroad, 2018), 62.

in the court and leaders and judges take bribes (v. 12). True religion, Amos reminds us, is to seek good for all according to the covenant (v. 14): "And so the LORD, the God of hosts, will be with you . . . Hate evil and love good, and establish justice in the gate" (4:14–15).

James writes with the same prophetic tone—sharp and direct, incisive and threatening:

> Come now, you rich people, weep and wail for the miseries that are coming to you. Your riches have rotted, and your clothes are moth-eaten. Your gold and silver have rusted, and their rust will be evidence against you, and it will eat your flesh like fire. You have laid up treasure for the last days. Listen! The wages of the laborers who mowed your fields, which you kept back by fraud, cry out, and the cries of the harvesters have reached the ears of the Lord of hosts. You have lived on the earth in luxury and in pleasure; you have fattened your hearts in a day of slaughter. You have condemned and murdered the righteous one, who does not resist you. (Jas 5:1–6)

Neither Amos nor James was against economic prosperity per se, nor did they promote poverty as a value or virtue. Here James recognized that as humans we participate together in a "limited good" economy where the overabundance of one has a direct and inverse effect on the other. Hoarding money is a form of abuse of the other; withholding or shortchanging payment to workers is a crime, because it needlessly increases suffering and deprivation. The big picture is that God is unwilling to sit idly by. Judgment is coming and, as James says, "You have fattened your hearts in a day of slaughter." Yikes!

To be clear, the heart of religion according to James is worship of God first and foremost. We find this emphasized throughout the letter: religion is pure service and devotion to God—James calls himself a "slave of God and the Lord Jesus Christ" (1:1 NET). Religion is also portrayed as faith and true commitment to the Lord Jesus Christ (2:1). The pious tongue should praise God (3:9) and submit to God (4:7). Christian brothers and sisters are called to draw near to God (4:8) and to pray with deep faith (5:13–18). But James also draws deeply from his Jewish heritage and sacred traditions that emphasize expressing respect for God by caring for other creatures, as James quotes Leviticus 19:18: "You shall love your neighbor as yourself" (Jas 2:8).[7] This is why James describes true religion as care for orphans and widows (Jas 1:27). These were the economically vulnerable ones in the first-century Greco-Roman world. The father (*paterfamilias*) was legally responsible for the well-being of his family. Those without a male guardian were dependent on the kindness and provisions of others. The Christian brother or sister who does not have compassion for other needy people, according to James, dishonors God's own grace and mercy toward sinful mortals. To be "religious" is to imitate the ways of God, not the ways of the world. James's letter reflects a wider biblical covenantal consciousness that conceives of true religion as holistic service to God that entails not only pure worship and devotion to God, but also service and compassion for one's own neighbors—loving others the way God loves them. Just as with the parable of the lost sheep, James's emphasis on the widow and orphan points to special concern for the most disadvantaged and most hurting.

OTHER NEW TESTAMENT VOICES
Acts 3:12; 10:2, 7; 26:5; Colossians 2:18; 1 Timothy 2:12; 3:16; 4:7–8; James 1:26–27; 2 Peter 1:3–7; 2:9

Matthew 23:23

In Matthew's Gospel, Jesus confronts and rebukes the Scribes and the Pharisees. The Jewish people look to them for guidance in worshiping God faithfully. Jesus credits them with knowing the law and caring passionately about its obedience. But sometimes they miss the forest for the trees when it comes to honoring God (Matt 23:1–4, 16–22).

---

7. Leviticus 19:18 is quoted often in the New Testament, probably a cherished Old Testament text by the apostles and NT writers *because* it was a favorite text of Jesus according to the Jesus tradition recorded in the Gospels (Matt 5:43; 19:19; 22:39; Mark 12:31, 33; Luke 10:27; Rom 13:9; Gal 5:14).

Jesus accuses them of meticulous observance of the minutiae of the law, like measuring out exactly a tenth of their spices for the tithe, but then ignoring the heart and soul of God's covenant, namely, *justice, mercy, and faithfulness* (23:23). As far as Jesus is concerned, *these* are the indicators of true religion. The religious leaders take the best seats at banquets, rather than offering them to others (Mat 23:6). They take pride in being greeted as "great teacher," rather than taking the posture of a humble servant (23:11–12). They seek to exclude the riffraff, acting as gatekeepers of God's mercy (23:13). Jesus recenters true religion on living out the grace of the gracious God. God's nature is to give and care for others, but the Pharisees are full of greed and pride (23:25). The righteousness they claim is false; they act wickedly.

In Matthew's gospel, Jesus continues after this discourse to talk about eschatological events that lie ahead, wherein his disciples will need to be vigilant and faithful so as *not* to fall into the false ways of the blind and hypocritical religious leaders. In a climactic teaching of this eschatological discourse, Jesus presents the heavenly king as blessing especially those who ministered to him when he was hungry, cold, sick, or alone (25:34–36). It is not that he himself was in these deprived situations per se, but that he is found in his people, especially the most vulnerable in society. Putting the pieces together of Jesus's gospel instruction from Matthew 23–25, we can say that what the Pharisees and Scribes lacked (justice, mercy, faithfulness) is precisely this: feeding the hungry, sheltering the homeless, providing for the naked, and tending to the sick (25:42–43). That is because "religion" is not a set of practices to appease a vain or fickle deity. Religion is living rightly with and before God, which involves living rightly in God's world and with respect to God's creatures.

Religion for Today

What Is Religion?

Throughout American history, there has been a strong tie between the President of the United States and religion, especially Christianity. Almost every president thus far has claimed to have had some faith, though obviously it seems more important to some than others.[8] In 2015 and 2016, when Vermont senator Bernie Sanders was making a strong run for the Democratic nomination, the media started to explore Sanders's religious views. While Sanders would have been the first Jewish president, he was often forthright in admitting that he was not "religious" and did not participate regularly in organized religion, Jewish or otherwise. His perspective is a secular one. But when pressed on his "religious beliefs" he would often repeat a humanist manifesto like this:

> It's very easy to turn our backs on kids who are hungry or veterans who are sleeping on the street, but I believe that what human nature is about is that everybody in this room impacts everybody else in all kinds of ways that we can't understand. . . . That's my religion. That's what I believe in.[9]

What Sanders means here is that he believes in the power of goodness in humanity to take care of each other out of compassion and justice. Sanders, while secular in his own perspective, has never shied away from talking to religious groups, acknowledging the positive contributions that churches, synagogues, temples, and mosques have made to the common good. Once in a while, Sanders has quoted or paraphrased the biblical golden rule taught by Jesus:

> Every great religion in the world—Christianity, Judaism, Islam, Buddhism—essentially comes down to "do unto others as you would

---

8. The Pew Research Center has an insightful study, listing Thomas Jefferson and Abraham Lincoln as the only two presidents with unclear relationships with churches and denominations. On the other end of the spectrum are Jimmy Carter and James Garfield, as the most religious, the latter a clergy member of the Disciples of Christ; see Aleksandra Sandstrom, "Biden Is Only the Second Catholic President, but Nearly All Have Been Christians," Pew Research Center, January 20, 2021, www.pewresearch.org/fact-tank/2017/01/20/almost-all-presidents-have-been-christians/; see also Forrest Wickman, "Who Was the Most Religious President of All Time?," The Slate, September 25, 2012, https://slate.com/news-and-politics/2012/09/most-religious-president-jimmy-carter-james-garfield-or-john-quincy-adams.html.

9. Alana Horowitz Satlin, "Watch Bernie Sanders' Moving Explanation of Why Faith Matters," Huffpost, February 24, 2016, www.huffpost.com/entry/bernie-sanders-religion_n_56cd8ad7e4b0ec6725e477ce.

like them to do unto you." And what I have believed in my whole life (is) that we are in this together. . . . The truth is, at some level when you hurt, when your children hurt, I hurt. And when my kids hurt, you hurt.[10]

Sanders has tried to highlight a common thread in all major world religions, namely that the purpose of humanity is to bring goodness and blessing to one another, and politics can play a role in this. I will be honest, while I do not agree with all of Sanders's political views, I have appreciated his passion for human rights and his willingness to threaten the political status quo to bring change. But when it comes to his personal definition of "religion," I find his statements misleading and confusing. Sanders describes the essence of religion as mutual respect. Of course, mutual respect is found in all world religions, I presume, but no Christian, Jew, Hindu, or Muslim I know would make that the center or foundation of their faith. Religion, as dictionary and dogmas both explain, is about God. To call common humanity or benevolent mutuality a religion is to redefine religion. Sanders's perspective is a philosophy, no doubt, but not really a religion, certainly not according to classic definitions.

I am not trying to judge Sanders harshly for his views; I respect his honesty. But I think what he means is that he does not turn to a higher power for spiritual guidance on how he should treat others. He finds that it is natural for all people to care for one another. These are beliefs, surely, but does this amount to the essence of religion?

I am not trying to split hairs. This relates to James in an important way. When James writes that "religion . . . is . . . to look after orphans and widows" (Jas 1:27 NIV), he wasn't *defining* religion as care for the vulnerable. James was writing in a kind of shorthand, explaining that relief for distressed widows and orphans is the proper *expression* of listening and responding to the covenantal God. Religion *must* manifest itself in loving service to the needy, but this in and of itself does not sum up religion.

---

10. John Fea, "In Bernie Sanders' Deeply Religious Message, an Echo of the Founding Fathers," *Religion News Service*, March 23, 2016, https://religionnews .com/2016/03/23 /bernie-sanders-deeply-religious-founding-fathers-181220/.

Do You Do Anything for Anyone?

My wife and I go out for a coffee date most weeks. During COVID 2020, we often looked for cafés with outdoor seating. On one occasion, a young gentleman, obviously down on his luck, approached us and asked, "Do you have any spare change so I can get a coffee?" I said, "No, sorry man." He initially turned around to walk away, but after taking a step, he stopped and said, "Do you do anything for anyone?" To be honest, my wife and I were both stunned; I managed to mutter a "Yeah" and then we sat in silence for a while, watching him walk away.

We do, in fact, give to charities of various kinds, but never have we been asked point-blank like that. It gave me pause to think—*What is my Christian obligation to this person?* Yes, I can give to my church's benevolence fund, to World Vision, or donate clothes to Goodwill. But the problem of poverty and economic injustice struck me in a different way when someone was standing twenty feet away, looking me in the eye, and saying, "Do you do anything for anyone?"

I am convinced that the biblically formed Christian ought to ponder this question as an important part of our "religion." There is a skewed form of religion that views faith primarily as a path to personal happiness and fulfillment without reference to others. That is an insular faith and James would condemn that as a counterfeit, an empty or dead faith. Mariam Kovalishyn introduced me to an insightful message from theologian Francis Schaeffer along these lines, in which he critiques American Christianity. Schaeffer argued that too many Christians he encountered were only interested in the values of what he calls "personal peace" and material benefit.[11]

> Personal peace means just to be let alone, not to be troubled by the troubles of other people, whether across the world or across the city—to live one's life with minimal possibilities of being personally disturbed. Personal peace means wanting to have my personal life pattern undisturbed in my lifetime, regardless of what the result

---

11. Francis Schaeffer, *How Then Shall We Live*, in *The Complete Works of Francis A. Schaeffer: A Christian Worldview*, 2nd ed. (Winchester, IL: Crossway, 1990), 211; as cited in Mariam Kamell (Kovalishyn), "James 1:27 and the Church's Call to Mission and Morals," *Crux* 46.4 (2010): 15–22, at 15.

will be in the lifetimes of my children and grandchildren. Affluence means an overwhelming and ever-increasing prosperity—a life made up of things, things, and more things—a success judged by an ever-higher level of material abundance.

Schaeffer wrote that several decades ago, but it seems relevant today. Elsa Tamez argues that if the letter of James were circulated secretly in certain countries today that are politically and economically corrupt, "it would very possibly be intercepted by government security agencies" for being a text that is dangerous to society, that threatens to disrupt the status quo.[12]

Just as I was uncomfortable having someone say to me, "Do you do anything for anyone?" so I think James's message about the Christian religion should prick our consciences and challenge our lifestyles. Sometimes, when I teach on James in the seminary classroom, I ask the students how it would go if they preached through James and especially focused on wealth and poverty. Imagine your preacher getting up front and reading out loud *The Message* text of James 5:1–6.

And a final word to you arrogant rich: Take some lessons in lament. You'll need buckets for the tears when the crash comes upon you. Your money is corrupt and your fine clothes stink. Your greedy luxuries are a cancer in your gut, destroying your life from within. You thought you were piling up wealth. What you've piled up is judgment.

All the workers you've exploited and cheated cry out for judgment. The groans of the workers you used and abused are a roar in the ears of the Master Avenger. You've looted the earth and lived it up. But all you'll have to show for it is a fatter than usual corpse. In fact, what you've done is condemn and murder perfectly good persons, who stand there and take it.

What would be some of the congregational responses? I hope many brothers and sisters would take time to reflect on James's needling rebuke. Others, hopefully, would immediately recognize their

---

12. Tamez, *Scandalous Message*, 1.

culpability and participation in systems of economic imbalance. But I honestly think there would be a substantial group that would take offense and offer a series of comebacks and excuses:

> *I earned my money fair and square, it is rightfully mine.*
> *I have earned comfort.*
> *I'm not hoarding, I'm investing in my family's future.*
> *If other people are lazy, they deserve to be poor.*
> *If I give my money to someone else, how do I know they will save it or*
> *   spend it wisely?*
> *It's not about how much money you have, it's about how you use it.*
> *There are a lot of people who have a lot more money than I do—*
> *   I'm not wealthy!*
> *The church should focus on Jesus, not my money.*

The topic of money is always an uncomfortable one to bring up at church because it is considered a private affair. For so many, they think of money in individualized terms. They operate in terms of individual ownership and personal property. *This is mine, not yours. This belongs to me.* Sometimes, when I have brought up this problem, I get criticisms to the effect that I am promoting socialism, or worse, Marxism! These are knee-jerk reactions to anything that might threaten someone's sense of what someone *deserves* to own or keep, even when it is more than what most others have, and far more than what the least have.

I encourage you to sit with James's words in 5:1–6, especially Eugene Peterson's *The Message* version, and consider what James would say about *your* practiced religion. In addition, I want to conclude with some reflections on economics from a Christian perspective via St. John Chrysostom's sermon on wealth in his reading of 1 Timothy.[13]

Chrysostom raises this question with the rich: *Where did your money come from?* Naturally, one might say, "From my father, and his from my grandfather." Chrysostom reasons that somewhere along the way it was acquired unjustly. Why?

---

13. The quotations included in the following are from Helen Rhee, *Wealth and Poverty in Early Christianity* (Minneapolis: Fortress, 2017), 99–103.

Because God in the beginning made not one rich and another poor. . . . Rather, he left the earth free to all alike. How come then, if it is common, you have acres and acres of land, while your neighbor has not a portion of it?

Chrysostom's economic perspective is shaped by his theology of creation (i.e., this is where, for him, "religion" and "money" meet). Chrysostom explains how God has given freely and equally to all sun, air, earth, water, heaven, sea, light, and stars: "Their benefits are dispensed equally to all as siblings. We are all formed with the same eyes, the same body, the same soul, the same structure in all respects, all things from the earth, all people from one human being, and all in the same habitation." These are signs that all should live with the same benefits and privileges in God's good world. No one "owns" the sun or the air. But sinful human nature tries to control these things for their own personal benefit: "Whereas God brings us together in every way, we are eager to divide and separate ourselves by appropriating things, using those cold words, 'mine and yours'." *Why do we not learn God's lesson when we breathe air or swim in the river or ocean*, Chrysostom wonders? Chrysostom concludes his message with words that are implicit in James's rebuke speech: "How can the rich be good? When they distribute their riches, they are good, so that they are good when they have ceased to have it, when they give it to others."

If this message from Chrysostom upsets you, if you find fault with the logic, if it seems risky and irresponsible, if it provokes your capitalistic sensibilities, ask yourself this: is it contrary to Scripture, is it contrary to James?

Suggested Reading

Crystal L. Hall. *Insights from Reading the Bible with the Poor*. Minneapolis: Fortress, 2019.

Elsa Tamez. *The Scandalous Message of James: Faith without Works Is Dead*. New York: Crossroad, 2018.

Carla Swafford Works. *The Least of These: Paul and the Marginalized*. Grand Rapids: Eerdmans, 2020.

CHAPTER 13

Holiness

A Glorious Otherness

1 Peter

"It's hard to define, but you'll know it when you see it." That famous phrase, or some variation of it, has been used in relation to wide-ranging concepts like leadership, frailty, beauty, and obscenity. I think it also fits for "holiness." When we talk about having a "holy" moment, what exactly does that mean? If someone who isn't religious asked you to define "holiness" using a synonym, what would you say? One way to get at this same question is through Bible translations and paraphrases. There are numerous translation projects that have tried to put the biblical text into words that make sense to unchurched folks today. For example, Genesis 6:9 says, in the NRSV, "Noah was a righteous man." Eugene Peterson's *The Message* paraphrases this as "Noah was a good man." Righteousness and goodness are not exactly the same thing, but they are related and close enough to represent pretty well what the author of Genesis was trying to say. But when you search for alternatives for holiness language, it gets quite a bit harder. Let's look at *The Message* again. Where the NIV says that the believers in Corinth have been "sanctified in Christ Jesus and called to be his holy people" (1 Cor 1:2a), Peterson explains this as "cleaned up by Jesus and set apart for a God-filled life." Does Peterson capture the essence of holiness and sanctification? Or take the example of something called the "Scholars Version Translation" which translates "sanctification" in 1 Thessalonians 4:3 as "the virtuous life."[1] Can holiness be equated with virtue? Or consider the way the Heidelberg Catechism explains what it means to "hallow" God's name according to the Lord's Prayer: "Help us to truly know you, to honor, glorify, and praise you for all your works and for all that shines forth from them."[2] Thus, to set apart God as holy is to honor, glorify, and praise God. Do these things fully capture God's holiness?

Hopefully, by now, you can see this is hard work to wrap our brains around the essential meaning of "holiness." But that is precisely what we should be trying to do, impossible as it is to accomplish fully. This book, *15 New Testament Words of Life*, is all about demonstrating how relevant and powerful the word of God is for life today if we are attentive to all the ways God is still working now as he did two thousand years ago. Even though we will fail to define holiness in a simple sentence, we can learn a lot about the values embedded in Scripture by giving some attention to key holiness texts.

Old Testament Background

There are many holiness texts in the Old Testament, and we might commence with the priestly duty of distinguishing "between the holy and the common, and between the unclean and the clean" (Lev 10:10). But I prefer to start with the familiar story of Moses and the burning bush. How Moses came to know about the luminous bush we don't know, but we are told his curiosity compelled him to move in closer (Exod 3:3). The divine voice warned him, "Remove the sandals from for your feet, for the place on which you are standing is holy ground" (3:5). It is clear that the ground is holy not because of the specific kind of dirt, but because of the concentrated presence of God. The "godness"

---

1. Arthur J. Dewey et al., *The Authentic Letters of Paul* (Salem, OR: Polebridge, 2010), 6.
2. "Heidelberg Catechism," Christian Reformed Church, www.crcna.org/welcome /beliefs/confessions/heidelberg-catechism.

of God creates a sort of proximity field, a spiritual radiation that affects its surroundings, making the space thick with numinous energy. There is something so pure and perfect and powerful there that Moses must show the proper care, humility, and respect.

We find a similar reaction to the holy presence of God in Isaiah 6 when the prophet finds himself in a heavenly throne room vision with the angels proclaiming "Holy, holy, holy is the LORD of hosts" (6:1–3). Isaiah's response is wondrous terror, "Woe to me! . . . I am ruined!" (6:5 NIV). At that moment, Isaiah recognized the overwhelming holiness of God, his senses were overloaded with divine glory, and he could not help but feel unfit to experience this sacred presence.

Holiness in Jewish perspective is about God, his glory, majesty, purity, perfection, and greatness all wrapped into something greater than the sum of these individual attributes. And just as God's holy mark affected the ground near Moses, so it was with the *holy* temple in Jerusalem, the special place for God's dwelling on earth. So also the special beings in close contact with God are his *holy* angels. Even though God alone is holy, in a sense, he can share this attribute and status with other things and beings as they come to be closely identified with him.

God called Israel to be special, set apart from the other peoples, a kingdom of priests and a "holy nation" (Exod 19:6). They must behave differently, imitate their God, because "You shall be people consecrated to me" (Exod 22:31; cf. Deut 28:9; Ps 34:9; Isa 62:12). This represents God's ownership of Israel as a treasure and special possession; when Israel was liberated from slavery in Egypt, they were not set free unto national independence, but rather for a new belonging of devotion and existence for YHWH.[3] They were covenanted into a holiness coterie, requiring exclusive commitment and faithful obedience.[4] But why? Walter Brueggemann explains that Israel was called to represent YHWH and embody his redemptive work on earth. This is a high calling indeed: "The notion of 'holiness' characterizes what is deepest,

---

3. See Walter Brueggemann, *Reverberations of Faith: A Theological Handbook of Old Testament Themes* (Louisville: Westminster John Knox, 2003), 99.

4. See Jo Bailey Wells, *God's Holy People: A Theme in Biblical Theology* (Sheffield: Sheffield Academic, 2000), 14.

most inscrutable, most marvelous, and most demanding in Israel's faith."[5] Israel was invited to be a people that reflects God's own holiness to a world devastated by sin. Through the covenantal law and bond, YHWH was forming his people into his special vehicle for redeeming the world he had created.[6] Christopher Wright puts it this way, "For Israel to be holy . . . meant that they were to be a distinctive community among the nations. . . . 'YHWH-like,' rather than like the nations. They were to do as YHWH does, not as the nations do (Lev 18:3–4). Holiness for Israel meant reflection on earth of the transcendent holiness of YHWH himself."[7]

We must get it out of our heads that the call to be holy was a burden on Israel. It was not. It was a privilege, like being invited to play for an Olympic team. While the training would be rigorous and the standards impossibly high, it was undeniably a rare and awesome honor. Of course, the Old Testament story of Israel presents a checkered history of holiness. Israel was all too often idolatrous, disobedient, and wayward. They looked to the Holy One, their God, to make things right (Isa 41:14; Ezek 39:7). Israel needed a greater purification to happen to them before they could properly reflect the holiness of God.

Focal Text: 1 Peter

A Different Kind of People

First Peter reflects all these distinctives of biblical holiness we have described and centers the biblical redemptive holiness project on the person of Jesus Christ. Before we get to the importance of holiness language in 1 Peter, let's briefly consider the context of this letter. In the background we can detect that the churches needing this apostolic instruction were suffering from rejection and persecution (1:6–7; cf. 1:11–12; 3:17–22; 4:1). They felt like "resident aliens," struggling with an erosion of their personal identity and social stability. Peter urges

---

5. Brueggemann, *Reverberations of Faith*, 98.

6. See Andy Johnson, *Holiness and the Missio Dei* (Eugene, OR: Cascade, 2016), 1–30.

7. Christopher J. H. Wright, *The Mission of God's People: A Biblical Theology of the Church's Mission* (Grand Rapids: Zondervan, 2010), 124.

them to live in hope, setting their minds and hearts on God's faithfulness to save them (1:5, 9–10; 2:2). When it comes to suffering and persecution, Peter does not sweep this problem under the rug. He presents suffering as an opportunity to stimulate growth, maturity, and resilience—to progress in virtue and demonstrate a life set apart for goodness and righteousness.

A foundational appeal that Peter makes to these struggling churches is that they should be holy in conformity to their holy God; he quotes Leviticus 11:44 verbatim: "You shall be holy, for I am holy" (1 Peter 1:15). This entails rejecting the ways of the world with its evil desires (1:14). The people of God, consecrated by the sprinkled blood of Jesus Christ (1 Peter 1:2; cf. 1:19), are called to a life set apart. If this invites some form of opprobrium, so be it. Then they must "live in reverent fear during the time of your exile" (1:17). Peter was not calling for a secluded life, far from the unholy and unbelieving world. He was challenging these Christians to be distinct and different in their lifestyle, not "holier than thou" in a snobby way. This holiness "difference" is not about being weird for the sake of being weird. As Jo Bailey Wells explains, according to Peter, believers "are estranged because they have a different intrinsic vision of reality. And because of this vision, they live differently."[8] Their holiness ought to look like transparency, integrity, and excellence in all things. Furthermore, they have been purified by the truth to display the character of God, especially evident in mutual love (1:23).

Priests and Sacrifices with Jesus

In chapter 2, Peter develops his holiness exhortation using metaphors from cultic life: temple, priesthood, and sacrifices—images familiar to both Jews and gentiles. For most people in the ancient world, temple and altar rituals were about placating the gods through material offerings, sacrifices, and prayers. These were gestures of goodwill, humility, submission, thanksgiving, and as necessary, penitence. Peter takes these common experiences and reorients them toward a transformed communal identity for Christians. Rather than trying

---

8. Jo Bailey Wells, *God's Holy People*, 224.

to conform to the identity and ways of the world, Christians ought to ground their being in the one God. "Come to him," Peter urges (2:4). *Come and be formed with the living Stone (Christ) into a new social structure, a Spirit-house and a holy priesthood (2:5a). Gather for worship, offering Spirit-sacrifices to God through Jesus Christ (2:5b).*

This second chapter of 1 Peter underscores the way believers naturally struggle with finding their way in the world. To identify with the crucified Christ *is* to be rejected by the world (2:7–8). There are only two paths before the believers—one road scoffs at the Stone of God (Christ); the other leads to conforming to the odd shape of that Stone, to be collected together into a special building. There is no hiding your identity as a Christian. In fact, Christians are called to come together to sing with one loud voice "the mighty acts of him who called you out of darkness into his marvelous light" (2:9).

Peter's use of holiness language and imagery is quite masterful in this letter. While cultic "holiness" can seem completely irrelevant to navigating life in the "real world," Peter turns this on its head. *Holiness is crucial in real life. Not bloody animals or plumes of smoke. No priests in robes or cultic structures of stone.* Biblical holiness is all about finding the essence of one's identity in the one God, through the purifying blood of Jesus Christ. But this holy life is not lived on one's own. It is lived together with the Christian community, a communal priesthood, as it were, who gather for worship and offering. In contrast to the kinds of priests, though, who leave the common space to move behind the curtain to serve God, these Spirit-formed priests have a strategic role to play in and for the sake of the world. They broadcast the goodness, justice, mercy, love, beauty, and glory of God—they conduct his holy light throughout the world.

Holiness and Suffering

Peter adds an important, but perhaps unexpected, dimension to holy living: the value, even the necessity, of suffering. The way our bodies and lives are naturally wired, we recoil from suffering. But Peter connects righteous suffering to godliness and holiness. To be holy is not to slip away to be with God, far from the rough and tumble of the world and its weakness and suffering. If the life and death of Christ has meant *anything*, it is that human suffering can demonstrate the perfect "otherness" of God, a way of living generously that one cannot find anywhere else (3:8–22, esp. 3:17–18). Put another way, Peter's revisioning of holiness should cause us to see Jesus's most "holy" moments, not as his episodes of quiet and private contemplation (important as those times are), but precisely those difficult events where he dared to live out a story of God's radical love and compassion for all, some of the very things that sent him to that unholy cross.

OTHER NEW TESTAMENT VOICES

John 17:17; Romans 6:22; 12:1–2; 1 Corinthians 3:17; Ephesians 4:24; Philippians 2:5; 1 Thessalonians 5:23; 2 Timothy 1:9; 2:21; 1 John 1:7; 3:6–10; Revelation 4:8

Matthew 5–6

"Be perfect, therefore, as your heavenly Father is perfect" (Matt 5:48). In Jesus's Sermon on the Mount, he clearly adapts the key Levitical command, "Be holy, for I am holy" (Lev 11:44; cf. 1 Peter 1:15). *Perfect? Is that what God wants, is that what Jesus was really teaching?* My friend Kent Yinger has made a strong case that we have mistranslated the underlying Greek word *teleios*. It doesn't refer to 100% perfection as in making no mistakes or being flawless, without blemish. Yinger contends that biblical language of this kind is about *wholeness* and *maturity*, singular devotion to God and integrity and wise thinking reflective of someone who is conforming to the character of God, especially as modeled by Jesus himself.[9] Jesus and Peter were teaching essentially the same thing about Christian holiness: we will reflect the unique identity of our God when we imitate his character.

Jesus's *teleios* command in the sermon is sandwiched by two teaching sections. The first one is on enemy love (Matt 5:43–47). The second

---

9. Kent Yinger, *God and Human Wholeness: Perfection in Biblical and Theological Tradition* (Eugene, OR: Cascade, 2019).

one is on transparent and authentic worship, devotion to God absent of any pious show, trying to gain attention and recognition from others (6:1–6). Holiness, perfection, maturity, whatever we choose to call it, is precisely identified with these things. "Perfection" in the way of God is not getting perfect grades, running a perfect marathon, or trying to please everyone in every way all of the time. Holy perfection of the children of the Father, the disciples of Jesus, is life lived oriented toward love of God and love of neighbor, just as the sermon teaches overall.

Not too much later in the sermon, Jesus shares with his disciples his model for prayer, the Lord's Prayer, which includes *sanctifying* (i.e., *marking as holy*) God's name (6:9c). Everything we have talked about so far in this chapter, from Peter and Matthew's Jesus, should make clear that this consecration of God's name doesn't happen solely in cathedrals and prayer closets. True religion, as the Bible describes it (see chapter 12 on James in this book), is an "everywhere-and-all-of-the-time" kind of thing. So, surely Jesus implies that we "hallow" God's name when we love God and love neighbor, when we are *teleios* in head, heart, and hands. We "hallow" God's name as salt and light in the world, not in any kind of escape from the world. If I can be permitted here a bit of theological license, I wonder if we could reconceive of the sermon's Beatitudes (5:3–11) as about not just demonstrating "blessedness" ("Blessed are the . . ."), but also holiness and wholeness (*teleios*-ness!).

> *Holy are the poor in spirit*
> *Holy are those who mourn*
> *Holy are the meek*
> *Holy are those who are hungry and thirsty for righteousness*
> *Holy are the merciful*
> *Holy are the pure in heart*
> *Holy are the peacemakers*
> *Holy are the persecuted*

These are blessed and holy because they march to the beat of a different drummer, the tune of the Holy God whose ways are righteous. And just as Peter connected holiness to suffering, so too does Jesus in his sermon: *Blessed (and holy) are you when you are persecuted* (5:11).

Suffer well, Jesus says, *turn the other cheek and love your enemies* (Matt 5:38–40), *because that honors the holy God. Suffer well*, Peter also says, *do not repay evil for evil* (1 Peter 3:9), *that honors the holy God.*

Holiness for Today

Holy Wonder

Recently, I found myself in a "showhole" (as many people do) looking for something to watch while I exercised. I happened upon a show sponsored by National Geographic called *The Right Stuff.* This eight-episode series is about the space race between the US and Russia in the 1960s, as both countries competed to put their best pilot sixty some miles beyond earth's atmosphere. As the story goes—I hope I'm not spoiling it for you!—the Russians beat the US by only a few weeks (April 12, 1961, cosmonaut Yuri Gagarin was the first human in space). The story itself is fascinating, but what really grabbed my attention was what was *unknown* to the world only a half century or so ago.

There is a gripping scene, when American astronaut-in-training John Glenn is shown a Russian image of the far side of the moon (taken by Luna 3, a Russian satellite). Several other people come over and stare at this amazing picture, something we would easily take for granted today. But imagine seeing, for the first time, what no one had ever seen before. Think about the work and energy it took to capture that image. The previously invisible (to us earthlings) had just been made visible. You couldn't help but marvel.

There was this feeling of awe and wonder that came over Glenn, evident in his face. At first, of course, he was upset that the Russians had beat them in this matter, but he immediately became aware of the privilege of even gazing upon something so great, so majestic, so beautiful.

In some ways, I envy a world before the Internet and computer-generated graphics. Before iPhones and Google. Sure, I'm gonna "selfie" at the Grand Canyon if I get the chance, but our impulse to put everything on social media or in a camera photostream, I confess, does rob these moments of wonder sometimes. My daughter performed in a school musical last year and I decided that I would watch it twice

(I actually went four times in the end). During the first viewing, I just sat and watched and enjoyed the show. Then, later, I brought a camcorder and filmed it. I didn't want to miss the emotional power of the performance by trying to "capture" it. It was nice to record the memory and share it with family, but we all know there *is* something special about "being there" and experiencing it fully.

I believe holiness may be the hardest concept to capture in our modern world, because we are the generation of "widely available, mass quantity, low quality" utility products and experiences. A while back I visited India with my wife and went to the Taj Mahal, as tourists do. There were some merchants offering to take our picture in front of the spectacle for a small fee. "No charge now, come to our shop after your tour and see the pictures, buy if you want." So we did. We went to their store later on, and they pulled up the pictures on a computer. We looked great, the Taj Mahal looked great, and the weather was spectacular. Something was wrong. They had airbrushed in good weather. The day we were there, it was overcast and gloomy. "You changed the picture," we said. "We made it better," they replied with a smile. *How can anything be "wonder"-ful if we can turn anything into anything else with a click of a button?*

I don't mean to be a curmudgeon or a Luddite. I love technology, I have a smartphone, and I definitely *don't* want to go back to the 1960s. What I am trying to say is that it is harder today than ever before in history, I think, to resonate with the biblical writers' appreciation for holy wonder. But it is not *impossible*. I go for a walk almost every day, and I am lucky to live in a hilly area of Oregon where I can see Mount Hood pretty well on a clear day. I often stop and enjoy looking at the majestic mountain. And sometimes I take out my phone and snap a picture. But I am *always* disappointed by the picture version. And I always think to myself, *There's just nothing that can replace looking at the real thing with my own eyes.*

This is one of the most powerful things the Bible can contribute to us modern readers. It can help us to reconnect with the power of holy wonder. To appreciate and have our breath taken away by God and some of the great and awesome things he has created. To be filled up with wonder and even a bit of dread, rather than try to capture it on a memory card, shrink wrap it in a factory, or try to improve upon it with Photoshop.

A Holy Difference

God's people are purified and sanctified by the blood of Jesus Christ to bring God's holy light to the world. As 1 Peter makes clear, it can be an uncomfortable scenario to live as Jesus followers in the world. Miroslav Volf reflects on this phenomenon in 1 Peter through the lens of sociological analysis. What does it mean for believers to live out a social holiness in society?

> Christians do not come into their social world from outside seeking either to accommodate to their new home (like second generation immigrants would), shape it in the image of the one they have left behold (like colonizers would), or establish a little haven in the strange new world reminiscent of the old (as resident aliens would). They are not outsiders who either seek to become insiders or maintain strenuously the status of outsiders. Christians are the *insiders* who have diverted from their culture by being born again. They are by definition those who are not what they used to be, those who do not live like they used to live. Christian difference is therefore not an insertion of something new into the old from outside, but a bursting out of the new *precisely within the proper space of the old.*[10]

Volf is rightly insistent that "difference" ought not to become an "us vs. them" dynamic, where Christians act superior to others. "Christian hope," Volf explains, should not correspond to "damnation of non-Christians. . . . It is Christian identity that creates difference from the social environment, not the other way around."[11] The Christian difference in society he describes as *soft* difference; not weak, mind you, but gentle and even inviting. This kind of "soft difference" holiness is at the core of the Christian missional ethos, seeking to win others, not with manipulation, but a beautiful life given to God for the sake of

---

10. Miroslav Volf, "Soft Difference: Theological Reflections on the Relationship between Church and Culture in 1 Peter," *Ex Auditu* 10 (1994): 15–30, at 18–19 (italics original).
11. Volf, "Soft Difference," 21.

the world.[12] Joel Green, portraying 1 Peter's holiness vision in similar terms, identifies the human "construction of life around God's [holy] character and purpose" to be the site of personal transformation where Christians become *different* in ways that ought to prompt others to be curious and inquisitive.[13] Lest believers become self-centered about holiness, Green reminds us that our holy life only exists because of God's grace. Green borrows from Jürgen Moltmann's definition of "sanctification" as a "divine act through which God chooses something for himself and makes it his own, thus letting it participate in his nature."[14]

Sometimes I hear Christians say, "I am nothing special. I am just a beggar telling another beggar where to find bread." Or they say, "I'm a sinner just like everyone else, but I know the Savior." Yes, these things are true in a sense, and Christians should never give unbelievers the impression that they are perfect or sinless. But I wonder if sometimes we are underselling the difference that Jesus has made in our lives. I wouldn't be a Christian at all if I hadn't *seen* a difference in the lives of those youth group kids in my school twenty plus years ago. I wasn't interested in their "theology." I was attracted to their lifestyles.

Using 1 Peter as a source for inspiration, we can consider several ways in which we are called, then and now, to represent this "glorious otherness," the holiness of the triune God.

Holy Worship (1 Peter 2:1–10)

Let us worship with dedication, authenticity, joy, lament, and service. Let our worship be beautiful and sonorous, contemplative, exuberant, and unified.

Hope and Holy Suffering (1:6–8, 13; 2:19–23; 3:14–18; 4:1, 13–19; 5:1, 9)

If we must suffer, may we suffer well, seeing challenges as opportunities for growth and trusting in the God who will right every wrong.

---

12. Volf, "Soft Difference," 24.

13. Joel B. Green, *1 Peter*, Two Horizons New Testament Commentary (Grand Rapids: Eerdmans, 2007), 206.

14. Green, *1 Peter*, 222; see Moltmann, *The Spirit of Life: A Universal Affirmation* (Minneapolis: Fortress, 1992), 174.

Holy Values (1:14–15; 2:11; 4:2–4; 5:1–2)

May we value and honor the holy God who calls us to the highest standards, not to threaten us with punishment for imperfection, but to enable us to reflect his glory more purely.

Holy Simplicity (1:17–18; 3:3–4)

May we live simple lives, finding value and significance in relationships, mission, worship, and helping God's creation to thrive. We do not need money or possessions to find fulfillment.

Holy Love (1:22; 2:1 [vice list]; 3:8; 4:8–11)

Above all, may we reflect the holiness of God through imitation of his holy love.

Suggested Reading

Stephen C. Barton. *Holiness: Past and Present*. London: Bloomsbury, 2003.

Kent Brower and Andy Johnson, ed. *Holiness and Ecclesiology in the New Testament*. Grand Rapids: Eerdmans, 2007.

Andy Johnson. *Holiness and the Missio Dei*. Eugene, OR: Cascade, 2016.

David Peterson. *Possessed by God: A New Testament Theology of Sanctification and Holiness*. New Studies in Biblical Theology. Downers Grove, IL: IVP Academic, 1995.

Jo Bailey Wells. *God's Holy People: A Theme in Biblical Theology*. Sheffield: Sheffield Academic, 2000.

CHAPTER 14

Love

Divine Affection, Loyalty, and Generosity

1 John

See How They Love!

Church father Tertullian (155–220 CE) spent fifty chapters supporting
and defending Christianity in his work *Apology*. It begins, "Magistrates
of the Roman Empire, seated as you are before the eyes of all, in almost
the highest position in the state to pronounce judgment: if you are
not allowed to conduct an open and public examination and inquiry
as to what the real truth is with regard to the Christians . . . then let
the truth reach your ears by the private and quiet avenue of literature" (*Apol.* 1.1).[1] His thirty-ninth chapter covers the testimony and
evidence of Christian love. He writes, "We form one body because of
our religious convictions, and because of the divine origin of our way
of life and the bond of common hope" (39.2a). When Christians come
together, Tertullian writes, they pray for world leaders, for the welfare
of all people, for peace, and for God's grace and mercy on the world.
Christians care about peace and prosperity for everyone in the world,
not just for themselves (39.2b).

---

1. All English translations are from Emily Joseph Daly, trans., *Tertullian, Apology* (New
York: Catholic University of America, 1950), 3–126.

Tertullian spends much time in his *Apology* talking about the responsible use of funds. Christians, he urges, are not compelled or coerced to give money to their own organization (i.e., the church). They do so at their own will and according to ability and conscience. And, unlike other associations at the time, the funds are not channeled into fancy feasts and "drinking parties." Rather, the money is used "for the support and burial of the poor, for children who are without their parents and means of subsistence, for aged men who are confined to the house; likewise, for shipwrecked sailors, and for any in the mines, on islands or in prisons" (39.6). Tertullian is quite bold in suggesting that when outsiders gossip about Christians, their hatred actually derives from jealousy. They see the deep love the Christians have for one another, and they despise it. "See how they love one another . . . and how ready they are to die for each other" (39.7). Tertullian claims that Christians commonly call each other "brothers" because they act like true family, "united in mind and soul [and] have no hesitation about sharing what we have. Everything is in common among us—except our wives" (39.11).

Tertullian explains the difference between the popular drinking parties of high society and the "Love Feast" of the Christians. Unlike the former (who overfill their bellies, pockets, and egos), the Christians welcome, care for, and feed the poor out of respect for their God who desires that "a greater consideration is given to those of lower station" (39.16).

Tertullian begs the instigators of persecution against Christians to produce any evidence of wrongdoing by the church: "But, for whose destruction have we ever held a meeting?" (39.21a). He concludes with this testimony: "We are the same when assembled as when separate; we are collectively the same as we are individually, doing no one any injury, causing no one any harm" (39.21b). His overall argument is that the Christian people are a good people, people who demonstrate the ideals of a good and just society, rich in mercy and love.

What's Love Got to Do with It?

I find Tertullian's *Apology* of Christian love both inspiring and humbling. I am inspired by his ability to point to concrete evidence of the early church's integrity, mutual affection, and commitment in love. I find humbling the fact that I rarely see *this* kind of love in the churches I visit today. Yes, churches sometimes carve out time for the "passing of peace" or a warm handshake and "hello" after the announcements. Yes, retreats and camps are planned and supported to kindle friendships. Yes, "love" is preached from the pulpit as the lectionary or sermon series dictates. Yes, many churches set aside a bit of the budget to support a local food pantry or shelter. But Tertullian paints a *radical* picture of deep and transformative love, for the benefit of those inside and outside the walls of the church; a picture, I must confess, that is hard for me to even imagine.

The modern church tends to fall into two problematic extremes when it comes to "love." In too many cases it does not really factor into the equation at all. "Church," in these communities, is about an orthodox and uplifting sermon and meaningful worship music. In other communities, we have the excruciating pattern of sexual abuse in the church by pastors and priests. "Love" is exchanged for manipulative power, control, and false intimacy. We have a tendency either to repel love or let it loose in unbridled and self- and other-destructive passion. *Is there hope? Is Tertullian's vision of love a mirage?*

I have had my moments of doubt, but my hope was renewed in part by the stirring wedding homily preached by Bishop Michael Curry at the British royal wedding in 2018.[2] Curry was speaking directly to the happy couple, Prince Harry and Meghan Markle. "Love" is an obvious theme for a wedding sermon, but Curry used that opportunity to remind the hearers (including 300,000+ YouTube viewers) of the centrality of love in the Bible, the gospel, and God's desire for the world he created.

Curry began by addressing the fact that we all know the jubilance of being loved and finding friendship. There is power in that. But Curry went on to exhort the royal couple to move love beyond their relationship to capture the Christian mission of love for the whole world, a ministry and movement "mandating to live that love [of God],

---

2. Maquita Peters, "Bishop Michael Curry's Royal Wedding Sermon: Full Text of 'The Power of Love,'" NPR, May 20, 2018, www.npr.org/sections/thetwo-way/2018/05/20/612798691 /bishop-michael-currys-royal-wedding-sermon-full-text-of-the-power-of-love.

and in so doing to change not only [your] lives but the very life of the world itself."

Curry pointed to Jesus as the model of love, a noble, sacrificial love that transforms. He exhorted the hearers to use their imagination:

> Imagine our homes and families where love is the way. Imagine neighborhoods and communities where love is the way.
>
> Imagine governments and nations where love is the way. Imagine business and commerce where this love is the way.
>
> Imagine this tired old world where love is the way. . . .
>
> When love is the way, then no child will go to bed hungry in this world ever again.

Curry ended his fiery and passionate message by returning to a quote by Martin Luther King Jr., "We must discover the power of love, the redemptive power of love. And when we do that, we will make of this old world a new world, for love is the only way."

Much like Tertullian, Curry preached that love, true love, transforming love, is at the heart of the Bible and in the heart of the triune God. For a moment, as I heard Curry's sermon on TV, my heart, often calloused to the notion that the church could really love, was softened. *Is it really true that the Bible is about love? Not sappy, here-today-gone-tomorrow "love," but the world-shaping love that Curry professed?*

Old Testament Background

Did you know "love" is found in the Ten Commandments? Yes, we think of these as laws and rules and "Thou shalt nots," but in Exodus 20:5–6 we find embedded within the prohibition against worshiping false gods the notion that YHWH is a *jealous* God. He will discipline his people if they turn away from him, but ultimately his default disposition toward Israel is love and compassion. Later on, when Moses received the new tablets of the law on Mt. Sinai, he came to know the identity of YHWH as "the LORD, the compassionate and gracious God, slow to anger, abounding in love and faithfulness, maintaining love to thousands, and forgiving wickedness, rebellion and sin" (Exod 34:6–7 NIV).

The very foundation of Israel's story is one of redemption by the covenant God, and this God knit together his people to himself through love, a bond and relationship of commitment, mutuality, compassion, and obligation to respect one another.

In the book of Numbers, we find an episode where this love is tested. On this occasion, the LORD is upset with his wayward people (again!) and he threatens to hand them over to their enemies. Moses steps in to warn YHWH that if he does this, other nations (like Egypt) will question his love for and loyalty to his own people. Moses reminds YHWH of those very words he heard on the mountain, "The LORD is slow to anger, and abounding in steadfast love . . ." (Num 14:18). Moses adds, "Forgive the iniquity of this people according to the greatness of your steadfast love, just as you have pardoned this people, from Egypt even until now" (14:19). The LORD relents from his plan to destroy and proclaims, "I do forgive, just as you have asked" (14:20).

But this is not a one-way street. Israel is called, likewise, to "love God," which includes utter devotion, committed service, and walking in obedience in heart and soul (Deut 10:12). The expectations are made crystal clear: "You shall love the LORD your God, therefore, and keep his charge, his decrees, his ordinances, and his commandments always" (Deut 11:1).

Today, Christians often have an unfortunate binary in their attitude toward the Bible. The New Testament is treated as the book of love, freedom, and faith; alternatively, the Old Testament is too often portrayed as the book of law, works, and ritual. But we must continually be reminded that when the New Testament writers talk about love, they often point back to the Old Testament (e.g., 2 John 1:5).[3]

Walter Moberly does an excellent job of demonstrating the centrality of love in his *Old Testament Theology*.[4] He points to the emphasis on Israel recognizing that God is *one* (Deut 6:4). This is not primarily a theological statement about the existence of only one deity. It is a call

---

3. See Victor Furnish, *The Love Command in the New Testament* (London: SCM, 1972).

4. R. W. L. Moberly, *Old Testament Theology: Reading the Hebrew Bible as Christian Scripture* (Grand Rapids: Baker Academic, 2013).

for Israel to direct all of its love and devotion to *this one* alone. Moberly notes that the same language is used of love in the Song of Solomon 6:9: "My dove, my perfect one, is the only one." Technically, there may be other women he could pursue, but this is his "one and only," as it were; she is unique and special to him. Correspondingly, Moberly explains, "If YHWH our God is 'the one and only,' then Israel's unreserved love is indeed the appropriate response."[5]

Continuing on with Deut 6:4 and the Shema, Moberly paraphrases the comprehensive call to love as this: "So you should love the Lord your God with all your thinking, with all your longing, and with all your striving."[6] This is total commitment; it includes the emotions and longings, but must also include the "striving" and acts of love, service, and obedience.

It is important to keep in mind this comprehensive vision of love (thinking, longing, striving) as we turn to the New Testament, particularly to the love-filled and love-focused letter known as 1 John.

Focal Text: 1 John

In the New Testament we find three letters associated with the apostle John, the first and longest (1 John) widely popular throughout Christian history for its stark expression, vivid imagery, and passionate theology. John Wesley exclaimed, "Here are sublimity and simplicity together, the strongest sense and the plainest language!"[7] Wesleyan scholar Franz Hildebrandt expanded upon Wesley's description of 1 John:

> Here is the perfect love which casteth out fear; here are the comfortable words for those who confess their sins and the uncomfortable texts about the reborn who cannot sin; here is the twofold test for all "real Christians" through the Spirit that confesses the incarnate Christ and the love that serves Him in the

---

5. Moberly, *Old Testament Theology*, 20.
6. Moberly, *Old Testament Theology*, 24.
7. Luke Tyerman, *The Life and Times of Rev. John Wesley*, 3rd ed. (London: Hodder & Stoughton, 1876), 2.537.

brethren; here is the Wesleyan note of assurance in the repeated "hereby we know"; and here again, as in John's Gospel, the end of it all is "that your joy may be full."[8]

Scholars have struggled to discern all of the background issues behind 1 John and why this letter was written. One view is that it was composed to refute emerging heresies. But better still is the view that the author was less concerned with fighting off enemies and more concerned with keeping believers focused on staying on the right path of walking with God through Jesus Christ in light and love.[9] When it comes to the "flow" or outline of 1 John, Walter Moberly (whom we quoted earlier about the Old Testament) offers a helpful perspective on the unique outlook and style of 1 John.

> John's pattern of thinking does not involve sequential logic in the manner of a conventional argument so much as the literary equivalent of musical variations on a theme—a constant circling around the basic issue, coming at it from a variety of angles, developing now this aspect and now that aspect, balancing one statement with another to clarify what is and is not entailed, returning to a point already made so that it may be seen afresh in the light of what has been said subsequently.[10]

What are the basic theological interests of 1 John? They appear to be the themes of walking in light, loving God and brothers and sisters rightly in sweet fellowship, confessing and rejecting sin, and behaving as true children of God through the Son Jesus Christ. "Love" binds all these elements together. As St. Augustine exclaimed in the prologue of his *Ten Tractates on the Epistles of John*, "Charity is above all commended

---

8. Franz Hildebrandt, "Can the Distinctive Methodist Emphasis Be Said to Be Rooted in the New Testament?" *London Quarterly and Holborn Review* 184 (1959): 238.

9. For a thoughtful discussion of background issues see Karen Jobes, *1, 2 & 3 John*, Zondervan Exegetical Commentary on the New Testament (Grand Rapids: Zondervan Academic, 2014), 23–30.

10. R. W. L. Moberly, "'Test the Spirits': God, Love, and Critical Discernment in 1 John 4," in *The Holy Spirit and Christian Origins: Essays in Honor of James D. G. Dunn*, ed. Graham Stanton, Bruce W. Longenecker, and Stephen C. Barton (Grand Rapids: Eerdmans, 2004), 298; Jobes, *1, 2, & 3 John*, 38.

[by John in 1 John]. He has spoken many words, and nearly all are about charity."[11] We will approach 1 John especially with Augustine's statement in mind.[12]

One Command: Believing and Loving

First John regularly returns to essential commitments of the Christian faith. It is stated no clearer than in 3:23: "And this is his commandment, that we should believe in the name of his Son Jesus Christ and love one another, just as he has commanded us." We can briefly unpack "believe" in 1 John by saying that this is not about "holding beliefs," but about profound interaction with the Son. We can point to the example of the author who talks about seeing with his eyes, gazing upon, and touching the "word of life" (1:1). This "word of life" is the gospel, but the gospel message cannot be separated from the person of Jesus himself, someone to know, experience, and love. When 1 John talks about "believing" in Jesus, this is discipleship, a "following-hard-after-him" kind of faith; seeing, hearing, touching, responding to, living with, and dying with the Word of Life. It is in this messy matrix of "life together" in faith that one experiences "eternal life"—not as a quantifying anthropological phenomenon of not aging, but as a transforming participation in the immortal life of God through Jesus the Son.

First John writes *one* command that involves two things: belief in the Son, and love for others. Isn't this more properly *two* command-ments? Not for 1 John. It is a singular phenomenon, one life expressed in two ways: faith and love.

Generous and Holy Love

All Christian love, 1 John makes clear, is responsive love, reacting to and imitating divine love for us. "In this is love, not that we loved God but that he loved us and sent his Son to be the atoning sacrifice

---

11. As cited in Judith Lieu, *The Theology of Johannine Epistles*, New Testament Theology (Cambridge: Cambridge University Press, 1991), 66.

12. Alicia Myers argues persuasively that 1 John's teachings on love resonate strongly with Jesus's teachings in John 13–17; see Alicia Myers, "Remember the Greatest: Remaining in Love and Casting Out Fear in 1 John" *Review & Expositor* 115.1 (2018): 50–61, at 54.

for our sins" (4:10). Divine love is more than a doctrine of salvation; 1 John portrays it as the lavish, gushy, emotion-filled love of the Father who names us and treats us as his children (3:1).

First John is clear, though, that not all kinds of love are holy. There is a selfish sort of love, a desire that is self-serving. This love is not purifying; it is toxic and destructive. He mentions specifically "the desire of the flesh, the desire of the eyes, the pride in riches" indicative of how the world chases after counterfeit forms of "love." These substitutes are cheap and fleeting (2:16–17), not to be confused with the real thing.

Over and over again, 1 John defines love for God as obedience to what God has commanded (2:5). And what is commanded? To do what is right and to love all God's children equally and unreservedly (3:10; 5:2). These expectations are not meant to be laws to observe per se, but rather a way of living in the world that counteracts the damaging effects of sin.

Jesus Is the Model of Sacrificial Love

The vast majority of "love" references in 1 John flesh out what Christian love looks like by pointing to the example of Jesus Christ. It is explicitly said that this is the perfect snapshot of world-transforming love: Jesus Christ "laid down his life for us," so "we ought to lay down our lives for one another" (3:16). Now, it is not the case that we will have everyday experiences that require us to *die* for one another. More realistically, Christian "sacrificial love" will come in many small acts of generosity and kindness. Like giving of money and resources to help the needy (3:17). True love must be more than "thoughts and prayers"; it takes shape and life in real action and personal commitment (3:18).

First John treats love of neighbor as more than "good Christian behavior." It is evidence of true Christian rebirth and true Christian wisdom (4:7). First John teaches a theology of communion with God through Jesus Christ which, in turn, connects believers to each other. The sonship of Jesus opens a pathway for believers to live in and through Jesus, and to share Jesus's love with each other (4:9). First John imagines a people who have interwoven lives, constantly giving and receiving love empowered by the first and greater love of God

(4:19). The reason why 1 John could famously state, "God is love," is because it is deeply embedded within his Life and constantly radiates out from him; he demonstrates the purest and most perfect form of love and teaches us how to love rightly.[13]

OTHER NEW TESTAMENT VOICES
Matthew 25:35–40; Luke 6:27–31, 35; John 15:9–10, 12–13; Romans 8:35–39; 1 Corinthians 13:4–8; 16:14; Ephesians 4:2–3; Colossians 3:14

Philippians 1:8

We have spent a good bit of time looking at love language in Scripture, so we will only briefly look at another text, Philippians 1:8. At the beginning of this short, affection-infused letter, Paul reminds the Philippian believers of the special bond he has with them and tells them how they have brought him encouragement in his imprisonment through their long-term partnership and, more recently, through the supply gift they sent through Philippian Epaphroditus (Phil 1:3–11). Paul shares openly with them that he longs for them "with the affection of Christ Jesus" (1:8 NIV). The Greek word Paul uses here, *splanchnon*, is a vivid term, referring to our emotional "guts." We would say today that Paul was "feeling all the feels" about the Philippians that Christ feels for them. This is a brief, but very important reminder that one thing that Jesus does for us is amplify our affections. We don't set aside feelings to commit to "Christian duty" as believers. We are given a special gift and opportunity to enter into the deep love and compassion Jesus has for others. Love is more than just feelings, but it is not bereft of feeling.

---

13. See Dirk G. van der Merwe, "'Lived Experiences' of the Love of God according to 1 John 4: A Spirituality of Love," *In die Skriflig* 51.3 (2017): a2169: https://indieskriflig.org.za /index.php/skriflig/article/view/2169/4358.

Love for Today

First John makes for nice sermon material, and it offers much theological thought about general Christian themes like light, walking in faith, fellowship, truth, sin, and righteousness. But when we try to process what "love" should look like today, how to be faithful to 1 John's repeated "love God" and "love one another" commands, it requires more than "side hugs" and platitudes fit for an inspirational poster. The kind of "love" that Deuteronomy demands, the kind of love that Tertullian pointed to as evidence of the beauty of Christianity, the kind of love that inspired Bishop Michael Curry's dream, and the kind of love that reflects the God who *is* love according to 1 John—that love is a rare gift and a difficult practice.

Being Loved by God

The Old Testament and the New Testament both underscore God as the first and best lover. As it is written, "The LORD did not set his affection on you and choose you because you were more numerous than other peoples, for you were the fewest of all peoples" (Deut 7:7 NIV). In some ways, that kind of statement can feel like a backhanded compliment, but what it is saying is that God didn't choose Israel in order to receive a status or material benefit back; in the same way we don't "choose" our children for what they can do for us. One answer to the question, *What does it mean to be a Christian?* is simply to say, *Someone loved by God through Jesus Christ*; someone who has accepted that love and responds with gratitude. That is not the whole story, but it must be the beginning.

But what does this look like? How are we "loved" by God today? Is it a passive thing that just happens, or are we more directly involved? We can begin with an easy affirmation that believers ought to rest in the knowledge and security of God's love for us. Theologian Donald W. Shriver was once asked to summarize the gospel in seven words. He chose this answer: "divinely persistent, God really loves us." He later expanded on this with a few more words:

The Spirit who raised Jesus from the dead is working to infiltrate the whole creation with God's love. Paul's testimony to the work of the

Spirit in Romans 8 is for me the key chapter in the New Testament. Dependence on—and receptivity to—the daily presence of the Spirit makes possible faith, hope and love in a human life.[14]

It should not be treated as a cliché, then, that humans need to be affirmed in love by God every day. I think about the ministry of the black housekeeper Aibileen in the 1960s-set novel and film *The Help*. The white family that Aibileen worked for had a little girl (Mae Mobley) who was emotionally and physically abused by her mother. Throughout the story, Aibileen loved and cared for Mae Mobley, including daily looking into her eyes and repeating, "You is good, you is kind, you is important." This is a nice parallel to the triune God who speaks to his people, saying, "You are loved, you are holy, you are mine" (see Exod 19:6). It is crucial that believers, young and old, begin and end their day with these kinds of divine words in mind and heart.

Loving God

How do we love God? As Deuteronomy suggests, it is with our thinking, longing, and striving—with all that is in us and with all that we do. This often involves putting God's desires and priorities above our own, or what we think is our own, "Yet not as I will, but as you will" (Matt 26:39 NIV). Love requires a unique and focused commitment, as in Solomon's dedication to his lover, his "one and only" (see Song 6:9). Or we could use Jesus's image of the slave who cannot serve two masters (Matt 6:24). We would never equate love with slavery, but for Jesus the one thing they have in common is devotion. In Jesus's time, a slave could literally not have two masters, because they served only one. So it is with the people of God, they are called to exclusive commitment. Love, according to the Bible, includes affection and enjoyment, but more than that, it involves allegiance and full devotion. First John sharpens this by calling for obedience to all that God commands, especially to love one another. To love God is to love what God loves, that is, to love his children.

---

14. Donald W. Shriver, "Divinely Persistent, God Really Loves Us," *Christian Century* (November 29, 2011), www.christiancentury.org/blogs/archive/2011-11/divinely-persistent -god-really-loves-us.

Loving One Another

When I was a student, our seminary president, Dr. Walter Kaiser, once began chapel with this comment on how church people treat pastors: "God's sheep bite!" Here he meant God's sheep bite the shepherds, but we might also say they bite each other (Gal 5:15). In Galatians, Paul urges Christians to have a spirit of grace and goodness toward all, but it must be especially seen and lived out in the family of the church (Gal 6:10). How do we "love one another"? If we have learned anything from Scripture about love, it is that it involves treating the other as family. For my kids, I regularly drop what I am doing to attend to their needs. If they get hurt at school, I leave work. If they need me at home, I stop and help them. I don't do that for just anyone, but because they are *my* kids, I do it. So it is with the "family of faith." We care for one another; we meet each other's emotional, physical, spiritual, and social needs.

I was at an academic conference some years ago while I was going through a very hard time in my life. A good friend could sense my lowness and he called a few other people together. We found an empty conference room and these four friends spent time praying over me with tears, with faith, with hope, and with love. Today, I continue to go back to that moment, their spontaneous and responsive act of concern and affection, as a glimpse of true Christian love.

Loving Strangers and Enemies

One of the amazing features of early Christianity is the emphasis on love of stranger and even love for enemies. When it comes to the stranger, we can think of Tertullian's comments about feeding the poor. Acts of generosity and kindness for the least of these. But how do you actually *love* your enemies? How do you love the person who abused you? How do you love the person who bullied you or called you names? How do you love the person who broke trust? How do you love the person who will never ask for forgiveness?

We can be clear about what is *not* being asked for. You are not being forced by the Bible to be friends with an abusive partner who continues to hurt you. You are not asked to be a doormat for jerks. Love is not a code word for letting other people walk all over you. But our resources, opportunities, and alternatives are not simply (1) hating your enemies or (2) enabling your enemies. I won't pretend to be Mr. Rogers and have nothing in my heart but pure love for my enemies. But we must strive to respond to Jesus's and the Bible's call for enemy-grace and enemy-love. Minister and theologian Sam Wells offers an exposition of Jesus's teaching on enemy-love in Luke 6:20–31 that is resonant with Jesus's challenging message. Wells captures the love-challenge of Jesus without sap or sentiment:[15]

"Do good to those who hate you." Wells urges, "Say by your actions, 'However much you hate me, I will never hate you.' Remember this will end. Don't let these people turn you into a monster. Repay evil with good."

"Bless those who hate you." Wells writes on this, "Mind your speech. Try not to lose your temper. Think of those who are hating and hurting you and see them as the tiny children they once were, longing for trust and safety, and speak to them as if they were still those children."

"Pray for those who abuse you." "Sometimes abuse is incredibly difficult to become disentangled from," Well explains. "Remember, God is always as much a part of any story as you are. In prayer, ask God to be made present not just to you but to your enemy."

"Offer the other cheek." Here Wells writes, "In other words, not just don't get into a fight, because then there'll be no difference between you and them, but don't let those who hate you think you can be intimidated by violence. Offering the other cheek means saying 'I'm not going to accept that violence trumps everything else.'"

"Don't withhold your shirt." "In other words, surprise your enemy with your generosity and thus show your enemies you have not become like them."

"Give to everyone who begs." "Remember that, even when you can only think of how you've been hurt, there is always someone worse off than you, and reaching out to them is a way of rescuing yourself from self-pity."

"Don't ask for your property back." Wells here says that "I think this means remember you will lose everything when you die, so start living

---

15. What follows in the next paragraphs is from Sam Wells, "Love Your Enemies: Luke 6.20–31," *Journal for Preachers* 38.4 (2015): 27–30, at 29–30; see too Laurie Brink, "Love Your Enemy?" *U.S. Catholic* 83.6 (2018): 28–33.

toward your possessions in such a way that they don't determine who you are."

Wells points out that Jesus was not just being preachy about love with his followers; he was preparing to be betrayed. Jesus himself was hated, cursed, abused, beaten, and shamed—and yet responded with love. Jesus could have hated; we might even believe he had that right. But those who hate become like their enemies. That doesn't make love easy, but Wells ends with words of encouragement that Jesus is with us in the hard work of enemy-love.

> We can walk the path Jesus walked [toward enemy-love] because he has first walked it for us. Sometimes we can't find it in us to forgive. Jesus shows us how still to love. We are people who are trying to learn what love really means. Thank God that, with Christ and the saints, we never walk alone.[16]

Suggested Reading

David G. Horrell. *Solidarity and Difference: A Contemporary Reading of Paul's Ethics.* London: Bloomsbury, 2016.

Jon D. Levenson. *Love of God: Divine Gift, Human Gratitude, and Mutual Faithfulness in Judaism.* Princeton: Princeton University Press, 2016.

R. W. L. Moberly. *Old Testament Theology: Reading the Hebrew Bible as Christian Scripture.* Grand Rapids: Baker Academic, 2015.

Francis J. Moloney. *Love in the Gospel of John: An Exegetical, Theological, and Literary Study.* Grand Rapids: Baker Academic, 2013.

Leon Morris. *Testaments of Love: A Study of Love in the Bible.* Grand Rapids: Eerdmans, 1981.

Christine Pohl. *Making Room: Recovering Hospitality as a Christian Tradition.* Grand Rapids: Eerdmans, 1999.

Willard Swartley. *The Love of Enemy and Nonretaliation in the New Testament.* Louisville: Westminster John Knox, 1992.

---

16. Wells, "Love Your Enemy," 30.

CHAPTER 15

Witness

Public Advocates for Jesus and His Way—No Matter What

Revelation

If there is an earthquake somewhere else in the country from where you live, how would you know it really happened? Perhaps you'd read about it in the newspaper (*are there still newspapers?*). Or you might see footage of houses shaking on the nightly news or the news feed on your phone. In the ancient world, you didn't have security cameras capturing information or underground sensors tracking seismic activity. The sources of truth for events were *eyewitnesses*. If an earthquake happened, you would hear about it via personal testimony, or else you might not know about it all. What about matters of crime and justice? How would you know if a crime really happened, and who committed the crime? The justice system of most ancient peoples depended heavily on trustworthy witnesses giving *testimony* about events that transpired.

Indeed, it might surprise you—but shouldn't really—that the Old Testament contains lots of instructions about eyewitness testimony. The death penalty should be given to a murderer, but the crime must have more than one witness (Num 35:30). And this doesn't just apply to heinous crimes: "A single witness shall not suffice to convict a person of any crime or wrongdoing in connection with any offense that may be committed. Only on the evidence of two or three witnesses shall a charge be sustained" (Deut 19:15). As you can imagine, there would be much to gain from hiring or becoming a false witness. "Witness tampering" was a serious problem. The psalmist cried out, "Do not give me up to the will of my adversaries, for false witnesses have risen against me, and they are breathing out violence" (Ps 27:12). (This happened to Jesus as well, of course; see Matt 26:60.) Jews did not just believe truth was "objective"; they also believed that it must be "recognized" and confirmed by trustworthy people. This has its origins in the village counsel or the law court, where a witness was called upon to give testimony to the truth (or perhaps to prove that something didn't happen). Because of how common this process was in society, it became a popular concept for validating truth beyond matters of legality. Thus, when used more metaphorically, the moon could serve as a witness to the faithfulness of God (Ps 89:37). Job calls upon God *himself* as a witness of Job's innocence and honor (Job 16:19). So, you could call anything a "witness" that points to truth.

But witnesses are not always needed. If I say, "I saw a bald eagle today when I went for a walk," my wife would be a bit surprised, but she would definitely believe my word. She would not call for other eye-witnesses to testify—the claim seems plausible enough, and the stakes are rather low. But what happens when the stakes are much higher, and the things you are saying are seemingly irrational and unfathomable? This is certainly the situation we have for the men and women who proclaimed Jesus as Messiah, who *testified* to the gospel. They were claiming to know this one great Truth, but it was something that seemed foolish, and even evil, to many of their neighbors and friends. To tell this kind of truth over and over again, to contradict and refute other ways of looking at the world—this was dangerous testimony. The Greek word *martys* means "witness," and is the common term for anyone who gives testimony about anything. But you may already know that our English word "martyr" comes from this Greek term, based on the history of Christian "martyrs" (witnesses to the truth of the gospel who gave their life). In Acts, Paul refers to his presence at the death of Stephen, "when the blood of your *martyr* Stephen was shed" (22:20 NIV). Should this be translated in English as "witness" or "martyr"? If we lived in Luke's time, the first century, it would make sense to retain the common translation "witness," but Stephen did lose his life because of his rejected testimony. I am reminded of the situation regarding Dietrich Bonhoeffer's famous book *The Cost of Discipleship*. The original title Bonhoeffer gave to the book was simply *Discipleship* (German: *Nachfolge*). But in retrospect, recognizing that eventually he was killed because of his Christian love for others and witness to the truth of the gospel, English publishers retitled it *The Cost of Discipleship*. Witness unto death, indeed.

Old Testament Background

We have already mentioned how there are numerous rules in the Pentateuch about how testimony should take place in legal proceedings. But here I want to look at the prophets, Isaiah in particular. First, we need to set the scene. In the ancient Mediterranean world, various peoples had their own gods. They pledged fidelity to their ancestral deities, and when they warred against other nations it was like one set of gods challenging another set of gods—a sort of clash of the Titans. But what happens when Israel enters someone else's land, into the territory of other gods (Canaan), settles down there, then is conquered and taken to yet another land (Babylon) with yet another set of gods? They start to have mixed allegiances. Numerous prophetic voices in the Old Testament indict Israel for being so easily wooed by foreign gods (e.g., Ps 81:9).

Isaiah raises concerns with and accusations against Israel because of their weak faith and their temptation to honor other gods. In chapter 43, the Lord, God of Israel, expresses exasperation at the problem of Israel being confused about who is supreme. "Which of their gods foretold [these prophesies] and proclaimed to us the former things? Let them bring in their witnesses to prove they were right, so that others may hear and say, 'It is true'" (Isa 43:9 NIV). While the Israelites were playing judge about which gods are worth their allegiance, YHWH turned the tables: "*You [Israelites]* are my witnesses . . . and my servant whom I have chosen, so that you may know and believe me and understand that I am he. Before me no god was formed, nor will there be one after me" (43:10 NIV).

Israel was the people rescued by YHWH from the power and hegemony of Pharaoh of Egypt. YHWH proved himself supreme, the truly highest God. Israel knew this to be true *then*, but later sowed and cultivated the seeds of doubt. The prophets regularly employed testimony language to reawaken Israel to the truth, that no god or "religion" could compare with the supremacy of YHWH.

This kind of prophetic conversation is important for thinking about the New Testament—and especially Revelation—because it is all about the truth going public and challenging any other claim to truth.

Focal Text: Revelation

The book called "Revelation" opens with a key statement that puts witnessing to truth at the center:

> The revelation of Jesus Christ, which God gave him to show his servants what must soon take place; he made it known by sending his angel to his servant John, who *testified* to the word of God and to the *testimony* of Jesus Christ, even to all that he saw. (Rev 1:1–2)

Before we address why and how Revelation uses testimony language, it is helpful to answer this question: *What kind of book is Revelation?* Scholars refer to this final book of the New Testament as a form of apocalyptic literature. This genre of writing offers a mediated heavenly vision of reality. A light shines down from the heavens and gives mortals a glimpse of a world beyond what our eyes can see. These "revelations" are sometimes necessary because either (a) believers have distorted the truth of God and mixed truth with false images, or (b) believers have lost sight of God and are stumbling around in the dark, looking for light and hope. And sometimes divine revelations offer both. John, historically called "John the Seer" or "St. John the Divine," is gifted with a powerful vision of history, the divine realm, and the future of the world, not so he could write down an eschatological timeline to follow like a time map, but so he could capture a fresh vision of the *truth* and then give testimony to it to bring hope and wisdom to the people of God—and also to challenge and convict those believers who have become accustomed to the darkness.

Revelation borrows this image of personal testimony to represent the faithful passing down and distribution of truth from God, through Jesus Christ, through an angel, and then through John. From the first verses of Revelation, we are reminded that the call to witness to truth is a call to point to Jesus, who points and testifies to his Father.

Jesus the Witness

To begin with, we can observe that John represents *Jesus Christ* as the "faithful witness" whose incarnated life demonstrates the extent to which he would go to bring his truthful message to us. Furthermore, Jesus was killed for bringing this rejected message, but God raised him up, "firstborn of the dead, and the ruler of the kings of the earth" (1:5). Later on, he is called the "Amen, the faithful and true witness, the origin of God's creation" (Rev 3:14). I am struck by this little title for Jesus, the "Amen." Jesus verifies the faithful and righteous presence of God in the incarnation. Jesus demonstrates the saving gift of God that fulfills his promises in his suffering and death. Jesus reveals the transforming power of God in his resurrection. And Jesus promises to return, as we see in the close of Revelation: "The one who testifies to these things says, 'Surely I am coming soon.' Amen. Come, Lord Jesus!" (22:20).

As the Amen of God, Jesus models not only God's promise to make good on his promises, but also what it means to trust God, even to the point of death (see Phil 2:6–11).

The Blood of Jesus's Witnesses

Revelation is clear that being a witness is dangerous business when people don't like the truth you are telling. There are few images in the Bible more grotesque than Revelation 17:6: "And I saw that the woman was drunk with the blood of the saints and the blood of the witnesses to Jesus. When I saw her, I was greatly amazed." The she-beast that John writes of here probably represents the goddess Roma, the patroness of the Roman Empire itself, which chewed Christians up and spat them out in the first and second centuries. We also learn about a certain Christian named Antipas who became a model of the truth teller who does not back down; he did not renounce his faith despite severe opposition and was put to death in Pergamum by the power of Satan (Rev 2:13).

The book of Revelation as a whole is not about the rapture; the end times are not *really* its primary concern. Rather, it is all about helping beleaguered and meek Christians to see the world through the eyes of God and know that their public witness is valuable, honorable, and effective—even if the world rejects, shames, tortures, and kills them.

OTHER NEW TESTAMENT VOICES
Acts 1:8; 1 Corinthians 15:15; 1 Thessalonians 2:10; 1 Timothy 6:12; Hebrews 12:1; 1 Peter 5:1

John 1

John the Baptist plays an important role in the Gospels. He was, in a way, the "opening act" for Jesus, getting the people ready for what was to come. He is often described by scholars as the "forerunner," an advance messenger previewing the Messiah's message. The Gospel of John explains that John the Baptist "came as a witness to testify to the light, so that all might believe through him" (John 1:7). John is a model in the New Testament of proclaiming hard truth to the world according to the revelation of God. There is one Lamb of God who can take away the sin of the world (John 1:29, 34, 36).

John could have testified to Jesus in many ways. He could have written books. He could have taught in synagogues. But all four gospels make reference to his unusual activities of preaching in the wilderness and dipping ("baptizing") people in the river. John wanted to embody his role as witness like a prophet. He had more than words to share.

He needed to make a big statement in word and deed to increase the reach and impact of his testimony.

Testimony for Today

Recently, a friend and I were swapping stories about how we were dreading being called upon for jury duty, our "civil service." We were thankful to live in America and for our system of law, but we both agreed that getting called for jury duty was a major inconvenience and a nuisance. But if you think about the ancient world, especially smaller people groups, trustworthy men were often called upon to give testimony. Being a faithful witness, even on a regular basis, was part and parcel of being an elder in society. They knew they had an *obligation* to speak and bear witness to the truth. All things being equal, to serve as a productive member of the justice system was considered an honor and a privilege, not a drudgery.

This is a helpful framework, I think, for the way the Bible talks about Christian "testimony." The world is a big court where truth is constantly on trial. Christians are called to point to Jesus publicly without shame. This was not easy for many Christians in the first century—many experienced suffering of various kinds, a few lost their lives. Most Western Christians today don't quite have these kinds of problems when it comes to testifying to the gospel of Jesus Christ, but it is still costly. Christians don't want to be seen as closed-minded, hostile, pushy, or condescending. So, the reality is that Christian testimony—what we call "evangelism" (which technically means "gospel-ing")—is dying.[1] Can it be revived in our times in the West?

I Saw the Light: Witnessing with Words

It is commonplace to share your "testimony" when there is an occasion to share about Jesus. "Testimony" has become a semitechnical

---

1. In 2013, a Barna Group report showed that evangelism is dying ("Is Evangelism Going out of Style?," Barna, December 17, 2013, www.barna.com/research/is-evangelism-going -out-of-style/); a more recent study (2019) indicates many young Christians think it is *wrong* to evangelize ("Almost Half of Practicing Christian Millennials Say Evangelism Is Wrong," Barna, February 5, 2019, www.barna.com/research/millennials-oppose-evangelism/).

term for "my Jesus story." That's fine, I don't want to nitpick, but the biblical concept aims a bit wider to involve "testimony" as truth at large. Not just the truth about "Jesus and me," but also the truth about Jesus and all things through the Christian lens. We need not get into all the ins and outs of a Christian worldview here, so let me just acknowledge my appreciation of Hank Williams's classic song "I Saw the Light" as an example in "testifying." Yes, Williams's song is about how Jesus changed his life. That is important, and definitely worth singing about. But the emphasis on light and darkness recognizes how Jesus opens our life up to a more complete understanding of the whole world. Williams sang about being lost and then found, about a darkness dispelled, about a newfound joy where there was sorrow. This is about more than going to heaven. It is about a real life changed by a gracious savior. Amazing how the simplest of songs can capture such profound experiences.

I Am the Light: Witnessing with Lifestyle

If we think of "witnessing" as pointing to Jesus Christ as Jesus Christ points to the Father, then believers are called to do this in both word *and* deed. It is not enough to say, "Do as I say, not as I do." We demonstrate the substance of our lives, our values and goals, by the way we live. But what counts as a "Christian lifestyle"? What testifies to the validity and value of our faith in Jesus Christ? We could walk through the whole Bible and catalogue the various virtues and vices that appear in Scripture. But we will stick with the focal text of Revelation and note that in Revelation's letters and messages to the seven churches, the Lord warns his people against three master vices: weakness of faith (cultural assimilation; 3:1–4), illicit sex (2:20), and greed (3:17–18). What is called for is the opposite: perseverance in faith and loyalty to God alone, purity, self-discipline, and faithfulness to our spouse. We can relate to all these today. How much would it mean to the world if *Christians* demonstrated generosity and not greed? What would it look like if pastors and Christian leaders were known for being safe people, rather than those who abuse others?

Revelation's wider message is embedded in these seven letters. The church as the "light of the world" must prove itself to be honest, consistent in word and deed, generous in love, and hating evil (2:2). To be

Christian is not just to be forgiven. Revelation has a hard message for many of these churches where believers are not willing to stick it out in tough times.

Again, we could fill many books with advice on how to "witness" to Jesus Christ with our lifestyle and acts, but here are four ways to reflect on for now.

Accountability

Too many people today live without any moral accountability, formal or even informal. This easily leads to abuse of power, abuse of relationships, and misbehavior unchecked. Christians ought to be willing and committed to accountability and to being transparent in leadership.

Justice and Respect for All

Throughout the years, Christians have often been at the forefront of justice and civil rights movements. That is because our Scriptures and our Lord have taught us the sanctity of life and the equality of all people. Of course, Christians and churches have also failed in this area. We must repent of laziness, apathy, and even prejudice.

Simplicity and Generosity

It makes me sick when I hear about filthy rich pastors and Christian leaders. God does not call all Christians to live in abject poverty, but Revelation portrays a vision of a church singularly focused on a self-given life in imitation of the holy, slaughtered Lamb. Personally, I find myself inspired by everyday Christians who reject the potential luxuries of life in order to share what they have with others. This honors God and testifies powerfully to the gospel of Jesus Christ.

Attempt Great Things for God

William Carey famously said, "Attempt great things for God, expect great things from God." I believe a key element of a lived testimony unto Jesus Christ is a faith that inspires us to dream big, to achieve big for the sake of caring about the things God cares about. *What can we invent, what can we imagine, what can we create, what can we make better in order to realize the dream of "Thy kingdom come"?* Repeatedly, Revelation uses the language of *conquer* and *victory* and *winning (nikaō).*[2] This could come across as triumphalistic, but we must keep in mind that "winning" is not about pushing others down. Evil, sin, death—these are the enemies to be overpowered. What we can take away from Revelation's exhortation to victory is faith, courage, and fortitude. To overcome evil with good, to triumph over death with the power of life and love. God's cruciform warriors must be dreamers; they must yearn and hunger too for the end of evil's reign. This will eventually make way for the benevolent reign of the Lord of lords and King of kings (Rev 17:14) and the realization of a new world—a kingdom of peace.

Suggested Reading

Richard Bauckham. *Bible and Mission: Christian Witness in a Postmodern World.* Grand Rapids: Baker, 2003.

Brian Blount. *Can I Get a Witness? Reading Revelation through African American Culture.* Louisville: Westminster John Knox, 2005.

Alexander S. Jensen. *John's Gospel as Witness.* New York: Routledge, 2016.

I. Howard Marshall, ed. *Witness to the Gospel: The Theology of Acts.* Grand Rapids: Eerdmans, 1998.

---

2. Rev 2:7, 11, 17, 26; 3:5, 12, 21; 5:5; 6:2; 11:7; 12:11; 13:7; 15:2; 17:14; 21:7.

Bibliography

Abernethy, Andrew T., and Gregory Goswell. *God's Messiah in the Old Testament*. Grand Rapids: Baker Academic, 2020.

Alexander, T. Demond, and Simon J. Gathercole, eds. *Heaven on Earth: The Temple in Biblical Theology*. Carlisle, UK: Paternoster, 2004.

Banks, Robert J. *Paul's Idea of Community*. Peabody, MA: Hendrickson, 1995.

Barclay, John M. G. "Pure Grace? Paul's Distinctive Jewish Theology of Gift." *Studia Theologica* 68.1 (2014): 4–20; online: http://dro.dur.ac .uk/12667/1/12667.pdf.

Barnouw, David, and Gerrold Van Der Stroom, ed. *The Diary of Anne Frank*. The Revised Critical Edition. New York: Doubleday, 2003.

Barth, Karl. *Dogmatics in Outline*. New York: Harper, 1959.

Barton, Stephen C., ed. *Holiness: Past and Present*. London: Bloomsbury, 2003.

Bates, Matthew W. *Gospel Allegiance: What Faith in Jesus Misses for Salvation in Christ*. Grand Rapids: Brazos, 2019.

———. *Salvation by Allegiance Alone: Rethinking Faith, Works, and the Gospel of Jesus the King*. Grand Rapids: Baker, 2017.

Bauckham, Richard. *Bible and Mission: Christian Witness in a Postmodern World*. Grand Rapids: Baker, 2003.

Beale, G. K., and Mitchell Kim. *God Dwells Among Us: Expanding Eden to the Ends of the Earth*. Downers Grove, IL: InterVarsity Press, 2014.

Beilby, James, and Paul R. Eddy, ed. *The Nature of the Atonement*. Downers Grove, IL: IVP Academic, 2006.

Bethge, Eberhard. *Dietrich Bonhoeffer*. English Translation. Minneapolis: Fortress, 2000.

Bird, Michael F. *Are You the One Who Is to Come? The Historical Jesus and the Messianic Question*. Grand Rapids: Baker Academic, 2009.

———. *Evangelical Theology: A Biblical and Systematic Introduction*. Grand Rapids: Zondervan Academic, 2013.

———. *The Saving Righteousness of God*. Eugene, OR: Wipf & Stock, 2007.

Blickenstaff, Marianne. "Pax Romana." Page 421 of vol. 4 of *New Interpreter's Dictionary of the Bible*. Edited by Katharine Doob Sakenfeld. 5 vols. Nashville: Abingdon, 2006–2009.

Blinkenberg, C., and K. Kinch, ed. *Lindos: Fouilles et recherches, 1902–1914*. Vol. 2: *Inscriptions*. Berlin: de Gruyter, 1941.

Blomberg, Craig L. *A New Testament Theology*. Waco, TX: Baylor University Press, 2018.

Blount, Brian. *Can I Get a Witness? Reading Revelation through African American Culture*. Louisville: Westminster John Knox, 2005.

Bock, Darrell. *Luke 1–9:50*. Baker Exegetical Commentary on the New Testament. Grand Rapids: Baker, 1994.

Boda, Mark J. *'Return to Me': A Biblical Theology of Repentance*. Downers Grove, IL: IVP Academic, 2015.

———. *A Severe Mercy: Sin and Its Remedy in the Old Testament*. Winona Lake, IN: Eisenbrauns, 2009.

Boda, Mark J., and Gordon T. Smith, ed. *Repentance in Christian Theology*. Collegeville, MN: Liturgical Press, 2006.

Bonhoeffer, Dietrich. *The Cost of Discipleship*. New York: Simon & Schuster, 1995.

———. *Life Together and Prayerbook of the Bible*. Minneapolis: Fortress, 1996.

Brink, Laurie. "Love Your Enemy?" *U.S. Catholic* 83.6 (2018): 28–33.

Brower, Kent, and Andy Johnson, ed. *Holiness and Ecclesiology in the New Testament*. Grand Rapids: Eerdmans, 2007.

Brown, Jeannine K., Carla M. Dahl, and Wyndy Corbin Reuschling. *Becoming Whole and Holy: An Integrative Conversation about Christian Formation*. Grand Rapids: Baker Academic, 2011.

Brueggemann, Walter. *The Prophetic Imagination*. Minneapolis: Fortress, 2018.

———. *Reverberations of Faith: A Theological Handbook of Old Testament Themes*. Louisville: Westminster John Knox, 2002.

———. *Worship in Ancient Israel*. Nashville: Abingdon, 2005.

Campbell, Constantine. *Paul and the Hope of Glory: An Exegetical and Theological Study*. Grand Rapids: Zondervan, 2020.

Carter, Tim. *The Forgiveness of Sins.* Cambridge: James Clarke, 2016.

Chalmers, Aaron. *Exploring the Religion of Ancient Israel: Prophet, Priest, Sage, and People.* Downers Grove, IL: IVP Academic, 2012.

Chennattu, Rekha. *Johannine Discipleship as a Covenant Relationship.* Peabody, MA: Hendrickson, 2006.

Clark-Soles, Jaime. *Reading John for Dear Life: A Spiritual Walk with the Fourth Gospel.* Louisville: Westminster John Knox, 2016.

Colijn, Brenda. *Images of Salvation in the New Testament.* Downers Grove, IL: InterVarsity Press, 2010.

Coloe, Mary L. *Dwelling in the Household of God: Johannine Ecclesiology and Spirituality.* Collegeville, MN: Liturgical Press, 2007.

Cook, John Granger. *Crucifixion in the Mediterranean World.* Tübingen: Mohr Siebeck, 2015.

Daly, Emily Joseph, trans. *Tertullian, Apology.* New York: Catholic University of America, 1950.

Dewey, Arthur J. et al. *The Authentic Letters of Paul.* Salem, OR: Polebridge Press, 2010.

Dunn, James D. G. *New Testament Theology.* Nashville: Abingdon, 2010.

Estelle, Bryan D. *Echoes of Exodus: Tracing a Biblical Motif.* Downers Grove, IL: IVP Academic, 2018.

Furnish, Victor. *The Love Command in the New Testament.* London: SCM, 1972.

Garland, David. *Luke.* Zondervan Exegetical Commentary on the New Testament. Grand Rapids: Zondervan Academic, 2011.

———. *A Theology of Mark's Gospel.* Grand Rapids: Zondervan, 2015.

Goldsworthy, Adrian. *Pax Romana: War, Peace and Conquest in the Roman World.* New Haven: Yale University Press, 2016.

Gombis, Timothy G. *Power in Weakness: Paul's Transformed Vision for Ministry.* Grand Rapids: Eerdmans, 2021.

Gooder, Paula. *Heaven.* Eugene, OR: Cascade, 2011.

———. *The Parables.* London: Canterbury Press, 2020.

Gorman, Michael J. *Abide and Go: Missional Theosis in the Gospel of John.* Eugene, OR: Cascade, 2018.

———. *Becoming the Gospel: Paul, Participation, and Mission.* Grand Rapids: Eerdmans, 2015.

———. *Cruciformity: Paul's Narrative Spirituality of the Cross.* 20th Anniversary Edition. Grand Rapids: Eerdmans, 2021.

Green, Joel B., *1 Peter*. Two Horizons New Testament Commentary. Grand Rapids: Eerdmans, 2007.

———, ed. *Dictionary of Scripture and Ethics*. Grand Rapids: Baker, 2011.

———. *Why Salvation?* Nashville: Abingdon, 2014.

Grieb, A. Katherine. *The Story of Romans: A Narrative Defense of God's Righteousness*. Louisville: Westminster John Knox, 2002.

Gupta, Nijay K. *A Beginner's Guide to New Testament Studies*. Grand Rapids: Baker Academic, 2020.

———. *Paul and the Language of Faith*. Grand Rapids: Eerdmans, 2020.

Hall, Crystal L. *Insights from Reading the Bible with the Poor*. Minneapolis: Fortress, 2019.

Harink, Douglas. *Resurrecting Justice: Reading Romans for the Life of the World*. Downers Grove, IL: InterVarsity Press, 2020.

Hays, Richard B. *The Moral Vision of the New Testament*. San Francisco: HarperSanFrancisco, 1996.

Hellerman, Joseph. *Embracing Shared Ministry*. Grand Rapids: Kregel, 2013.

Henderson, Suzanne Watts, "The 'Good News' of God's Coming Reign: Occupation at a Crossroads." *Interpretation* 70.2 (2016): 145–58.

Hengel, Martin. *Crucifixion in the Ancient World and the Folly of the Message of the Cross*. Philadelphia: Fortress, 1989.

Hildebrandt, Franz. "Can the Distinctive Methodist Emphasis Be Said to Be Rooted in the New Testament?" *London Quarterly and Holborn Review* 184 (1959): 230–39.

Hill, Wesley, and John M. G. Barclay. "What's So Dangerous about Grace." *Christianity Today*. December 31, 2015. www.christianitytoday.com /ct/2016/january-february/whats-so-dangerous-about-grace.html.

Horrell, David G. *Solidarity and Difference: A Contemporary Reading of Paul's Ethics*. London: Bloomsbury, 2016.

Humphreys, José, and Adam Gustine. "An Ecclesiology of Shalom." *The Covenant Quarterly* 77.1 (2019): 36–52.

Jensen, Alexander S. *John's Gospel as Witness*. New York: Routledge, 2016.

Jipp, Joshua W. *The Messianic Theology of the New Testament*. Grand Rapids: Eerdmans, 2020.

Jobes, Karen. *1, 2 & 3 John*. ZECNT. Grand Rapids: Zondervan Academic, 2014.

Johnson, Andy. *Holiness and the Missio Dei*. Eugene, OR: Cascade, 2016.

Johnson, Luke Timothy. *The Creed: What Christians Believe and Why It Matters*. New York: Doubleday, 2003.

———. *Sharing Possessions: What Faith Demands*. 2nd ed. Grand Rapids: Eerdmans, 2011.

Kamell (Kovalishyn), Mariam. "James 1:27 and the Church's Call to Mission and Morals." *Crux* 46.4 (2010): 15–22.

Kinney, Jeff. *Diary of a Wimpy Kid*. New York: Amulet Books, 2007.

Konstan, David. *Before Forgiveness: The Origins of a Moral Idea*. Cambridge: Cambridge University Press, 2012.

Levenson, Jon D. *Love of God: Divine Gift, Human Gratitude, and Mutual Faithfulness in Judaism*. Princeton: Princeton University Press, 2016.

———. *Resurrection and the Restoration of Israel: The Ultimate Victory of the God of Life*. New Haven: Yale University Press, 2008.

Lewis, C. S. *The Great Divorce*. New York: HarperOne, 2009.

———. *Mere Christianity*. London: HarperCollins, 2017.

Lieu, Judith. *The Theology of Johannine Epistles*. New Testament Theology. Cambridge: Cambridge University Press, 1991.

Lincoln, Andrew T. "'I Am the Resurrection and the Life': The Resurrection Message of the Fourth Gospel." Pages 122–145 in *Life in the Face of Death*. Edited by Richard N. Longenecker. Grand Rapids: Eerdmans, 1998.

Longenecker, Richard N., ed. *Life in the Face of Death*. Grand Rapids: Eerdmans, 1998.

Marshall, I. Howard. *New Testament Theology: Many Witnesses, One Gospel*. Downers Grove, IL: IVP Academic, 2004.

———, ed. *Witness to the Gospel: The Theology of Acts*. Grand Rapids: Eerdmans, 1998.

Matera, Frank J. *New Testament Theology: Exploring Diversity and Unity*. Louisville: Westminster John Knox, 2007.

McKnight, Scot. *A Fellowship of Differents: Showing the World God's Design for Life Together*. Grand Rapids: Zondervan, 2014.

———. *Pastor Paul: Nurturing a Culture of Christoformity in the Church*. Grand Rapids: Baker, 2019.

McNall, Joshua M. *The Mosaic of Atonement: An Integrated Approach to Christ's Work*. Grand Rapids: Zondervan, 2019.

Miller, Patrick. *The Religion of Ancient Israel*. Minneapolis: Fortress, 2007.

Moberly, R. W. L. *Old Testament Theology: Reading the Hebrew Bible as Christian Scripture*. Grand Rapids: Baker Academic, 2013.

———. "'Test the Spirits': God, Love, and Critical Discernment in 1 John 4." *The Holy Spirit and Christian Origins: Essays in Honor of James D. G. Dunn*. Edited by Graham Stanton, Bruce W. Longenecker, and Stephen C. Barton. Grand Rapids: Eerdmans, 2004.

Moloney, Francis J. *Love in the Gospel of John: An Exegetical, Theological, and Literary Study*. Grand Rapids: Baker Academic, 2013.

Moltmann, Jürgen. *The Spirit of Life: A Universal Affirmation*. Minneapolis: Fortress, 1992.

Morales, L. Michael. *Exodus Old and New: A Biblical Theology of Redemption*. Downers Grove, IL: IVP Academic, 2020.

Morris, Leon. *Testaments of Love: A Study of Love in the Bible*. Grand Rapids: Eerdmans, 1981.

Myers, Alicia. "Remember the Greatest: Remaining in Love and Casting Out Fear in 1 John." *Review & Expositor* 115.1 (2018): 50–61.

Nouwen, Henri J. *Adam: God's Beloved*. Maryknoll, NY: Orbis Books, 1997.

O'Day, Gail R. "The Gospel of John." Pages 491–865 in *New Interpreter's Bible*, vol. 9. Nashville: Abingdon, 1995.

Perrin, Nicholas. *Jesus the Temple*. Grand Rapids: Baker Academic, 2010.

———. *The Kingdom of God: A Biblical Theology*. Grand Rapids: Zondervan, 2019.

Peterson, David. *Possessed by God: A New Testament Theology of Sanctification and Holiness*. New Studies in Biblical Theology. Downers Grove, IL: IVP Academic, 1995.

Pitre, Brant, Michael P. Barber, John A. Kincaid. *Paul, a New Covenant Jew: Rethinking Pauline Theology*. Grand Rapids: Eerdmans, 2019.

Pohl, Christine. *Making Room: Recovering Hospitality as a Christian Tradition*. Grand Rapids: Eerdmans, 1999.

Porter, Stanley E., ed. *The Messiah in the Old and New Testaments*. Grand Rapids: Eerdmans, 2007.

Rutledge, Fleming. *Crucifixion: Understanding the Death of Jesus Christ*. Grand Rapids: Eerdmans, 2017.

Schaeffer, Francis. *How Then Shall We Live*. 2nd edition. Winchester, IL: Crossway, 1990.

Schreiner, Patrick. *The Kingdom of God and the Glory of the Cross*. Wheaton, IL: Crossway, 2018.

Senior, Donald. *The Gospel of Matthew*. Interpreting Biblical Texts. Nashville: Abingdon, 1997.

Shriver, Donald W. "Divinely Persistent, God Really Loves Us." *Christian Century*. November 29, 2011. www.christiancentury.org/blogs/archive /2011–11/divinely-persistent-god-really-loves-us.

———. *Why the Cross?* Nashville: Abingdon, 2014.

Smith, Daniel Lynwood. *Into the World of the New Testament*. London: Bloomsbury, 2015.

Snodgrass, Klyne. *Stories with Intent: A Comprehensive Guide to the Parables of Jesus*. Grand Rapids: Eerdmans, 2008.

Spicq, Ceslas, and James D. Ernest. *Theological Lexicon of the New Testament*. Peabody, MA: Hendrickson, 1994.

Stewart-Sykes, A., trans. *Tertullian, Cyprian, and Origen: On the Lord's Prayer*. New York: St. Vladimir's Seminary Press, 2004.

Swartley, Willard M. *Covenant of Peace: The Missing Peace in New Testament Theology and Ethics*. Grand Rapids: Eerdmans, 2006.

———. *The Love of Enemy and Nonretaliation in the New Testament*. Louisville: Westminster John Knox, 1992.

Talbert, Charles. *Learning through Suffering: The Educational Value of Suffering in the New Testament and Its Milieu*. Collegeville, MN: Liturgical Press, 1991.

———, and Jason A. Whitlark. *Getting "Saved": The Whole Story of Salvation in the New Testament*. Grand Rapids: Eerdmans, 2011.

Tamez, Elsa. *The Scandalous Message of James: Faith without Works Is Dead*. New York: Crossroad, 2018.

Tyerman, Luke. *The Life and Times of Rev. John Wesley*. 3rd ed. London: Hodder & Stoughton, 1876.

U2. *U2 by U2*. London: HarperCollins, 2006.

van der Merwe, Dirk G. "'Lived Experiences' of the Love of God according to 1 John 4: A Spirituality of Love," *In die Skriflig* 51.3 (2017): a2169: https://indieskriflig.org.za/index.php/skriflig/article/view/2169/4358.

van der Watt, Jan G., ed. *Salvation in the New Testament: Perspectives on Soteriology*. Leiden: Brill, 2008.

Volf, Miroslav. *Exclusion and Embrace: A Theological Exploration of Identity, Otherness, and Reconciliation*. Nashville: Abingdon, 2019.

———. "Soft Difference: Theological Reflections on the Relationship between Church and Culture in 1 Peter." *Ex Auditu* 10 (1994): 15–30.

Weima, Jeffrey. "'Peace and Security' (1 Thess 5.3): Prophetic Warning or Political Propaganda?" *NTS* 58 (2012): 351–59.

Wells, Jo Bailey. *God's Holy People: A Theme in Biblical Theology*. Sheffield: Sheffield Academic, 2000.

Wells, Sam. "Love Your Enemies: Luke 6.20–31." *Journal for Preachers* 38.4 (2015): 27–30.

Wenham, Gordon. *Genesis 1–15*. Word Biblical Commentary. Waco, TX: Word, 1987.

Westfall, Cynthia Long and Bryan R. Dyer, ed. *The Bible and Social Justice: Old Testament and New Testament Foundations for the Church's Urgent Call*. Eugene, OR: Pickwick, 2016.

Whitmarsh, Tim. *Battling the Gods: Atheism in the Ancient World*. New York: Knopf, 2015.

Wieland, George. *The Significance of Salvation: A Study of Salvation Language in the Pastoral Epistles*. Eugene, OR: Wipf & Stock, 2006.

Winter, Bruce W. *Divine Honours for the Caesars*. Grand Rapids: Eerdmans, 2015.

Wolterstorff, Nicholas. *Justice: Rights and Wrongs*. Princeton: Princeton University Press, 2010.

Works, Carla Swafford. *The Least of These: Paul and the Marginalized*. Grand Rapids: Eerdmans, 2020.

Wright, Christopher J. H. *The Mission of God's People: A Biblical Theology of the Church's Mission*. Grand Rapids: Zondervan, 2010.

Wright, N. T. *Evil and the Justice of God*. Downers Grove, IL: IVP Academic, 2013.

———. *How God Became King: The Forgotten Story of the Gospels*. New York: HarperOne, 2012.

———. *Simply Good News: Why the Gospel Is News and What Makes It Good*. New York: HarperOne, 2015.

———. *Surprised by Hope: Rethinking Heaven, the Resurrection, and the Mission of the Church*. New York: HarperOne, 2007.

Yinger, Kent L. *God and Human Wholeness*. Eugene, OR: Cascade, 2019.

Acknowledgments

This book was born of a seminary professor's profound desire to see his students deeply changed by encountering the God of the gospel in the pages of Scripture. Many of these chapters were "field tested" with my students at Portland Seminary and Northern Seminary. I am grateful for their feedback and encouragement. My Zondervan editor Katya Covrett enthusiastically supported this project from beginning to end and gave me much helpful direction toward producing a better resource for readers. Chris Beetham at Zondervan helped me make sure what I wanted to communicate was clear and accurate.

Two Northern students, Susy Flory and Cody Matchett, assisted me in some of the research needs for this book, I want to register how much I value their input and contributions. Also, I am deeply grateful for the foreword written by my friend Paula Gooder. It is a great honor to have these words of support. Finally, this book is dedicated to my wife, a seminary-trained pastor who is for me a model of theology lived out in real life.

Subject Index

Scripture Index

Other Ancient Literature Index